EVERY DAY WITH JESUS

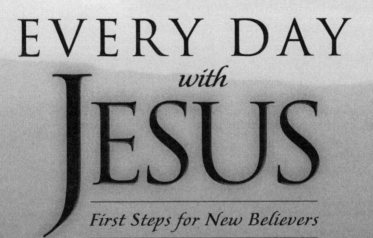

EVERY DAY
with
JESUS

First Steps for New Believers

GREG LAURIE

Tyndale House Publishers, Inc.
WHEATON, ILLINOIS

Visit Tyndale's exciting Web site at www.tyndale.com

Designed by Ron Kaufmann

Edited by Jeremy Taylor

Previously published by Harvest House Publishers, Copyright © 1993 by Harvest House Publishers,
ISBN 1-56507-058-5.

First printing by Tyndale House Publishers 2004.

Library of Congress Cataloging-in-Publication Data

Laurie, Greg.
  Every Day with Jesus / Greg Laurie.
    p. cm.
  Originally published: Eugene, OR : Harvest House, © 1993.
  ISBN 1-4143-0075-1
  1. Bible. N.T. Gospels—Meditations. 2. Devotional calendars. I. Title.
BS2555.54.L38 2004
242'.2—dc22   2004001580

Printed in the United States of America

09 08 07 06 05 04
7   6   5   4   3   2   1

ACKNOWLEDGMENTS

To the congregation of Harvest Christian Fellowship:
A pastor couldn't ask for a more supportive
and responsive flock of committed believers.
Special thanks to Karen Dagher, Carol Faulkner, and Steve Halliday
for their invaluable help in the preparation of this book.

CONTENTS

Every Day with Jesus

PART ONE
The Man Who Was God
Walking With The Master 2
Christmas, B.C. 5
With God, All Things Are Possible 9
The Story Of Stories 12
The Highest To The Lowest. 15
Have You Lost Him? 19
Behold The Lamb! 23
Why Did He Come? 26
On The Mountaintop 30
The King Arrives 33
Dark Storm Rising 36
Popularity Plus 39
In The Shadow Of The Cross. 42
A Terrible, Holy Moment 45
From Moriah To Calvary 48
By His Stripes We Are Healed. 51
The Last Prayer 55
No Contradiction 58
The Greatest Love Story 62
The Darkest Hour 65
When God Was Thirsty 69
The Ultimate Battle Cry 72
You Can't Keep The God-Man Down 75
Surprise! 78
Up, Up, And Away! 81
A Divine Blockbuster. 85
Home Sweet Home 89
What Do *You* Think Of Jesus Christ? 92

PART TWO
Working Out What God Has Worked In

Growing God's Way 99
The Secret Of Contentment. 103
God's Answer To Burnout. 106
A Changed Life 110
Power Under Constraint 114
A Craving For Holiness. 117
Matters Of The Heart. 121
The Christian's Badge Of Honor. 124
When The World Doesn't Like You 128
Count Your Blessings. 132
It's Not Easy 135
You Can't Outgive God 138
Specks And Planks 141
Caught In The Act. 144
Where Are Your Accusers? 147
The Problem Of Worry. 151
Even Sea Gulls Go To Work 154
That Sinking Feeling 158
The Grass *Isn't* Always Greener 162
Hope For The Prodigal 165
A New People. 169
How To Be A Kingdom Builder. 173
A Life Of Prayer 177
Father Knows Best 180
Hindrances To Answered Prayer 184
Carte Blanche 188
Where Are The Other Nine? 191
Making Our Heart His Home. 194

PART THREE
Maintaining And Shining

Do You Love The Lord? 198
The Christian's Strategic Role. 201
Shining Hearts. 205
Our Marching Orders 208
How To Be An Effective Witness 212
No Compromise. 216
Pass It On 220

That's Fine For You, But 224
A Spiritual Litmus Test 227
Posers 231
Choosing To Stay Upright. 235
Spiritual Heartburn. 239
What Are You Waiting For? 243
The Bigger Picture. 247
The Good Shepherd 251
The Shepherd's Voice. 255
Life Abundant 259
No Time Off 263
When God Wept. 267
God's Cure For Heart Trouble 271
After The Mountaintop 274
Real Success 278
How To Wait For The Lord's Return 282
Like A Thief 286
Signs Of The Times. 290
The Parable Of Equal Opportunity 294
Judgment Day 298
Served By The King 301

EVERY DAY WITH JESUS

As I worked on this book, I was continually reminded of how many practical lessons Jesus left with us concerning how to live a productive, fruitful, joy-filled Christian life. It's amazing how often we take His life for granted when it comes to our day-to-day living.

We may look back with a bit of envy at the original disciples, who had the unique privilege of literally walking and talking with Jesus during His earthly ministry. But I have good news for you! You can still walk and talk with the Master where you are right now.

John was one of those privileged to walk with the Lord during His earthly ministry. He wrote:

> That which was from the beginning, which we have heard, which we have seen with our eyes, which we have looked upon, and our hands have handled, concerning the Word of life—the life was manifested, and we have seen, and bear witness, and declare to you that eternal life which was with the Father and was manifested to us—that which we have seen and heard we declare to you, *that you also may have fellowship with us; and truly our fellowship is with the Father and with His Son Jesus Christ.* And these things we write to you that your joy may be full (1 John 1:1-4, emphasis added).

You can have the same kind of complete joy that John experienced as you walk with Jesus today!

I've centered this devotional on Philippians 2:3-14, a passage that paints a wonderful picture of Jesus' life and example. In Part

One of this book, "The Man Who Was God," I consider who Jesus is and how that should impact the way we live. In the second section, "Working Out What God Has Worked In," we will look at Jesus' lifestyle and teachings concerning what it takes to be one of His true disciples. Finally, in the last section, titled "Maintaining And Shining," we'll discover what Jesus taught us about persevering in our Christian life.

Each chapter, I'll leave you with a thought or a passage of Scripture for further study. I have added these little sections to challenge you to live out what you've just read.

In an era that has seen so many Christian counterfeits, it's time we went back to God's original design. It is my hope that this book will encourage you and instruct you, giving you the help and resources you need to tackle the unique situations you face every day.

Greg Laurie

PART ONE

THE MAN WHO WAS GOD

*"Let this mind be in you which was also in Christ Jesus, who,
being in the form of God, did not consider it robbery to be equal with God,
but made Himself of no reputation, taking the form of a servant,
and coming in the likeness of men. And being found in appearance
as a man, He humbled Himself and became obedient to the
point of death, even the death of the cross."*

—PHILIPPIANS 2:5-8

All of history hinges on Jesus Christ. Who is He? What did He do? Why did He come? How should we respond to Him? ✍
What we believe about Jesus not only has a profound effect on the way we live today, but seals forever our eternal destiny. It is therefore crucial that we have a clear answer to the question Jesus Himself asked in Matthew 16:15: "Who do you say that I am?" ✍
This section focuses on the Master Himself. It listens in to crucial conversations between Jesus and His disciples. It watches as the Savior demonstrates before friends and foes alike that He is God in the flesh. And it calls us all to respond to the Lord in a way that honors Him for who He truly is.

1

WALKING WITH THE MASTER

≤

*"That which we have seen and heard we declare to you, that you also
may have fellowship with us; and truly our fellowship is
with the Father and with His Son Jesus Christ."*

—1 JOHN 1:3

IF I COULD HAVE PICKED any period in history to be alive, I
would have chosen the time of the earthly ministry of Jesus.

What a privilege it would have been to walk alongside Jesus
as He ministered to the needs of countless thousands in ancient
Israel. What a time that must have been to be alive! No doubt it
was a primitive era in comparison to ours. They certainly didn't
have the creature comforts that we do. No cars. No telephones.
No fax machines. (Come to think of it, it's sounding better all
the time!)

Though you would have to forego many modern conve-
niences, just think what you would have gained by spending
time with Jesus Himself. Imagine what it would have been like to
hear His voice with your own ears. To reach out and touch Him
with your own hands. To watch with your own eyes the miracles
He performed and to ask Him your personal questions.

Then, of course, I would like to have seen His face. I wonder
what Jesus looked like? What color was His hair? His eyes? How
tall was He?

It's interesting that in Scripture, God never chose to reveal to us what Jesus looked like. Couldn't Matthew, Mark, Luke, or John at least once have given us a physical description of Him? "Jesus was about 6′2″, had wavy brown hair, and hazel eyes." Surely one of them could have given us some kind of report. But there's not a single physical description of Him in the Bible except the one in Revelation, which is a symbolic depiction of Jesus with hair like wool and eyes like flaming fire.

Throughout history our greatest artists have done their best to portray how Jesus may have appeared. I have yet to see any artistic depiction of Him that I feel comes close to capturing who He really was. I especially object to the anemic, weakling version that has been presented of the Master by some misdirected artists. He didn't walk around with a permanent halo above His head or a lamb wrapped around His neck.

Why didn't God give us a picture? I think it's because He knew our tendency to gravitate toward idols, pictures, and things instead of the true and living God. There's something in us that wants tangible objects that we can touch. If we can't touch it, we grow frustrated and make some kind of an image and imagine it represents God. Pretty soon we're bowing before the representation of Him—and that looks a lot like idolatry to me.

So we don't have any real descriptions of the physical Jesus. *But we can still see Him.* Oh, we can't *physically* see Him. If God were to roll away the heavens right now, poke His face through and say, "Hello, how are you? I'm God," no doubt we would all drop dead on the spot. No one can see God and live. All of His holiness and perfection would overwhelm all our unholiness and imperfection.

But in a real sense we *can* see Jesus. The apostle John had this very thing in mind when he told us, "That which we have seen and heard we declare to you, that you also may have fellowship with us; and truly our fellowship is with the Father and with His Son Jesus Christ. And these things we write to you that your joy may be full" (1 John 1:3-4).

John's wording in the original Greek text is interesting. His phrase "that which we have seen" could be rendered literally, "What we still see in our mind's eye." What John saw was still glowing on the canvas of his mind. What he heard was still ringing in his ears. "Yes," John wants us to know, "I was an eyewitness of Jesus. I was there."

John was privileged to be with Jesus throughout His earthly ministry. We read that he was the one leaning on the Master's chest, taking in His every word, even His whispers. That's the reason he was called "the disciple whom [Jesus] loved" (John 19:26).

It was this same John who said, "That which we have seen and heard we declare to you, that you also may have fellowship with us; and truly our fellowship is with the Father and with His Son Jesus Christ." In other words, "Yes, we had the privilege of walking and talking with the Master—but you can know Him in an intimate way just as we knew Him!"

Don't miss the phenomenal promise that John is giving us here. To *see* the Master—it was not just for a privileged few! All of us can know Him in this deeper sense. All of us have the unbelievable privilege of walking with the Lord of the Universe, of talking with Him daily, of asking Him to guide us, and expecting Him to enter into every facet of our lives.

Every Day with Jesus was written and designed to help you "see" Jesus in just this sense. As you walk with Him through the pages of this book, never lose sight of the fact that it's Jesus Christ Himself who invites you to look deeply in His loving eyes and take firm hold of His strong hands. He wants to keep you company as you walk through all of life.

So let's take this journey together as we spend every day with Jesus!

To find out why it is so important to spend time with Jesus, studying His life and words, read 1 John 2:1-6.

2

CHRISTMAS, B.C.

✄

*"In the beginning was the Word, and the Word
was with God, and the Word was God."*

—JOHN 1:1

THE CHRISTMAS STORY is far more profound than many of us may realize.

Long before there was a planet earth, long before a man named Adam and a woman named Eve ate of the forbidden fruit in a garden named Eden, long before Bethlehem was founded . . . a decision was made in eternity that Jesus Christ would come to this earth as a man and walk among us, die on the cross, and rise again on the third day.

The stunning truth is, God designed the Christmas story to make provision for our sins and failures even before there was a you and me!

Revelation 13:8 makes this clear: "The Lamb [was] slain from the foundation of the world." And C.S. Lewis succinctly explained why this was necessary when he wrote, "The Son of God became a man that men might become sons of God." Adam and Eve's sin in the garden didn't surprise God; even before He created the world He knew He would have to make provision for us.

Allow me to illustrate this with the procedure I once used

with my son Jonathan whenever he sat down with a bowl of cereal. I knew he was going to make a mess. I'm a father and I'd seen this before. So I made provision for his mess by placing a bib around his neck or putting a plastic tarp beneath his high chair (or perhaps even getting a nearby garden hose cranked up and ready to go—you get the idea). As a parent, I made provision for the mess I knew my son was going to make.

In the same way, God made provision for the mess that man was going to make. He knew before Adam sinned that he would do so and He knew it would be necessary for Jesus to come to this earth.

Think of it! Long before Bethlehem existed, everything was decided. Before Ruth gleaned wheat in the fields of Boaz. Before David grew up and lived as a young boy and later became the king of Israel and an ancestor of Jesus. Some 650 years before the birth of Christ, the prophet Micah said of Bethlehem, "But you, Bethlehem Ephrathah, though you are little among the thousands of Judah, yet out of you shall come forth to Me the One to be ruler in Israel, whose goings forth have been from of old, from everlasting" (Micah 5:2)—literally, "from the vanishing point."

When Jesus finally came, it had been more than 400 years since Israel last heard from a prophet, 400 years since the last miracle, 400 years since the appearance of an angel. The people were waiting. They were spiritually hungry. They were reaching out.

And when the time was just right, "God sent forth His Son, born of a woman, born under the law, to redeem those who were under the law, that we might receive the adoption as sons. And because you are sons, God has sent forth the Spirit of His Son into your hearts, crying out, 'Abba, Father!'" (Galatians 4:4-6).

We think of Christmas as the celebration of a great arrival, and so it is. But it's also the celebration of a tremendous *departure*. Never forget that Jesus came because a decision had been made that He should leave heaven.

Did you know we have a record of His good-bye message? Hebrews 10:5-7 says, "When He came into the world, [Jesus] said: 'Sacrifice and offering You did not desire, but a body You have prepared for Me. In burnt offerings and sacrifices for sin You had no pleasure.' Then I said, 'Behold, I have come—in the volume of the book it is written of Me—to do Your will, O God.'" Those were the words of Jesus to His Father. The animal sacrifices pointed to what Jesus would ultimately accomplish as the Lamb of God who takes away the sin of the world. God must become a man; there must be a final and complete sacrifice.

This should give you great comfort. God has always known that you could never measure up to His perfection. He never expected you to! Instead, He provided you with His spotless, pure Son, who came to earth and died in your place—and you need to do nothing else but accept His gift of salvation.

Are you struggling with sin? Is there a part of your past that keeps coming back to haunt you? Do you feel as though the Christian life is too difficult?

If so, then may I remind you that God never intended for you to live up to His standards on your own? He made provision for you—and your messes—through His Son. And once you accept that provision, your life is hidden in Christ. As Paul wrote in Galatians 2:20, "I have been crucified with Christ; it is no longer I who live, but Christ lives in me."

If by faith you have placed your trust in Jesus Christ, that truth should give you tremendous strength and courage. It does me! The Lord does not want us to rely on *our* strength, but on *His* strength. He knows that we are but dust (*see* Psalm 103:14).

It's exactly for that reason that when Jesus came to earth the first time, He came as a servant, not a king. He had to clean us up and take care of our messes before we would be fit to be seated at the marriage supper of the spotless Lamb.

"No man ever loved like Jesus. He taught the blind to see and the dumb to speak. He died on the cross to save us. He bore our sins. And now God says, 'Because He did, I can forgive you.'"

—*Billy Graham*

3

WITH GOD, ALL THINGS ARE POSSIBLE

✦

"For with God nothing will be impossible."

—LUKE 1:37

GOD WORKS IN AN ASTONISHING number of ways in our world. Sometimes He works through miraculous means; at other times through normal means. Unfortunately, when He chooses the supernatural, we often have trouble believing it. The virgin birth is a classic example of this.

Some people today say you don't need to believe in the virgin birth. They say if you believe merely in the death and resurrection of Jesus, that's sufficient. They claim the virgin birth is not really important and it's probably just some early fable or myth to be easily discounted.

I reject that completely. If Jesus was not supernaturally conceived in the womb of Mary, then He may have been a great teacher and a wonderful prophet, but He was still merely a man. That means that when He died on the cross, it would have been only a man dying—a sinful man who could do nothing for the condition of our lost souls.

No, the supernatural conception and birth of Jesus was both unique and miraculous. The doctrine of the virgin birth is a foundational truth, a bedrock teaching. It is an absolutely essential Christian belief.

God had to walk among us, for we are told in Isaiah 9:6, "Unto us a Child is born, unto us a Son is given; and the government will be upon His shoulder. And His name will be called Wonderful, Counselor, Mighty God, Everlasting Father, Prince of Peace."

Jesus was not merely God's Son. He was God the Son. Philippians 2:6-7 tells us that He emptied Himself and took upon Himself the form of a servant, coming in the likeness of sinful flesh. Note that He was not sinful flesh; He was in the *likeness* of it only. Why? Because the Father of Jesus was God.

The blood that flows in your veins right now is the same blood type as your father's. In the same way, the blood that flowed in the veins of Jesus was the blood that God had given to Him. When His blood was shed on the cross, no blood like it had ever been shed at any time on earth. John writes, "If we confess our sins, He is faithful and just to forgive us our sins and to cleanse us from all unrighteousness" (1 John 1:9). It's that special blood shed by God the Son that cleanses us, and no other. Thus it is essential not only to believe in the death and resurrection and bodily return of Jesus, but also that He was supernaturally conceived in the womb of the virgin.

Joseph was not Jesus' natural father. It is true that Jesus had to come from the tribe and lineage of David, and Joseph was in this line. But Joseph was not the only descendant of David; Mary descended from David, too! In Jesus' veins flowed the blood of a direct descendant of David through Mary, because she too was of this line.

The Pharisees, like many liberal theologians of our day, questioned Jesus' supernatural conception. In John 8:41 they told Jesus, "We were not born of fornication; we have one Father—God." That was an insult. They were implying to Jesus, "At least we weren't illegitimate."

They knew Mary had become pregnant before marrying Joseph. And since they refused to believe He was the Messiah, they claimed He was illegitimate. They did not want to believe that He really was God the Son.

Is this a problem for you, too? Is it too hard to believe that God could have a virgin give birth? The way I look at it, if you can believe Genesis 1:1, the rest of the Bible is easy: "In the beginning God created the heavens and the earth." Now, is that hard for you to believe? If it isn't, then the virgin birth isn't going to be hard. Nor is any other miracle we read of in Scripture.

You say, "But how could it be?" The answer is found in Luke 1:37: "With God nothing will be impossible." I can't logically explain it to you. I can't medically explain it to you. I can't scientifically explain it to you. Quite simply, the virgin birth was a supernatural miracle of God, one that He performed uniquely in this situation.

Luke 1:35 does add one interesting detail. To Mary it was prophesied, "The Holy Spirit will come upon you, and the power of the Highest will overshadow you." The word "overshadow" was a term applied to the presence of God in the Holy of holies in the Jewish tabernacle and temple. Think about that! Mary's womb became a Holy of holies for the Son of God, where He was conceived supernaturally. With God, all things are possible.

No wonder the angel Gabriel instructed Mary to call her son "Jesus." To Joseph, Gabriel said, "You shall call His name JESUS, for He will save His people from their sins" (Matthew 1:21).

The name *Jesus* means "Yahweh is salvation." It was a common name at the time—many little boys were running around with the name. But there was only one person who ever fully embodied the meaning of the name, and He was born in a stable to a virgin named Mary.

We call Him Jesus of Nazareth, but we could also call Him Jesus of Heaven. And it is this virgin-born Son of God who saves *us* from our sins. This one, and no other.

To better understand the uniqueness of Christ's birth, read Luke 1:26-55, which chronicles Mary's response to the message that she would bear the Messiah.

4

THE STORY OF STORIES

*"The book of the genealogy of Jesus Christ,
the Son of David, the Son of Abraham."*

—MATTHEW 1:1

SOMETIMES WE WONDER if God could ever use people like us. With all our flaws, shortcomings, and sins, it seems unlikely, if not impossible.

But one look at the genealogy of none less than Jesus Christ should show us that indeed, there is hope.

Jesus' genealogy features many unsavory characters, all of whom demonstrate God's grace from the word go. Flawless men and women do not populate this list.

Consider both David and Abraham. David, though a great king, was guilty of adultery and murder. Abraham, rightly called the father of faith, suffered a number of lapses in his own faith when he fell into the habit of deception. Yet God included both David and Abraham in the Messianic line.

Other names in Matthew's genealogy also call for attention. Notice especially the women. Five are listed, including Mary. The other four all were saddled with questionable reputations. These were sinful women, not known for their virtue or godliness. They weren't even Jewish, yet God included them in the Messianic line.

First we read of Tamar (Matthew 1:3). Tamar's story is filled with deception and blemished by sordid accounts of prostitution—certainly she was not a godly woman. Nonetheless, by the grace of God she was included in the line of the Messiah. You can read her story in Genesis 38.

Then there's Rahab (Matthew 1:5). She was a prostitute working in Jericho when she met two Jewish spies sent ahead to check out the city prior to the Israeli invasion. Rahab took in these men and hid them from the other inhabitants of Jericho. As a result, when the city fell to Israel, Rahab's life was spared. God in His grace not only spared her, but brought her into the Messianic line as the wife of Salmon, the mother of the godly Boaz, who was David's great-grandfather.

Then there's Ruth (Matthew 1:5). Ruth was a Moabitess. Her people resulted from an incestuous one-night fling between Lot and his daughters. One of the children born of that ungodly union was a man named Moab, whose tribe came to be known as the Moabites. They were idol worshipers, not believers in the true God.

Ruth left her people when her Jewish husband died, choosing to return with her mother-in-law Naomi to Israel. Ruth said to Naomi, "Wherever you go, I will go; and wherever you lodge, I will lodge; your people shall be my people, and your God, my God" (Ruth 1:16). Ruth the Moabitess went with Naomi the Jew back to Naomi's homeland, back to Bethlehem. In time Ruth met Boaz, who married her and became her kinsman-redeemer. Ruth became the grandmother of Israel's greatest king, David, and thus was included in the Messianic line.

We also read of Bathsheba, although she is not mentioned by name (Matthew 1:6). She is identified as "her who had been the wife of Uriah." David took her from her husband and engaged in an adulterous relationship with her, yet she was included in the Messianic line.

Now, what's the point of rehearsing all this? It shows that

the genealogy of Jesus proves not only His full humanity, but that God's grace was operative from the very beginning.

When we have sinned—and we all do—sometimes we wonder, *Is there any hope for me? Is there any forgiveness for me?* The answer is found in one look at the line of the Messiah Himself! God's grace was at work from the beginning.

Matthew's genealogy of Jesus repeatedly emphasizes the grace of God. God extended His grace to the likes of Abraham and David, who despite their shortcomings, were included in the Messianic line. He extended His grace to Tamar, Rahab, Ruth, and Bathsheba. And He extends it to you, today.

The genealogy of Jesus paints an awesome picture of all that God has done for us. And while you can't become a part of the physical line of Jesus, you can become part of His family. Right where you are. Whatever your history. Whatever your heritage.

My guess is, you'll fit right in.

To see how God changes people and uses them for His purposes, read the apostle Paul's testimony in Acts 26:1-29.

5

THE HIGHEST TO THE LOWEST

⚔

*"Then the shepherds returned, glorifying and praising God for
all the things that they had heard and seen, as it was told them."*

—LUKE 2:20

IT'S FUN TO SPECULATE what the angels might have discussed when choosing who should first hear about the birth of Jesus.

Perhaps their discussion went something like this: "To whom shall we go? To Caesar's court to tell Augustus he'd better move over? Or perhaps to that paranoid Herod to tell him the King has been born and there is nothing he can do to stop it? Maybe we should go to the religious people who ought to be studying the Scriptures about the coming of Messiah. No, no, that won't do. Say, let's go to the lowest of the low. Let's go to the people no one else even talks to. Let's go to the ones who are hurting. Let's go to the shepherds."

Whatever the case, the fact that God directed them to a group of shepherds is super significant. We don't realize how much shepherds were despised and hated. I can't even think of a contemporary analogy. Let me just put it like this: God chose those who occupied what was perhaps the lowest rung on the social ladder.

Shepherds were hated in those days. They were thought to be shady, dishonest, and unscrupulous. The testimony of a shepherd was not even admissible in a court of law. They were pushed out and shunned by the religious people because they were unable to observe the ceremonial hand washings practiced in the temple. Shepherding was looked upon as the vilest kind of work possible. Despite the fact that both Moses and David had been shepherds, somehow through the years the profession had been demoted to the lowest of the low.

Try to imagine the shepherds' surprise, then, when the angels appeared to them. They must have thought, *Oh, we're in trouble now! Even the angels are mad at us. Everyone else hates us and now the angels have come to get us!*

But that's not what happened. In essence, the angels said, "We have good news for you! Though you may be despised and rejected and outcasts in your society, a Savior is born—and we wanted to tell you first!"

The message was unbelievably good news. Glad tidings. It was a message of peace to a people who had known much war. Even though the *Pax Romana*, the Roman peace, had been in effect for many years, there was nothing but emptiness in the hearts of the people. Their hearts knew no peace.

In fact, one philosopher of that day said, "While the emperor may give peace from war on land and sea, he's unable to give peace from passion, greed and envy. He cannot give peace of heart, for which man yearns more than even for outward peace."

How right he was! The emperor could not give anyone peace inside. During this time taxes were high. Unemployment was rampant. Rome ran a military state and public morals were slipping lower with each passing day. Neither Roman law, Greek philosophy, nor even Jewish religion could meet the needs inside of the people. What emptiness; what turmoil!

In such a context, it's easy to see why the angelic message was welcomed as such good news: "Behold, I bring you good tidings of great joy which will be to all people. For there is born to you this day in the city of David a Savior, who is Christ the Lord" (Luke 2:10-11).

If no human being understood the significance of this event, the angels did. While men saw only Jesus' arrival, the angels also saw His departure. They knew how much He left behind, how much He gave. They knew the first Christmas gift was not that which the wise men gave to the child Jesus, but the gift of God to us in the Person of His beloved only Son.

It's been said that love can be measured by gifts—not by how much they cost, but how much they cost *you*. Some people are so well off financially they could write out a check for a thousand dollars and not even notice it. Such a check for others would represent their entire life savings. The first group gives out of their abundance; the other gives everything they have.

God could have given out of His abundance to us. He could have sent us galaxies of gold—but what kind of sacrifice would that have been? Gold lines the streets of heaven; it's the asphalt of paradise. And it would have been no great sacrifice.

But when God gave His only Son, the ultimate gift, it became impossible to miss how much our redemption really cost. Love is known by the obstacles it overcomes. God overcame the obstacle of our sin and loved us and presented us with this infinitely precious gift.

I don't know how much of this the shepherds grasped, but it's quite possible they understood it better than anyone else. It may well be that these shepherds keeping watch over their flocks by night were caring for the very sheep that would be used in the temple sacrifices. If so, in one sense you could say they were making it temporarily possible for God and man to have communion. Thus, it was appropriate that Jesus' birth was first announced to them.

In any event, the outcast shepherds were the first to receive the message that the Good Shepherd had come. To men who watched these lambs came the message that the Lamb of God who would take away the sin of the world had arrived on planet

17

earth. And they responded just as we all should: by glorifying and praising God for His matchless gift. It's the only response that makes sense.

After the shepherds heard this wonderful message, they couldn't contain themselves. Luke 2:17 tells us "when they had seen Him, they made widely known the saying which was told them concerning this Child." Consider how God in His grace has reached out to you. Today or tomorrow, why don't you follow the example of the shepherds and tell at least one person about Jesus?

6

HAVE YOU LOST HIM?

❧

"And the Child grew and became strong in spirit, filled
with wisdom; and the grace of God was upon Him."

—LUKE 2:40

A LITTLE BOY ONCE VISITED an old, ornate church and
saw candles lit all around the inside of the building. He thought
it was a birthday party for Jesus, so he started blowing out the
candles and singing, "Happy Birthday" to God. Just as the boy
was leaving, a minister caught sight of what he was doing. The
minister thought, *It's about time this young man learned to have re-*
spect for God. He knew where the boy's family lived and decided to
pay a visit to his mother.

When the minister arrived at the boy's house, he told the
mother, "I want to talk to your son." The mother went upstairs
and brought down the little boy. The minister looked at the boy
square in the eyes and asked, "Young man, where is God?" The
question startled the lad and his eyes got big, but he said nothing. So the minister said again, "Where is God?" The question
made the little boy edgy and his eyes got even bigger, but still he
made no reply. For the third time the minister said, "Tell me,
where is God?" The boy was scared now and fled upstairs to his
mother. Breathlessly, he cried out, "Mommy, mommy, they lost
God at that church and they think I took Him."

Have you ever "lost God"? Don't be too quick to answer in the negative—it's much easier to do than it might seem. In a sense, even Jesus' parents were guilty of it; it happened when Jesus was about twelve years old. But before we look at that story, it might be helpful to consider the early days of Jesus' life.

In reality, Scripture doesn't speak much about the first dozen years of Jesus' time on earth. Some don't like that and want to try to fill in the blanks. One nonbiblical book called the Gospel of Thomas contains some very strange stories about the childhood of Jesus. One tells how Jesus was fond of throwing little clumps of mud into the air and then watching them turn into birds and fly away. Another describes how Jesus cursed a bully who harassed Him. But the Jesus we read about in the Gospels would never have done such things. That is one of the reasons why the Gospel of Thomas is not in our Bibles.

Still, most of us are curious about what Jesus was like as a child. It's interesting that God gives us a big blank—we just don't know. God did not choose to reveal that to us.

Of course, we do know a few things about His childhood. We know that when He was about two years old the wise men came to visit Him. Contrary to popular manger scenes, they did not visit the stable in Bethlehem. Scripture says they came when He was a child living in a home.

We also know that Jesus was the son of a carpenter. He learned that trade and probably built plows, furniture, even homes. We know He was schooled in the Scripture. He observed the law and went to the temple.

We know that He was the only child who ever grew up without the handicap of original sin. He did not grow as we do when we become Christians, from sinfulness to obedience. He grew from obedience to higher levels of obedience, from faith to faith, from grace to grace, from strength to strength. How that happened I don't know; Scripture doesn't tell us.

Only one story is related to us about Jesus as a youth—the

one where Mary and Joseph lost Him at the temple when He was twelve years old.

It happened like this: In those days travelers would send the women ahead a day's journey; the men joined them later. When it was time for Jesus' family to leave Jerusalem, Mary went ahead, thinking Jesus was with Joseph. Meanwhile, Joseph thought Jesus had accompanied Mary. When the pair finally rejoined each other, they discovered Jesus wasn't with either of them. So they hurriedly returned to Jerusalem and found Jesus in the temple, listening to the scribes and asking questions (*see* Luke 2:46).

When they found their son, Mary asked Him, "Son, why have You done this to us? Look, Your father and I have sought You anxiously" (Luke 2:48). She didn't understand who it was she had growing up beneath her roof. That's why Jesus responded to her, "Why is it that you sought Me? Did you not know that I must be about My Father's business?" (Luke 2:49). It's clear that even at this young age Jesus knew who He was. Nevertheless, He submitted to His parents' authority and returned to Nazareth with them.

I think it's fascinating that Jesus' parents had breakfast, lunch, and dinner without taking note of Jesus. Oh, they hadn't stopped loving Him. They hadn't lost their faith in Him. They just lost Him. They had allowed Jesus to be crowded from their thoughts because they had been so involved in all the religious activities: going to the temple, celebrating the feasts, attending the services. They just forgot all about Him.

We also can lose sight of Him. We can forget about God. Oh, we don't stop loving God. We don't stop believing in God. But quite honestly, we forget about Him.

Remember that no matter how noble or good a certain thing is in and of itself, anything that comes between us and Jesus can become sin. We must not become so preoccupied with religious activity that we forget about Jesus. We should hate to take a single step without Him. Like Jesus, we too must be about our

Father's business—and we won't manage that unless we walk with Him every moment of our lives.

Read the story of Jesus' visit to the home of Mary and Martha in Luke 10:38-42. It seems Martha missed an important lesson which Mary learned. What was it?

7

BEHOLD THE LAMB!

✧

"The next day John saw Jesus coming toward him, and said,
'Behold! The Lamb of God who takes away the sin of the world!'"

—JOHN 1:29

IN OUR CULTURE, if you were to say of someone, "He's a real Superman!" it's a sure bet everybody would know what you meant. In the same way, when John the Baptist said of Jesus, "Behold! The Lamb of God who takes away the sin of the world," his meaning was not lost on his listeners.

Every Jew immediately understood what John meant by the Lamb of God. The law taught them to atone for their sins by bringing an animal sacrifice, perhaps a lamb or a ram. A priest would take the animal, kill it, then symbolically take the sin of the worshiper and place it on the animal. Everyone knew what it was to see lambs slain to atone for their sins.

Jews would think back to the Passover when God told them to take a lamb, slay it, and put the blood on their doorposts. Many Jewish homes would take this lamb into the house as a pet. Can you imagine having to sacrifice your dog? Or your favorite cat? But they intentionally did it so that real affection would develop, thus heightening the sense of loss when the animal was finally killed. They would feel the pain of it and realize the pain God felt when they sinned against Him.

Incidentally, there is an interesting progression in the commands about the Passover lamb (*see* Exodus 12:3-5). First God said take "a" lamb. Then "the" lamb. Then "your" lamb. It moves from the impersonal to the personal.

That's how we come to know God. First He is "a" god. A lamb. There's a god out there and Jesus is one among many. Then one day we realize that He's "the" Lamb of God. Not just a god, not just one among many, but the one and true God—and Jesus is the one and true way to get to the Father. Last, I realize He's "my" Lamb. I take Him as my own.

That's the progression John started in his disciples when he said, "Behold! The Lamb of God who takes away the sin of the world!" He was announcing a new covenant, a new opportunity to know God whereby we no longer had to offer animal sacrifices. Only one, final sacrifice remained: Jesus, the Lamb of God.

It's as essential for us to believe John's testimony as it was for his own disciples. Jesus Christ is the Lamb of God who takes away the sin of the world. The Bible says that one day all those who have rejected Jesus will stand at the judgment seat of God, and only those who have their names written in the Lamb's book of life will enter in.

John was such a credible witness that several of his disciples immediately left him to follow Jesus. They realized it wasn't enough merely to recognize the uniqueness of Jesus. They had to act on it. They could have said, "John, that's great. He's the Lamb of God who takes away the sin of the world. So what do you want to do now?"

It's not enough to know Jesus is God, however. It's not enough to believe He died on the cross for your sin and rose again from the dead. *You must follow Him.*

But don't do so without thinking. When Jesus saw these new followers, He turned to them and asked, "What do you seek?" (John 1:38). In other words, What is it you're after? What do you boys want?

There is more to this question than immediately meets the

eye. Jesus did not mean to ask them only what they were seeking at that moment, but for all time. It's a question God is asking every one of us. What are you seeking in life? What do you desire in life? What do you want?

The question made these men uncomfortable, and they reacted like many of us would in a similar situation: They tried to change the subject. "Rabbi, where are You staying?" they asked.

These men probably thought Jesus lived in some palatial castle or beautiful mansion with servants waiting upon Him. But the Lord had no mansion. He had no castle. He Himself said, "Foxes have holes and birds of the air have nests, but the Son of Man has nowhere to lay His head" (Luke 9:58).

"Come and see," Jesus told them. He meant more than, "Come and see where I live." He was drawing them closer—and without a doubt they saw.

It is believed John the apostle was one of these two men. John watched Jesus closely during His earthly ministry and at the end of his life testified that he had indeed seen. He saw the Lord for the three years of His earthly ministry. He saw Him in the years that followed as he grew closer to the Lord. And he saw Him when Jesus unveiled to him the events of the last days in the book of Revelation. Jesus had said, "Come and see," and John did just that.

Now it's your turn. *You* can come and see. *You* can come and know God. Don't let anything hold you back. Come and see! You won't be disappointed.

"The greatest proof of Christianity for others is not how far a man can logically analyze his reasons for believing, but how far in practice he will stake his life on his belief."

—*T.S. Eliot*

8

WHY DID HE COME?

✻

"The Spirit of the LORD is upon Me, because He has anointed Me to preach the gospel to the poor. He has sent Me to heal the brokenhearted, to preach deliverance to the captives and recovery of sight to the blind, to set at liberty those who are oppressed, to preach the acceptable year of the LORD."

—LUKE 4:18-19

SOMETIMES WE BECOME so familiar with spiritual things that we become immune to them. It's almost as if we are inoculated against the truth.

That is my greatest concern for children being reared in the homes of committed Christians. From the crib they've heard about Jesus. They've listened to stories from Scripture. They know about God's plan for their lives. Yet somehow they become immune to all of it and forget why Jesus came.

Why did He come? What was the purpose of His coming? Jesus states it plainly in Luke 4:18-19.

First, He talks about the "poor." This does not mean those who are poor in the material sense, but describes the bankruptcy of one's spiritual condition. Jesus came to preach the gospel to the spiritually dead, those who are not alive in the spiritual dimension, anyone who has not yet been born again.

Jesus is saying, "God has called me to speak to these who are spiritually dead." We all fit in that category before we knew the Lord.

Next He says He came "to preach deliverance to the captives"—prisoners of war, if you will. Before you knew the Lord, you were a captive of Satan. The Bible says you were held captive by him to do his will. You were taken alive. You were his prisoner of war (POW). Then Jesus came and delivered you from Satan's POW camp. He brought you to life and you became His servant.

It's as if Jesus says to you today, "I've come to preach deliverance to the prisoners of war. I've come to free you from that bondage. I've come to redeem you."

The word "redeem" is a powerful term. It can be translated "to buy out of a slave market." In ancient times it was used in that context. Slavery was commonplace, as were slave auctions. Auctioneers would put shackled slaves up on a pedestal and interested buyers would stand around and make bids.

From Jesus' perspective, it was as though you were on that pedestal, shackled, the bidding started for you . . . and Jesus outbid everyone in the place. Then He took you down from that place of shame, unlocked your handcuffs, and said, "All right, you can go now. You're free." He bought you out of a slave market. He bought you out of sin. He freed you from all the things that used to shackle you. He brought deliverance to the captives.

He also brought "recovery of sight to the blind." He came to open wide the eyes of the prisoners. After He took you out of prison and released you from being a POW, He opened your eyes to see new things. Life began to look different. You started seeing what was really going on around you. You started seeing the spiritual conflict raging on all sides. Your eyes were opened.

Last, Jesus says He came to bring freedom to the oppressed: "to set at liberty those who are oppressed, to preach the acceptable year of the LORD." The word "oppressed" or "bruised" could also be translated "those who are crushed with life"—those who are shattered, broken down, mistreated.

It's quite possible someone is reading these words right now whose own life is shattered. You've been mistreated, broken down. If that's you, I have good news for you: Jesus knows just how you feel. The Bible says He looked at the multitudes who gathered around Him and saw them as sheep without a shepherd, distressed and downcast. "Distressed" was a term used of sheep which had been lacerated and bruised by fleecing. "Downcast" described someone who was exhausted and ready to quit.

Jesus saw people as ripped off, bruised, taken advantage of, exhausted, and ready to quit. And not only did Jesus see us that way, but as the Son of God, He knew what it was to suffer that kind of treatment Himself.

To these people—people such as us—Jesus came. To the poor, the spiritually bankrupt. To the brokenhearted. To the prisoners of war. To those who lack spiritual sight. To those who have been crushed with life. To all of us, He came. He came for *you*.

May I ask, is it time now that you came to Him?

If you don't yet know Christ, you are that person who is spiritually blind. You're that POW of sin. You're the one who is brokenhearted. You're the one who needs life in the spiritual dimension. You're the stray sheep that He's after.

Jesus is saying to you, "Come to Me, all you who labor and are heavy laden, and I will give you rest." He wants to give you relief and refreshment for your soul. He wants to give you life.

Don't let the familiarity of this story blind you to its spiritual, eternal, and *personal* significance. Jesus came for *you*.

Are you safe within His care?

Excellency of Christ

He is a path, if any be misled;
He is a robe, if any naked be;
If any chance to hunger, he is bread;

If any be a bondman, he is free;
If any be but weak, how strong is He!

To dead men life is He, to sick men, health;
To blind men, sight, and to the needy, wealth;
A pleasure without loss, a treasure without stealth.

9

ON THE MOUNTAINTOP

✴

"He took Peter, John, and James and went up on the mountain to pray.
And as He prayed, the appearance of His face was altered,
and His robe became white and glistening. Then behold,
two men talked with Him, who were Moses and Elijah."

—LUKE 9:28-30

HAVE YOU EVER HAD a mountaintop experience with God? A moment during worship or prayer when you felt so near to God it was as though you could reach out and touch Him? A moment when the spiritual seemed more real than the physical?

Peter, James, and John never forgot their mountaintop experience when Jesus took them to what we call the Mount of Transfiguration. The Greek word used to speak of the transfiguration also underlies the English term "metamorphosis," which describes a change on the outside that comes from the inside.

We tend to think of the transfiguration as a miracle because Jesus shone like the sun. But that wasn't the miracle at all. The miracle was not that He shone on the mountain, but that He didn't shine the rest of the time! The transfiguration merely gave the disciples a glimpse of who Jesus really was. Here on the mountain, just for a moment, He pulled back the veil, so to speak, on His deity.

Just so the disciples didn't miss the significance of the occasion, no less than Moses and Elijah appeared with Jesus, chatting with Him. This is noteworthy because Moses and Elijah occupy unique positions in the Old Testament. Moses symbolizes the law; Elijah, the prophets. The New Testament often referred to the Old Testament by the phrase "the law and the prophets," and here were the chief representatives of the law and the prophets, speaking with the One who fulfilled everything they pointed to.

What did they discuss? We read in Luke 9:31 that they spoke about His coming execution. The text calls it "His decease." It's noteworthy that the word "decease" means "exodus." Thus it's related to the word used to describe the departure (or exodus) of Israel from Egypt. Moses was talking to Jesus about the exodus!

Moses knew about an exodus, too. He led approximately 3 million whining people through the wilderness for 40 years to a promised land that he himself was not allowed to enter . . . until this glorious meeting with the Savior. It took him awhile—in fact, hundreds of years—but Moses finally did make it to the promised land. And what an arrival! To finally set foot on that sacred soil, accompanied by no less than the Lord of Glory Himself!

I doubt they spoke much about the ancient exodus, however. The topic at hand was a greater exodus—*His* exodus. An exodus that would take place through Jesus' death, resurrection, and ascension. An exodus where God's people would be freed from bondage and led through the gates of heaven.

No doubt it was a bittersweet meeting, both sober and joyous. Joyous because Moses and Elijah recognized they stood in the presence of their Maker. Bitter and sober because they realized the horrific suffering He would have to undergo.

Incredibly, Peter was catching a little shut-eye for most of this. Waking up and rubbing his eyes, he saw Moses and Elijah there with the transfigured Jesus. In a moment of excitement, Peter blurted out, "It is good for us to be here" (Luke 9:33).

One wonders what might have happened behind the scenes when this sleepy disciple spoke up. Did Moses turn to Jesus and say, "Who's that?" Jesus might have replied, "Oh, that's Rock. He's one of my disciples." The only thing we know for sure is that the Bible reports Peter said this because he did not know what to say.

Have you ever said something regrettable because you did not know what to say? You wanted to make a great impression. You went in for that job interview and wanted to impress everyone with your prodigious abilities, but you blurted out something you immediately regretted. "Why did I say that?" you chided yourself. Or perhaps on that first date you stuck your foot in your mouth. There's an old Swedish proverb that says, "Better to be silent and thought a fool than to open your mouth and dispel all doubt."

Peter dispelled all doubt. He was so moved by the scene, he did not know what to say. But he said it anyway: "Let us make three tabernacles: one for You, one for Moses, and one for Elijah" (Luke 9:33).

No one ever responded to Peter's comments. But Someone did speak on the heels of Peter's suggestion, and His words put the capstone on the entire event. No sooner had Peter spoken up than a cloud overshadowed the group and a voice boomed out of the cloud, saying, "This is My beloved Son. Hear Him!" (Luke 9:35).

And then, just as suddenly as the transfiguration had begun, it was over. The cloud disappeared and Moses and Elijah with it. Jesus will not shine again on this earth until the day He returns in power and great glory.

When that day comes—and it may not be far off—take care that you don't follow Peter's example. Don't stick your foot in your mouth. In fact, don't say anything. Not a word.

Just stand in awe of the King of the Universe. I guarantee you, it won't be hard.

David loved worshiping God, and he often wrote about it in the Psalms. Read Psalm 27 and notice how often David mentions his desire to seek the Lord.

10

THE KING ARRIVES

"The next day a great multitude that had come to the feast, when they heard that Jesus was coming to Jerusalem, took branches of palm trees and went out to meet Him, and cried out: 'Hosanna! "Blessed is He who comes in the name of the LORD!" The King of Israel!'"

—JOHN 12:12-13

CELEBRATIONS CAN BE A LOT OF FUN. Just watch the next time a football team wins the Super Bowl or a presidential candidate secures enough votes to win the electoral college. People will be screaming, clapping, crying, jumping up and down, and kissing each other. They'll be clapping each other on the back, gathering for group hugs, and just generally carrying on. They're happy and they don't care who knows it.

It was exactly that kind of atmosphere that greeted Jesus the day He made His way into Jerusalem on a donkey. The people were in a frenzy. They laid palm branches at His feet and cried out, "Hosanna!" There was excitement in the air, a sense of celebration. It was so thick you could feel it.

Jesus had just performed perhaps the most dramatic of all of His miracles, the resurrection of a man who had been in a tomb for four days. Jesus had become the talk of the town—everyone was interested in Him. There was only one problem:

The people believed Christ was coming to establish His earthly kingdom.

And it wasn't only the multitudes who were swept up into such an expectation. The disciples also believed it. They thought they were going to share in His kingdom. They hoped Christ was going to overthrow the tyranny of Rome and take immediate control. His true purpose in coming seemed to go over their heads.

That's why they decided to celebrate. They laid out palm branches and began to cry, "Hosanna!" to the son of David. That word "hosanna" is both a word of praise and a word that means "save now." In effect, the people were saying, "All right, Lord, do it! Now is the time. Seize the opportunity. You're very popular, very big. Momentum is working for you. This is the moment! Go for it! We're behind you."

Without question this was the high point of Jesus' human popularity. And few could miss the deep significance of this event.

The Romans would immediately note its symbolism. When a Roman hero returned to his hometown from the battlefield, the townspeople would lay palm branches at his feet and sing his praises. The Romans would look at Jesus on this day and ask, "What does this mean? They're treating Him like a military hero. He's marching through the streets like a king."

The Jews would instantly recognize this event as a fulfillment of Bible prophecy. Zechariah 9:9 says, "Rejoice greatly, O daughter of Zion! Shout, O daughter of Jerusalem! Behold, your King is coming to you; He is just and having salvation, lowly and riding on a donkey, a colt, the foal of a donkey." The Jews would understand He was coming as their Messiah, fulfilling a Messianic prophecy.

And of course, Jesus fully understood the day's significance. He had entered the city on this day in a way specifically designed to draw attention to Himself. His hour had finally come.

How many times we read of Jesus saying in the Gospels, "My hour has not yet come"! But now His hour *had* finally come. On at least one other occasion the people tried to make Him king, but He had rejected their advances. Now, in a deliberate attempt to call attention to Himself, He arrives with pomp and encourages the people's praise and adulation.

In a sense, Jesus was forcing the hands of the authorities. A warrant had already been issued for His arrest. He was a marked man. Annas, the high priest, had demanded that any information as to the whereabouts of Jesus be reported to the authorities. Despite that, Jesus deliberately chose to enter the city as a king. Instead of laying low and hiding, Jesus came openly and publicly, forcing the authorities to respond.

He would not enter the city as a victim, but as a victor. He was in complete control of His circumstances, knowing that His ultimate goal was to get to the cross.

However, the people's cries of "Hosanna!" were misdirected. He was not coming at that time to establish an earthly kingdom; He was coming to die on a cross. He wasn't going to be placed on a throne of gold; He would be placed on a cross of wood. He wasn't going to wear a crown of jewels; He was going to wear a crown of thorns.

Jesus knew the real score. He saw beyond the euphoria and adulation and knew full well that His crucifixion lay just around the corner. He knew He was coming to die.

Yes, it's true that on this day many people went after Jesus. It's true they sang His praises. But it is also true that a few days later many of those same fickle people cried out, "Crucify Him!"

How about you? Do you cry out, "Hosanna!" when things look promising, but, "Crucify Him!" when they don't? Or are you committed to Jesus of Nazareth whatever your personal circumstances? The answer you give will determine the quality of your entire spiritual life.

John Wesley said, "If I had 300 men who feared nothing but God, hated nothing but sin, and were determined to know nothing among men but Jesus Christ, and Him crucified, I would set the world on fire." Would you be one of those 300?

11

DARK STORM RISING

✤

"Now as He drew near, He saw the city and wept over it."

—LUKE 19:41

CHARLES DICKENS created one of literature's most memorable first lines when, in his novel *A Tale of Two Cities*, he wrote, "It was the best of times, it was the worst of times." He was writing about the French Revolution, but he might as well have been describing the events surrounding Jesus' final visit to Jerusalem.

In the middle of a joyous, frenzied celebration, filled with shouting, palm-waving, and loud rejoicing, Jesus moved off to one side . . . and wept.

Of course, this is not the only time that Jesus wept. The shortest verse in the Bible is John 11:35, "Jesus wept." It describes the scene just before Jesus raised His friend Lazarus from the dead.

But here as Jesus comes to Jerusalem, He weeps. The word "wept" in Luke 19:41 is different from the Greek term used in John 11:35. It means he audibly sobbed, as one who mourns for the dead. In Lazarus's case He quietly wept; here He openly sobs.

Imagine the surprise of the disciples. They've joined with the crowd in singing, "Hosanna to the son of David!" This is their moment in the limelight. They're celebrating. They're exulting. And suddenly they look over to Jesus, and He's staring at the city of Jerusalem and weeping openly. *What is wrong with You, Lord?* they must have thought. *Why are You doing this?*

Why did He weep? Possibly because His ministry was almost over. His time was short. By and large He had been rejected. He had healed their sick, raised their dead, fed their hungry, and forgiven their sins. Yet they had rejected Him and turned away. Isaiah 53 says He was "despised and rejected by men . . . and we did not esteem Him" (verse 3).

Imagine how Jesus felt. He had just poured Himself out. He realized that in a few days the very people who were crying out, "Hosanna!" would be screaming, "Crucify Him!" The same lips that uttered His praises would soon be saying, "His blood be on us and on our children" (Matthew 27:25).

He realized that in a short time one of His very own disciples, who had seen His miracles and heard His teachings, would turn on Him and betray Him for 30 pieces of silver. He knew that in a little while Herod and Pilate, formerly mortal enemies, would come together to plot how they might rid themselves of Jesus. He knew it was just a short time until Peter would deny Him three times. He knew all of this. And it broke His heart.

No doubt He wept not because of what the people were doing to Him, but what they were doing to themselves. He realized the consequences of their disobedience, the judgment they would bring upon themselves because they did not know the time of their visitation (Luke 19:44).

Jesus knew the future. Looking ahead, He saw the destruction that was coming. He prophesied to them, "For the days will come upon you when your enemies will build an embankment around you, surround you and close you in on every side, and level you, and your children within you, to the ground; and they will not leave in you one stone upon another" (Luke 19:43).

Forty years later, this all took place just as He had predicted. In A.D. 70 Titus and the Roman legions rode to Jerusalem and in a siege lasting 143 days killed 600,000 Jews and took thousands more captive.

The Jewish historian Josephus tells how rivers of blood flowed through the gates of the city. Many Jews fled from building to building, finally seeking a hiding place in the temple. Some drunken Roman soldier threw a torch into the temple, igniting it. The gold covering the temple melted and oozed into the crevices between the stone blocks. The greedy Romans, lusting after every bit of that gold, dismantled the temple stone by stone, thus literally fulfilling Jesus' prophecy.

Why did Jesus weep? He wept because of the unbelief of the people, just as He weeps at our disbelief today. He wept about the consequences of their disobedience—and still weeps about our disobedience today. He loves us, just as most parents love their children and would gladly exchange places with them if they were in danger. In a sense, at Calvary that's exactly what happened. God changed places with us and took the judgment we deserved.

It breaks God's heart when we sin against Him. Not just because of what we've done, but because of what it will ultimately do to us and how it will harm our spiritual life.

That is why Jesus wept. That is why He went to the cross. And that is why the smartest thing for you to do is to throw yourself into the arms of the God who wept.

Read Romans 8:28-39, paying close attention to verses 37-39, which describe the depth of Christ's love for you. Remember this great promise when you encounter times of opposition.

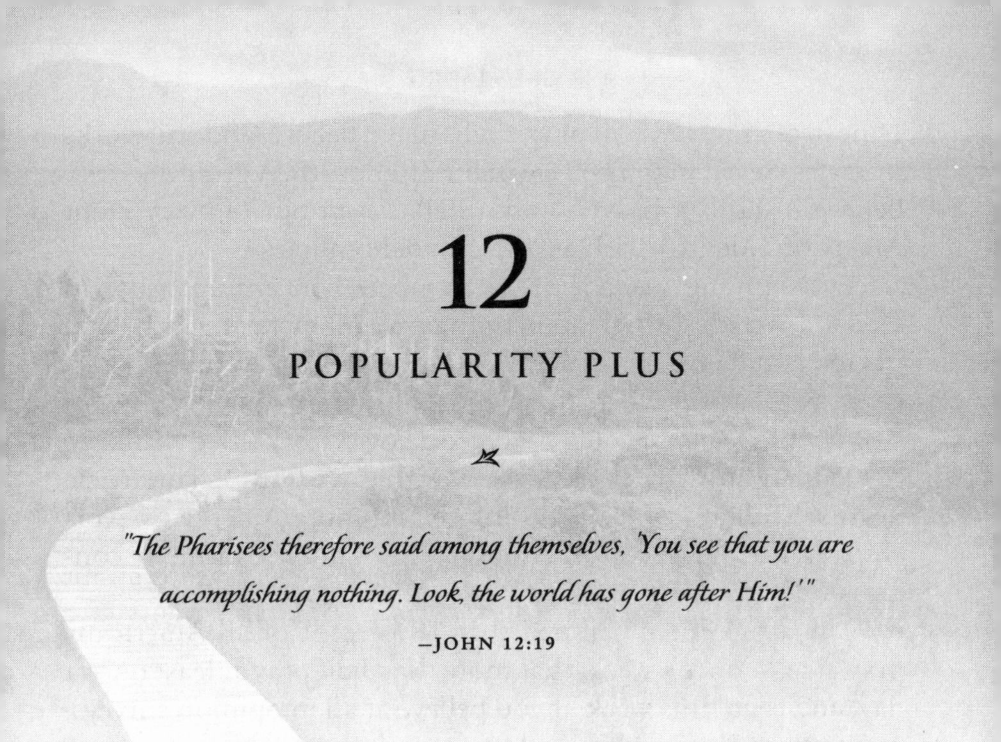

12

POPULARITY PLUS

"The Pharisees therefore said among themselves, 'You see that you are accomplishing nothing. Look, the world has gone after Him!'"

—JOHN 12:19

YOU KNOW YOU'RE UPSETTING SOME APPLE CARTS when even your enemies admit to your popularity.

The comment, "Look, the world has gone after Him!" was not a compliment but an expression of alarmed concern. The Pharisees wanted to eliminate this man Jesus, but that would be hard to do as long as adoring crowds thronged the one targeted for murder.

Jesus' popularity had skyrocketed because people were eager to find someone who could lead them from shame to glory, from the backwater to prominence. "Look, the world has gone after Him!" But sadly, most of the enthusiasm was only skin-deep.

Things haven't changed much in 2,000 years.

As you look at the soaring numbers of Americans who claim to believe in God, it still looks as if "the world has gone after Him!" A flurry of recent surveys have found that most Americans believe in God and identify themselves as strongly religious.

Nine in ten Americans say they have never doubted the existence of God. Ninety-six percent of Americans believe in Him.

Nine in ten say they still pray. Eight in ten believe God still works miracles. Seven in ten believe in life after death. A great majority believe in both a heaven and a hell. Seven out of every eight Americans identify with a Christian denomination.

Even among teenagers the numbers concerning belief in God are incredibly high. Ninety-five percent of teenagers believe in God and 93 percent believe God loves them. Seventy-five percent say they pray when alone, most of them frequently.

A news magazine once featured a cover story titled "Talking to God: An Intimate Look at the Way that We Pray."* The article begins, "Talking to God. For more and more Americans, worship services are no longer enough. They want the intimate contact of personal prayer."

The article then claimed that 78 percent of all Americans pray at least once a week, that more than half pray at least once a day, and that "this week, if you believe at all in opinion surveys, more of us will pray than will go to work or exercise or have sexual relations, according to recent studies."

Such statistics might seem to indicate that America is a believing country. But analysts who have studied the data say the spirituality of most Americans is shallow at best. One historian, Will Herberg, put it this way: "The paradox is that the United States is at once the most religious and also the most secular society in the western world."

The reason so many went after Jesus 2,000 years ago is that they did not understand His purpose. They did not understand His terms and His mission. But when that was revealed, they quickly disappeared.

The same is true today. People say they want to know God. They say they want to pray and have a relationship with Him . . . until He lays out His terms. Then many beat a quick path in the opposite direction.

Happily, not everyone fits in that category. There are always a

---

*K.L. Woodard, "Talking to God," *Newsweek*, January 6, 1992, pp. 38-44.

few people, both then and now, who genuinely thirst for a real relationship with God. Even in Jesus' day, some people had come to Jerusalem seeking God and had found only religion. Instead of finding a vibrant faith such as in the glory days of David and Solomon, they found only an empty shell laden with rules and regulations laid down not by God but by man.

This is typical of religion. Religion never satisfies. Religion will never meet your deepest needs.

I once received a letter from a woman who said her heart was like stone. As a young girl her parents divorced and she sought out a church to talk to the minister. The man was cold and indifferent toward her and she vowed she would never return to church or have anything to do with religion. But the emptiness inside pushed her to search for meaning. That search led her into the occult, then into the New Age movement, and down several other dead ends. After years of enduring these very dark things, she heard our radio broadcast and God began to speak to her heart. Eventually she made a commitment to Jesus Christ—not to religion, but to Jesus.

Religion won't ever meet our needs. It can't. But today, as in Jesus' day, there are a few people searching for a relationship with the true God, the God of Abraham, Isaac, and Jacob. When people like this hear about Jesus—this man who performed miracles, who taught with such profound depth, who raised the dead, who Himself conquered death—their search is over. They're home.

"Look, the world has gone after Him!" Yes, it has—but there's a wrong way to go after Him and a genuine way. Which way have you chosen?

"Religions are man's search for God; the gospel is God's search for man. There are many religions, but one gospel."
—*E. Stanley Jones*

13

IN THE SHADOW OF THE CROSS

"Father, if it is Your will, remove this cup from Me;
nevertheless not My will, but Yours, be done."

—LUKE 22:42

NEXT TO THE CROSS ITSELF, I think the loneliest moment in the life of Jesus occurred in the Garden of Gethsemane. It was there Jesus experienced a depth of loneliness no man or woman could ever know. It was there the decision was reaffirmed that took Him to the cross. The ultimate triumph that was to take place at Calvary was actually accomplished first beneath the gnarled old olive trees of Gethsemane.

The name "Gethsemane" literally means "the place where the olive is pressed." It was here, where olives were pressed to get oil, that Jesus was pressed to make the decision to give His life. It was here He decided He would go through with it.

Not that the prospect of Calvary took Him by surprise. From the moment of His birth Jesus lived in the shadow of the cross. He knew exactly what was coming.

From the time He was dedicated in the temple and the prophet Simeon said to Mary, "This child is destined for the fall and rising of many in Israel" (Luke 2:34) to His death, He always lived under the shadow of the cross.

Jesus spoke of the cross constantly. In John 3 He said, "As

Moses lifted up the serpent in the wilderness, even so must the Son of Man be lifted up, that whoever believes in Him . . . [will] have eternal life" (verses 14-15). In John 10 He said, "I am the good shepherd. The good shepherd gives His life for the sheep" (verse 11). And to His disciples He had proclaimed, "The Son of Man must suffer many things, and be rejected by the elders and chief priests and scribes, and be killed, and be raised the third day" (Luke 9:22).

Yet here in the garden there was a struggle. His petition was no idle request: "If it is Your will, remove this cup from Me." When the moment finally came for Jesus to go to the cross, He shrank from it. He recoiled from the moment of decision. Why?

I personally don't think it was because of what lay ahead physically. Jesus, as God, knew they were going to rip open His back with a whip. He knew they were going to tear the beard from His face. He knew they were going to pound spikes through His hands and crucify Him.

But that was not what He most dreaded. He didn't shrink from the cold indifference of Pilate as the governor gave the order for His execution. It wasn't the heartless soldiers who would kill Him without thinking twice, or the knowledge that His own disciples would soon desert Him, or that Judas Iscariot would betray and turn on Him. None of that caused His wrenching anguish of soul. No, what hurt Him the most was this cup itself—a cup that would pour the sin of the world on His spotless head.

It was from that that He recoiled.

Think of it: He who was holy, righteous, and pure was about to take upon Himself everything that was unholy, unrighteous, and impure. All of the depravity and sinfulness of every person who would ever come to faith was about to be dumped on His perfect and blameless soul.

Here was a man who had obeyed God perfectly. He never entertained an impure thought, never hated a single person, never had been angry in a sinful way. In fact, never in His life had He sinned in any manner at all.

Yet within hours of His departure from Gethsemane, sin in

all its vileness would attach itself to His very body. And He who was God shrank from bearing such filth and corruption.

But as awful as that was, even that was not the worst of it.

What Jesus most abhorred was that soon His fellowship with God would be broken temporarily. He knew that in just a few hours He would cry out, "Eli, Eli, lama sabachthani?" which means, "My God, My God, why have You forsaken Me?" Isaiah describes the cup that Jesus was to drink as the cup of God's fury (*see* Isaiah 51:17). The Savior would drink the dregs of the cup, drain dry the cup of trembling.

By drinking that cup, the judgment that should have fallen upon us would instead pour on the spotless Son, and in that horrible moment the Father would turn away and Jesus would bear our guilt . . . alone.

That, I believe, was the bedrock reason for Jesus' cry in the garden. Nothing repulsed the Lord more than being out of communion with the Father.

His anguish at this horrifying thought was so great that Luke tells us He sweat, as it were, great drops of blood. It's possible Luke was describing a rare phenomenon known as *hematidrosis*, a medical condition caused by great emotional stress in which tiny blood vessels in the sweat glands rupture, producing a mixture of blood and sweat. Jesus' anguish reached such proportions that night that His cry ripped the still air: "If it is possible, let this cup pass from Me" (Matthew 26:39).

But there was no other way. It was the Father's will that Jesus, the spotless Lamb of God, should become sin for us. And so the anguish of Gethsemane led to the peace of the cross.

Your peace, by the way. Bought at the cross but decided in Gethsemane. *For you.* He was forsaken that you might be forgiven. He entered the darkness that you might walk in the light. He did it for you.

Sometimes we forget just how great a price Jesus paid for our sins—for our salvation. Read Isaiah 53 and thank Christ for His incredible sacrifice on your behalf.

14

A TERRIBLE, HOLY MOMENT

✠

*"Jesus therefore, knowing all things that would come upon Him,
went forward and said to them, 'Whom are you seeking?' They
answered Him, 'Jesus of Nazareth.' Jesus said to them, 'I am He.'
And Judas, who betrayed Him, also stood with them. Then—when He
said to them, 'I am He,'—they drew back and fell to the ground."*

—JOHN 18:4-6

YOU WOULDN'T EXPECT God and the devil ever to be working toward the same objective, but for one, brief moment, in a sense they were.

Two forces in the Garden of Gethsemane moved simultaneously toward the same destination. On one hand marched the devil with his cronies; on the other side moved God. That's right: God.

We don't often think of it this way, but God was at work to bring Jesus to the cross. Acts 2:23 says, "Him, being delivered by the determined counsel and foreknowledge of God, you have taken by lawless hands, have crucified, and put to death." It's a curious thing that God and the devil would ever work toward the same goal. But here, for a moment, they did just that.

Obviously, they had two vastly different purposes. The devil wanted to destroy Jesus. The Lord had made havoc of the devil's kingdom and Satan wanted to stop Him in His tracks.

God the Father had a different purpose. He too wanted to see Jesus die, but only because of what His death would accomplish. Through Jesus' death, countless millions would live. Those who had been separated from Him by sin would now have free access into His presence. Through Jesus' death, God would take up residence in the hearts of all who turned from their sin and trusted in Christ.

At last, all the players had been assembled. The devil had gathered a mob to arrest Jesus. But before He was taken away, we are given one last glimpse of Jesus' true nature. He said to the crowd, "Whom are you seeking?" They answered, "Jesus of Nazareth," and He replied, "I am."

You may have noticed I did not use the word "He," though it may be printed in your Bible. That's because it is not there in the original Greek text. Jesus did not say, "I am *He*." He said, "I am." Jesus spoke the same words that thundered from the burning bush to Moses when God said, "Tell them 'I am that I am'" (*see* Exodus 3:14). This was a claim of deity.

When Jesus spoke those two words, He demonstrated His power one last time. In an instant, everyone in the mob fell backward. There was chaos—torches, spears, and swords went flying. People were falling on top of each other—all at the mighty words of the God-man.

Some might be tempted to think, *Poor Jesus—they were taking Him away*, but their concern would be misplaced. Jesus could have said, "I am and you *were*. Bye!" and that would have been it. The same God who spoke creation into existence could certainly have taken care of an angry rabble. But He didn't. He came to die for those people, the very ones who were intent on nailing Him to a cross.

Judas delivered the last insult by betraying Jesus with a kiss. And there's one little element in Matthew's Gospel that we often miss. As Judas was betraying Him, Jesus said, "Friend, why have you come?" (Matthew 26:50). Imagine—He called him "friend." But Judas was so blinded by his own sin he missed that Jesus was giving him one last chance to repent.

Peter stood by watching all of this and growing frustrated and angry. He couldn't stand it. Finally he pulled out his sword, took a wild swing, and an ear went flying. He cut off the ear of the high priest's servant, a man named Malchus. Jesus immediately touched the man's ear and healed him. It is worth noting the last miracle Jesus performed during His earthly ministry was to heal the ear of a man who had come to crucify Him.

Jesus then said to Peter, "Put your sword into the sheath. Shall I not drink the cup which My Father has given Me?" (John 18:11).

So they took Jesus away. But He was not taken against His will. He purposefully went. It would not have been hard for Him to put a stop to this at any moment He chose. He Himself said to Peter, "Do you think that I cannot now pray to My Father, and He will provide Me with more than twelve legions of angels?" (Matthew 26:53).

That must have been a hard day for the angels. Here was the One they loved so dearly, and they could not come and deliver Him. Angels are powerful beings. One move and they could have airlifted Jesus out of this dilemma quicker than you could blink an eye. I'm sure those angels were ready with swords drawn, saying, "Please say the word. Let us lop off some Roman heads. We would gladly comply. Let us deliver You. Call out to us." You might say the angels were on red alert, ready to go.

But Jesus would not use His executive privilege. Jesus would not call upon them. They were under orders not to intervene at this terrible, holy moment. They had to wait. He had to go through with this. If He had called for their help, you and I could not have been saved. He had to go through this for us.

Nothing happened in this garden by accident. This was no interruption in an otherwise incredibly successful ministry. It was Jesus' goal and purpose from the very beginning.

And at last, the stage had been set for the final act.

Jesus came at just the right time to save *you*. Read Romans 5:1-11. Remember, you are precious to God!

15

FROM MORIAH TO CALVARY

✻

"Isaac spoke to Abraham his father and said, 'My father!'
And he said, 'Here I am, my son.' And he said, 'Look, the fire and the wood,
but where is the lamb for a burnt offering?' And Abraham said,
'My son, God will provide for Himself the lamb for a burnt offering.'"

—GENESIS 22:7-8

I THINK ONE OF THE clearest illustrations of what God the Father went through as Jesus approached the cross is the Old Testament story of Abraham and Isaac. I believe one of the reasons God put that story in Scripture is to help us see the crucifixion from the Father's perspective.

Remember that Abraham fathered his son Isaac late in life and he dearly loved that boy. This son was the delight of his life. How his heart must have trembled when God said to him one day, "Take now your son, your only son Isaac, whom you love, and go to the land of Moriah, and offer him there as a burnt offering on one of the mountains of which I shall tell you" (Genesis 22:2).

Despite his anguish, Abraham did not drag his feet. He did not argue with God but obediently took his son to Mount Moriah. I am sure that great agony consumed his soul as he and his beloved son made their long way up that hill. Deep inside, Abraham must have grieved over what he knew his son was about to undergo.

"My Father!" said Isaac, "Look, the fire and the wood, but where is the lamb for a burnt offering?" Abraham prophetically answered, "My son, God will provide for Himself the lamb for a burnt offering." Abraham couldn't have known it, but he was prophesying not only about imminent events on Moriah, but also about events hundreds of years in the future on another hill called Calvary. Ultimately, God Himself would provide the sacrifice of His only Son.

Isaac was probably in his teens or early twenties at this point. As he was on his way up the hill with his father, he no doubt got the drift of what was going on. Especially when he was laid on the altar. He might have said, "Dad, I don't know about this. Let's reconsider this for a moment. You're an old guy. You haven't got that much longer. Why don't we offer *you* as a sacrifice?"

Isaac wasn't some helpless little child. He was a full-grown man who could have gotten out of that predicament easily. But he willingly laid down. The father's heart was broken, but he was willing to give up his son, and the son submitted to the father. Isaac willingly went along with this plan.

We don't know what was said between Abraham and Isaac in those final moments before Abraham stretched the knife over his son's prone body. Perhaps nothing was said at all. Perhaps Abraham's heart was so heavy that he could not bear to speak.

But we do know that as Abraham raised the dagger, he believed in his heart that God would raise his son from the dead. Hebrews 11:19 says Abraham acted in the confidence that "God was able to raise [Isaac] up, even from the dead."

His strong belief was never fully tested, however. Before the dagger came down, God told Abraham to stop. Abraham had passed this stiffest of tests and God provided for the burnt sacrifice a ram caught in a thicket of thorns. His beloved son Isaac had been spared.

That's where the analogy between Moriah and Calvary breaks down. There was no reprieve for Jesus. God the Father did not stop at the last moment. God Himself took the great knife of His own fierce wrath against sin and brought it in full fury upon His only Son. He did it reluctantly. He did it sorrowfully. But He did it. There was no other way. The Scripture says, "Without shedding of blood there is no remission [of sin]" (Hebrews 9:22). It also says, "Nor is there salvation in any other, for there is no other name under heaven given among men by which we must be saved" (Acts 4:12).

The Father reluctantly offered His Son for us as a sacrifice. But let's not forget that the Son willingly went all the way to Calvary. The Bible says that He set His face like a flint to go to Jerusalem, knowing full well what awaited Him there (see Isaiah 50:7).

God loved His Son Jesus. He didn't want to give Him up. It broke the heart of God to pour all of the sin of the world upon His Son. But the Son submitted. The Son went along with it.

God has said that we're all sinners and that is why He took such drastic measures and sent His own dear Son to die on that cross. We don't know the details of what happened for the three hours Jesus took the sin of the world upon Himself, any more than we know what Abraham and Isaac might have talked about as Abraham prepared to sacrifice his son. It's a divine mystery.

But it's no mystery what Jesus accomplished. He made it possible for us to live forever in God's family, free from all guilt and shame, enjoying at God's right hand pleasures forevermore.

The next time you read the book of Genesis, pay special attention to chapter 22. And remember: While Isaac was spared the sharp, smooth edge of the blade, Jesus was not spared the rough surface of the cross. It's precisely because He wasn't that we can enjoy eternal life in the holy and joyful presence of God Almighty.

"Christ on the cross is the way Calvary really reads. For he died for us—in our place. We, then, are debtors. Strange, that so often we act like we owe nothing."

—C. Neil Strait

16

BY HIS STRIPES WE ARE HEALED

✄

"So Pilate, wanting to gratify the crowd, released Barabbas to them;
and he delivered Jesus, after he had scourged Him, to be crucified."

—MARK 15:15

WHAT EXACTLY HAPPENED when Jesus was scourged and crucified? Believe me, it's not material for the weak of stomach.

When a man was scourged in Roman times, his hands were tied over his head to a post, his body dangling and taut. The torturer's whip featured a short wooden handle with several leather thongs attached, each embedded with jagged pieces of metal, glass, and bone. As the whip struck a person's back, it would rip deep through the outer skin. Muscles would be lacerated and veins and arteries would be torn open. Even the kidneys, spleen, and other organs could be exposed and slashed.

The Roman rule was 40 lashes minus one for mercy. Most people didn't make it to 39. Normally, because of the severity of the whipping, a prisoner would quickly confess his crimes after only a few cruel lashes.

But Jesus had no crime to confess. He had nothing to say to defend Himself. So He took 39 lashes. You can be certain of this: His body was a bleeding mass when they were done. We know He was so weakened by the whipping that He fell under the weight of the cross when He was forced to carry it to Golgotha. I'm surprised He was able to stand up, much less carry a cross. His loss of blood would have been incredible.

When the scourging was done, He was brought before a mocking contingent of soldiers and a sharp crown of thorns was pressed upon His head, cutting deeply into His forehead and causing severe lacerations. Then they took turns striking Him, hard, with hands toughened by battle. At last Pilate presented Him to the people, announcing, "Behold the Man!" (John 19:5).

This shows you one thing about Jesus: He was a man. Don't believe those anemic portraits you see of Jesus that have been handed down to us through the centuries. Our Savior was no pale, thin, wispy-looking man. He was strong. He was muscular. He walked the dusty roads of Israel from Galilee to Jerusalem. He was raised in the shop of a carpenter under His father Joseph. He overturned tables of marble in the temple, not thin card tables that fold up. He was a man's man. He was tough. The suffering He went through seems such a cruel waste. But it wasn't.

Isaiah 52:14 says, "His visage was marred more than any man, and His form more than the sons of men." You could not even tell He was a man. His face was beaten and bloated and puffed beyond recognition. His beard had been ripped from His face. The crown of thorns gouged into His forehead. It was hard even to tell who He was. You could not recognize Him.

I don't know if you've ever seen a traumatized person, but when someone has been in a severe accident, the body often reacts in such a way that you can hardly recognize the victim. I've gone to hospitals and visited people who have been in horrible accidents, and I couldn't identify them. This is how Jesus appeared at this moment.

But it got worse.

When it came time to crucify Him, His ripped-open back was laid on the cross and metal spikes five to seven inches long were pounded through His wrists and feet. The left foot pressed backward against the right foot and a spike was driven through both.

Then the cross was raised and dropped into a hole deep enough to keep it upright. And there He hung. The increasing inflammation of the wounds in His back, hands, and feet; the congestion of blood in His head, lungs, and heart; and the swelling of virtually every vein in His body all combined to make crucifixion the cruelest of deaths.

It's important to note that crucifixion was a form of punishment reserved for the vilest of crimes, for criminals of the worst type. It was not designed simply to put a person to death—there are easier ways to kill a man than by crucifixion. Rome's primary method of execution was decapitation. They would simply behead a man. Crucifixion, on the other hand, was designed to humiliate and torture an individual. The person crucified could live for hours, even as long as three days, on the cross.

The Romans crucified hundreds, sometimes thousands of men at a time and lined them up on each side of the roads leading into a city. As visitors rode in, they would see hundreds of crosses on each side with men hanging on them—some dead, some alive. The statement Rome intended to make was clear: Don't defy Roman authority! If you commit a capital crime, this will be your fate.

The Gospels tell us that soldiers came to Jesus to break His legs. Do you know why? Crucifixion was death by exposure and suffocation. It didn't kill by spikes in the wrists and feet, though that was painful. It most often killed by suffocation because the condemned's diaphragm was compressed in such a way that he could not breathe. A little step was often built beneath the feet of the condemned. By using that step, the victim could lift himself up to get a much-needed breath. But if his bones were broken, he lost the ability to push himself up. When the soldiers came to break Jesus' legs, they intended to hasten His death. But He had already died.

You might wonder why I've taken time to describe even a small portion of the horrors of the cross. I've done it for one reason only: that we might pause in gratitude and wonder at the sacrifice of the Son. We didn't deserve it. We didn't earn it. But then, He knew that before He ever left the glories of heaven.

Look at the apostle Paul's words in Galatians 2:20. Paul identifies why Jesus went through this horrible process of the crucifixion.

Remember, you can say the same thing as Paul in regard to your life.

17

THE LAST PRAYER

"Father, forgive them, for they do not know what they do."

—LUKE 23:34

THE SCOURGING WAS OVER, the spikes had been driven through His wrists and feet, and His cross had been raised. Now Jesus, barely able to breathe and in excruciating pain, decides to utter a word.

It would be very painful to speak in this condition. To get a breath was difficult, to speak even more so. His tongue was swollen, His mouth parched with thirst. When He raised His body the spikes would rip anew into His flesh, sending flashes of stabbing pain up and down His arms and legs. Despite this, Jesus now raises Himself up—His mangled back scraping across the rough cross—opens His mouth, and with a bloated tongue utters His first words from the cross.

What were they? We know He spoke seven statements. What's the order? It has to be significant. If He had said first of all, "Eli, Eli, lama sabachthani?" which means, "My God, My God, why have You forsaken Me?" we would understand (Matthew 27:46). If His first words had been, "I thirst" (John 19:28), that would have made sense. Or if He had said, "Father, *condemn* them for what they have done to Me," we would surely understand that.

But His first words were, "Father, forgive them, for they do not know what they do."

Jesus' public ministry opened with prayer at His baptism and it closed with prayer at His crucifixion. But some might say, "Who wouldn't pray at a time like this? Only a fool would not call upon God when facing his death." It has been said there are no atheists in foxholes. When a man is facing death he *will* turn to God, unless his heart is so hardened he no longer can.

Jesus called on God like all of us would. If I were in this predicament, I would have prayed, "God, take away the pain." Or even, "Lord, quicken my death. Make it come faster." I'm certain I also would have said, "Lord, may Your judgment fall and a double portion on those who have done this to me. In fact, why don't You start now!"

In this dark hour, the Savior prayed, as most people in such circumstances would do. But His prayer was not for His disciples. It wasn't for His mother standing at the foot of the cross. He didn't even pray for Himself. His prayer was for His enemies.

Jesus modeled exactly what He taught. Years earlier on a bright day during what is called the Sermon on the Mount, He told His disciples, "Love your enemies, bless those who curse you, do good to those who hate you, and pray for those who spitefully use you and persecute you" (Matthew 5:44). What He spoke on that sunny Mountain of Beatitudes He modeled here at Mount Calvary. He prayed for His enemies.

When He uttered the words, "Father, forgive them, for they do not know what they do," He emphasized one simple truth: No one is beyond the reach of prayer. He prayed for the very men who had crucified Him.

We might have supposed that soldiers hardened enough to drive spikes through a man as pure and innocent as Jesus would be beyond the point of no return. We might think such men could never believe. But Jesus prayed for them all and thus demonstrated that no one is beyond the reach of prayer.

On each side of Jesus hung a criminal. The Greek word for

"criminal" means "one who uses violence to rob openly." This stands in contrast to the thief who secretly enters into the house to steal. The two men crucified with Jesus were not only guilty of robbery, but probably were murderers as well. Considering their punishment, I assume they had committed such heinous crimes on more than one occasion.

Obviously, there were some significant differences between Jesus and the two criminals. They were being punished for their personal crimes; Jesus suffered for the crimes of all humanity. They had been sent to their crosses against their will; He willingly chose the horrors of Calvary. They could not have escaped; He could have freed Himself from that cross with a single word. They were held to their crosses by nails; He was held to His cross by love.

It's fascinating to see how these three men faced death. They were looking death squarely in the face; it was only days away, perhaps hours. As Jesus was raised on His cross these two men momentarily forgot their personal pain and joined the chorus of jeers from the onlookers. They said, "He saved others; Himself He cannot save. If He is the King of Israel, let Him now come down from the cross, and we will believe Him. He trusted in God; let Him deliver Him now if He will have Him; for He said, 'I am the Son of God'" (Matthew 27:42-43).

How this mockery and unbelief must have pained Jesus! He was dying for the sin of the very people who dared to hurl these insults in His face. And yet He says, "Father, forgive them, for they do not know what they do."

If nothing else had convinced His enemies that He truly was the Son of God, this prayer should have. "Father, forgive them, for they do not know what they do." It was a prayer of power . . . and it would be answered almost immediately.

Read Colossians 2:13-14. There you will find the ultimate example of forgiveness. Can you claim it in your life today?

18

NO CONTRADICTION

✦

"Assuredly, I say to you, today you will be with Me in Paradise."

—LUKE 23:43

THERE ARE PEOPLE WHO SAY the Bible is full of contradictions, and the Lord's second word from the cross appears to be one example.

Matthew's Gospel tells us that both of the criminals crucified with Jesus cursed and mocked the Lord. But Luke's Gospel tells us that one of these thieves rebuked the other one and then turned to Jesus and said, "Lord, remember me when You come into Your kingdom" (Luke 23:42).

Is that a contradiction? Did the Bible make a mistake? No. It's not a contradiction; it's a *conversion*. The Holy Spirit simply moved with blinding speed to answer Jesus' prayer on the cross (*see* Luke 23:34).

It's important to remember that this repentant criminal was not just a petty thief. He was being executed because of insurrection or rebellion against Rome. He believed Rome was wrong, that it was running an empire by tyranny. He tried to do something about it and now was paying the ultimate price.

But then he saw a man who was willing to forgive those who would kill Him. The sight was impossible to dismiss. And in an amazing turn of events, he who had such a hardened and rebellious heart suddenly felt it quiver, soften, and melt—and he believed. Let's consider the events that brought about his conversion.

The thief had been watching Jesus with keen interest. He could see this "King of the Jews" had been beaten severely. It's doubtful the thief had received 39 lashes, that he had been beaten, that his beard had been ripped from his face, or that a crown of thorns had been pressed to his head. That was not the norm for crucifixion; these were added tortures for Christ alone.

The thief also noticed that Jesus did not curse those who pounded the spikes through His hands, nor did He curse God, as might have been expected. Instead, He was silent. Quiet. He said not a word. Perhaps the thief even recalled the words of Isaiah 53:7: "He was oppressed and He was afflicted, yet He opened not His mouth; He was led as a lamb to the slaughter, and as a sheep before its shearers is silent, so He opened not His mouth."

Then he saw Jesus readying Himself to speak. He strained to hear the words. *What's He going to say?* he probably thought. And when the Lord finally pulled His pain-wracked body up and prayed, "Father, forgive them, for they do not know what they do," I believe the words reverberated through this man's hardened heart. All the rebellion, bitterness, and anger that had driven him for years suddenly dissolved. His heart melted.

No doubt this thief had been exposed to religious hypocrisy his whole life. His only example of God's representatives were probably the Pharisees and Sadducees and high priests. At best these men misrepresented God and at worst they drove people away from Him. If that was the only exposure the thief had to God, it's no wonder he was hardened against anything spiritual. He had dealt with religion—but he had never dealt with Jesus.

This man's life was transformed by one single statement from Jesus. Something happened to him, something of great importance. In Luke 23:40 we read that he turned to the other criminal and rebuked him: "Do you not even fear God, seeing you are under the same condemnation?"

This is amazing. This man has a faith just moments old and already he is speaking up for God. Then he says, very truly of both himself and of Jesus, "And we indeed justly, for we receive the due reward of our deeds; but this Man has done nothing wrong" (Luke 23:41). Even a thief attested to the spotless character of Jesus.

Last, this thief turns to Jesus and says, "Lord, remember me when You come into Your kingdom" (Luke 23:42). Notice how much faith this man had! He didn't say, "Lord, remember me *if* You come into Your kingdom." His statement was absolute. He *knew* Jesus was going to a kingdom. How did he know that? Because Jesus had already spoken to the supernatural realm and said, "Father." The thief immediately realized there was a higher kingdom, a different realm—and he wanted to go with Jesus when He returned to His kingdom.

It would appear that this thief who had trusted Christ just moments before he made his request possessed more spiritual insight than any of the closest followers of Jesus. Much later Simon Peter would preach on how Jesus atoned for our sins on the cross, but this thief saw and understood these things even while Peter was running for his life. John had leaned on the breast of Jesus and had been closer to Him than anyone, but this thief grasped more in a few moments than John apparently understood in three years.

Then Jesus replied, "Today you will be with Me in Paradise" (Luke 23:43). Can you imagine the comfort those words must have brought to this man? *Today.* To think that he could have the assurance that he was forgiven. Redeemed. Reborn. Loved. It was almost too good to be true. But it was true. The man had a new address: Paradise.

Someday you and I will be able to meet that man—no longer as a thief, but as a child of God. And all because of Jesus.

"The cross is rough, and it is deadly, but it is effective. It does not keep its victim hanging there forever. There comes a moment when its work is finished. . . . After that is resurrection glory and power, and the pain is forgotten for joy that the veil is taken away and we have entered in actual experience the Presence of the living God."

—*A.W. Tozer*

19

THE GREATEST LOVE STORY

"When Jesus therefore saw His mother, and the disciple whom He loved standing by, He said to His mother, 'Woman, behold your son!' Then He said to the disciple, 'Behold your mother!' And from that hour that disciple took her to his own home."

—JOHN 19:26-27

WE COME NOW to the greatest love story ever told. Not Romeo and Juliet. Not the story of the love of a man for a woman or of a woman for a man. Not even the love of a parent for a child.

It's the love of God for mankind.

This incident shows how much God loves us and wants to have fellowship with us. If you have ever been tempted to doubt that God loves you, pay careful attention to this story. It shows beyond a shadow of a doubt how much He cares.

Jesus looks down at the foot of the cross and there He sees His mother. His eyes feed upon the face that first greeted Him when He came into the world. He gazes upon her, somehow gestures toward the man standing beside her, and speaks His third word from the cross: "Woman, behold your son!"

Imagine the anguish Mary felt at this moment. I doubt you can begin to appreciate how hard this must have been for her unless you're a parent, especially a mother. This woman bore that child. From her own womb. Yes, He was the Son of God. Certainly, He was the Messiah. But still, He was the firstborn she held in her own arms—and she loved her son.

The crowds stood by mocking, the soldiers milled about, calloused and indifferent, the priests jeered. And there on the cross hung her son. She had kissed that once-small forehead, now crowned with thorns. She had guided those once-tiny hands, now nailed to the cross. Though His disciples forsook Him, she stood by His side until the very end.

I wonder if Mary reflected on the day long ago when she and Joseph dedicated Jesus in the temple. Like every Jewish couple, they brought in their newborn son to dedicate to the Lord. They were greeted by an old man named Simeon, who said, "Lord, now You are letting Your servant depart in peace, according to Your word; for my eyes have seen Your salvation which You have prepared before the face of all peoples, a light to bring revelation to the Gentiles, and the glory of Your people Israel" (Luke 2:29-32). Then he turned to Mary and said, "Behold, this Child is destined for the fall and rising of many in Israel, and for a sign which will be spoken against (yes, a sword will pierce through your own soul also), that the thoughts of many hearts may be revealed" (Luke 2:34-35).

I wonder what Mary thought of such a statement. Perhaps she asked herself, *Who is this man? What does he mean that my child is set for the fall and rising of many in Israel? What does he mean when he says a sword will pierce my own soul?*

I think she knew now.

As she stood at the foot of the cross and looked up at her son, no doubt the sword Simeon spoke of in Luke 2:35 went all the way in. Could it be that a revelation came to Mary's mind as she gazed upon Him and perhaps for the first time realized that He was not her child, but she was His? That the One she bore in her womb was her Creator? That it was almighty God in human form hanging on that cross? Perhaps for the first time she understood the whole picture.

I wonder if now she realized there really was a master purpose, a master plan. Perhaps now she understood that this was always what God had called her son to do. Perhaps. But I doubt it took away any of the pain she felt inside.

At last Jesus removed His gaze from His mother and fixed His eyes on His disciple John. "Behold your mother!" He cried. He was telling John, "Friend, take care of her for Me."

Jesus was the firstborn, the eldest son. It was His responsibility to care for His mother since it appears that Joseph, her husband, already had passed from the scene. It is thought by most Bible scholars that Joseph was dead by this time, and common sense would point out that Mary needed the care and protection of another.

Jesus was nearly ready to depart. Before the day was over He had much more to accomplish, yet right now He took the time to think of His own mother. "Woman, behold your son!" And to John, "Behold your mother!" The Scripture tells us that from that hour forward John took Mary into his own home.

It's amazing: Jesus was nailed to a Roman cross, yet His first thought was for the very ones who crucified Him. Then He thought of the thief hanging next to Him. Next He saw His mother, realized there was no one to take care of her, and gave instructions designed to see to her welfare.

Truly, this is the greatest love story ever told. If ever you doubt God's love for you, look back to the cross. Watch as Jesus forgives those who murder Him. Listen as He welcomes an undeserving sinner into His kingdom. And marvel as He compassionately makes arrangements for the care of His dear mother.

This is a Creator who loves His creation. Which, by the way, includes you.

God truly cares for you. Read all of Psalm 91, and meditate on the promises God gives you concerning His protection. How has He cared for you in recent months? Thank Him for what He has done.

20

THE DARKEST HOUR

✠

" 'Eli, Eli, lama sabachthani?' that is, 'My God, My God,
why have You forsaken Me?' "

—MATTHEW 27:46

THE FOURTH STATEMENT Jesus proclaimed on the cross is the darkest one of all. In fact, it's the darkest statement in the Bible, the darkest statement in all of history. This was the moment He feared more than any other. In a voice choking with agony, Jesus cried out, "My God, My God, why have You forsaken Me?"

We have to ask, What was going on here? Was this a lapse of faith on Jesus' part? It seems impossible that He who just a few moments earlier had so confidently told the thief, "Today you will be with Me in Paradise," would now cry out, "My God, My God, why have You forsaken Me?" I believe this was a cry of deep despondency, punctuating a moment at once infinitely holy and utterly dark.

It was this very moment He was dreading in the Garden of Gethsemane when He sweat, as it were, great drops of blood and three times pleaded, "If it is possible, let this cup pass from Me" (Matthew 26:39, cf. verses 42, 44). Jesus shuddered at the thought that all the depravity and sin of mankind would be poured upon

Himself. He recoiled at it. And now at the cross He cries out in desperation, "My God, My God, why have You forsaken Me?"

Some listening at the foot of the cross thought they heard Jesus call for Elijah. They misunderstood His first words, "Eli, Eli," and supposed He was pleading with Elijah to come and help Him. That's why they said, "Let us see if Elijah will come to save Him" (Matthew 27:49).

But Jesus was not asking for Elijah. The crowd should have recognized He was crying out the first line of Psalm 22, which reads, "My God, My God, why have You forsaken Me?" Later in that same psalm David predicted the suffering of the coming Messiah: "All those who see Me laugh Me to scorn; they shoot out the lip, they shake the head, saying, 'He trusted in the LORD, let Him rescue Him; let Him deliver Him, since He delights in Him!' . . . I am poured out like water, and all My bones are out of joint; My heart is like wax; it has melted within Me. My strength is dried up like a potsherd, and My tongue clings to My jaws. . . . The assembly of the wicked has enclosed Me. They pierced My hands and My feet" (22:7-8, 14-16). Jesus, of course, was fulfilling Scripture. But what a somber prophecy to fulfill!

Darkness fell on the land for three long hours when Jesus spoke these words. What happened during the silence?

Scripture doesn't spell out exactly what happened, but it would seem that this was the moment when the sin of the world was poured out upon Him. I know that at some point during His crucifixion sin engulfed Him; the Bible says He who had known no sin became sin for us. This could have been the moment.

I believe that at this moment, the Father turned away from His Son. Jesus was bearing the wages due His people. The Scripture says in Isaiah 53:5, "The chastisement for our peace was upon Him," or quite simply, "The punishment to obtain our peace with God was placed upon Jesus." Thus Jesus cried out in despondency. At that moment, He was bearing the sin of the entire world. There was no other way to deal with the sin issue.

Why not? Because God is holy. So holy that the angelic beings veil their faces before Him. So holy that His friend Abraham, standing before Him, said, "I am nothing but dust and ashes" (Genesis 18:27, NIV). So holy that when Job came into His presence, the patriarch said, "I abhor myself" (42:6). So holy is God, we are told in Habakkuk 1:13 that He is "of purer eyes than to behold evil, and cannot look on wickedness."

The holy Father *had* to turn His face away from His Son when He poured the wrath of the world upon Him. On the cross, Jesus received the wages due us sinners. He took the punishment that you and I should have received. Isaiah says, "The LORD has laid on Him the iniquity of us all" (53:6).

Try to imagine not only the pain that Jesus suffered at that moment, but also the pain of the Father. Only a father could understand this. Most dads would gladly put themselves in harm's way to spare their child. If most dads knew that by dying they could save their child's life, they would do it without a moment's hesitation. Why? Because they love that child and want what's best for him or her. When that child is sick, they hurt inside. They wish they could take the sickness on themselves.

But try as we might, all these analogies ultimately fail. We simply cannot imagine what a sacrifice this moment must have been for the Father.

Consider this: There was never a thought in the mind of Jesus that lay outside the Father's mind. Jesus never entertained an idea out of harmony with the Father. Jesus never spent a moment outside the conscious presence of His Father.

Yet in that moment He took on Himself all the filth and corruption of the world . . . and His Father broke their perfect communion and turned away.

We must never forget that Jesus was forsaken by God for a few moments so we don't have to be. Jesus was forsaken by God for a time so that we might enjoy His presence forever. Jesus was forsaken that we might be forgiven. Jesus entered the darkness that we might walk in the light.

He did all of that for me. He did all of that for you. And none of us can fully understand what it cost Him.

"The Cross of Christ does not make God love us; it is the outcome and measure of His love for us."

—*Andrew Murray*

21

WHEN GOD WAS THIRSTY

⚹

"I thirst!"

—JOHN 19:28

FOR THREE AGONIZING HOURS Jesus hung on the cross, taking the punishment you and I deserved. Finally, He uttered His fifth word—the first word of a personal nature. John writes, "After this, Jesus, knowing that all things were now accomplished, that the Scripture might be fulfilled, said, 'I thirst!'"

Jesus' mission was done at this point. Finished. Complete. Only then did He think of His own needs. "I thirst!" His tremendous blood loss had sent His body into shock, creating an intense and even desperate thirst.

It is hard to imagine. The Creator of the universe is saying He needs a drink. The One who created water, who spoke liquids into existence, was thirsty.

He could have done a miracle so easily. In the Old Testament, hadn't God brought water out of rocks in the wilderness? Wasn't Jesus' first public miracle turning water into wine? It would have been a simple thing for Him to speak water into existence to quench His raging thirst. He could have spoken the word and torrents of water would have cascaded from heaven.

But He refused to do it.

It's important to remember that Jesus never once performed a miracle for His own benefit or comfort. His miracles were always on behalf of others. When He was hungry, He sought out food. When He was tired, He slept. When He was thirsty, He would get something to drink. He exposed Himself to the same limitations of humanity that you and I face.

Remember when He was tempted by Satan in the wilderness to turn rocks into bread (*see* Matthew 4:2-4)? A song that was popular a few years ago portrayed this story inaccurately. One of the lines in "We Are the World" says, "As God has shown us by turning stones to bread." The first time I heard that, I thought, *What Bible did they get that from?* Jesus never turned the stones to bread—that was the devil's idea and Jesus didn't go along with it. He never did a miracle for His own benefit.

Jesus refused Satan's temptation by saying, "Man shall not live by bread alone" (Matthew 4:4). Instead, He chose to bear the physical limitation of hunger. It was His habitual practice.

The Bible says of Him, "Being found in appearance as a man, He humbled Himself and became obedient to the point of death, even the death of the cross" (Philippians 2:8). And Hebrews 4:15 tells us "we do not have a High Priest who cannot sympathize with our weaknesses, but was in all points tempted as we are, yet without sin."

Here on the cross, as the time for His departure grew near, Jesus became thirsty. Surprisingly, perhaps, His request was not only heard but honored. John writes, "Now a vessel full of sour wine was sitting there; and they filled a sponge with sour wine, put it on hyssop, and put it to His mouth" (John 19:29).

Don't confuse this drink with the concoction mentioned in Matthew 27:34. That was a mixture of vinegar and gall, often given to numb victims to pain. Jesus, tasting what they were offering, refused that drink. He did not want a drug that would even slightly deaden His pain; He wanted no drug to cloud His mind for the task He was undertaking. He was determined to be in full control of His faculties and fully conscious to the end.

His refusal to drink the mixture of vinegar and gall might strike us as odd, but it shouldn't. Everything Jesus did, He did for our benefit and God's glory. And even His extreme suffering is a potent reminder to us of His ability and willingness to sympathize with our needs.

It was this Jesus who willingly bore our griefs and carried our sorrows, according to Isaiah 53:4. It was this Jesus who was called "a Man of sorrows" (Isaiah 53:3). The implications of these truths are both staggering and personal.

Is your body wracked with pain right now? So was His. Have you ever been misunderstood or misjudged or misrepresented? So was He. Have your closest friends turned away from you and deserted you and abandoned you? His friends turned from Him as well.

In other words, there is a God right now who understands what you're going through. You may say, "He couldn't know what I'm going through." But He does.

No matter how great your need or difficulty, you can be sure He understands. No matter what your circumstances, you can be certain that you have His full attention. No matter how rough your road or difficult your dilemma, you can be confident that Jesus Christ cares, that He loves you with a furious affection, and that He will walk with you through whatever troubles may come your way.

That's why we're told in 1 Peter 5:7 to cast "all your care upon Him, for He cares for you." I think that's one of the most delightful commands in Scripture. Don't you? And the more I get to know Jesus, the more delightful it becomes.

Won't you join the mighty throng of Christians through the ages who have discovered this delight for themselves?

No one understands your situation like Jesus. Read Hebrews 12:1-4. May Christ be your example and your friend!

22

THE ULTIMATE BATTLE CRY

✄

"It is finished!"

—JOHN 19:30

THROUGHOUT HISTORY certain battle cries have taken their place in the common culture. We recall the battle cry of Texans: "Remember the Alamo!" Then there was the battle cry of the Japanese as they attacked Pearl Harbor: "Tora, Tora, Tora!" The Revolutionary War had its own battle cry: "Don't shoot 'til you see the whites of their eyes!"

But the greatest and most far-reaching battle cry ever heard in the universe was the one that fell from the lips of the Son of God as He hung on a Roman cross 2,000 years ago: "It is finished!"

These words not only rang in the ears of those who stood close to the cross, but also throughout the kingdoms of both hell and heaven. In the presence of the Father, the words, "It is finished!" were a victory cry as a new covenant and relationship with God was made possible through what Jesus had accomplished on the cross.

But imagine how the disciples might have misread Jesus' statement. At that moment their dreams were shattered, their hopes destroyed. They probably thought, *That's it. It is finished, just as He said. It's over for us. We had hoped that He would build His kingdom. We had hoped that He was the One who would deliver Israel. But now look what they've done to Him! Oh, where did everything go wrong?*

But it was the disciples who were wrong, not the events leading to the cross. Jesus' words were not those of a victim, but a victor. This was a victory shout affirming that the battle had been finally and completely won. *It is finished!*

This word "finished" is an important word in the original Greek text. It can be translated "it is made an end of," or "it is paid," or even "it is accomplished." Every one of those words describes a different facet of what was won at the cross of Calvary.

What was made an end of? Our sin and the guilt that accompanied it.

What was paid? The price of our redemption.

What was accomplished? The work the Father had given Jesus to do.

The decisive blow was delivered against the devil and his forces when Christ spoke these words from the cross. Colossians 2:14-15 says that through the cross Jesus "wiped out the handwriting of requirements that was against us, which was contrary to us. And He has taken it out of the way, having nailed it to the cross. Having disarmed principalities and powers, He made a public spectacle of them, triumphing over them in it."

At Calvary, Satan tried to do away with Jesus once and for all, but instead, his own fate was sealed.

Matthew's Gospel also tells us that at this moment, the veil in the temple was ripped from top to bottom (*see* Matthew 27:51). This was not some sheer membrane you could look through; this was a veil of thick woven material that some scholars believe could have been as thick as 36 inches.

I wish I could have been in the temple for that moment. Can you imagine the priest walking along? All of a sudden he hears a big tear, the veil ripping from top to bottom. It's not as though man were saying, "Let's get rid of the veil." It's as though God were saying, "This is no more. This veil used to separate you in the temple from the Holy of holies. Only the high priest could come in once a year, and then only with a sacrifice.

"But now I'm ripping that veil. You have access. You can come in. You can know Me, have fellowship with Me. The barriers are gone; you don't need a priest anymore. Now My Son Jesus will be your mediator. You don't need to meet Me in a building or in a temple; now I'll take up residence in your heart. You don't have to come in fear and trembling before Me, but now you can come through My Son Jesus Christ and can call Me Father and have free access to Me at any time." God ripped the veil.

The world rejoiced when the Berlin Wall dividing East and West Germany fell years ago. That wall stood for communism, which trapped its people in and shut others out. People grew excited as the wall began to crumble.

But what happened in the temple was something far greater than that. The wall separating man from God was broken down and we were given free access to Him.

When Jesus cried, "It is finished!" He meant the devil's stranglehold on humanity was broken. The storm had passed. The cup had been drained. Satan had done his worst and the Lord had bruised his head. The darkness was lifted. It was over with. Finished. Never again would Jesus' heel be bruised at the evil hands of Satan. Never again would He even momentarily be forsaken by God. *It was finished!*

The disciples may not have understood these words. But I believe they reverberated through hell and through the ranks of the demons because they heralded a whole new ball game, so to speak. Jesus pulled Satan's teeth at the cross. Oh, the devil may gum you real hard, but he can't leave teeth marks. Satan may roar and taunt and tempt and harass you, but he can't beat you. He can't because . . . IT IS FINISHED!

Read Romans 3:21-26. There you will find God's purpose behind the crucifixion. What personal significance does the crucifixion have for you?

23

YOU CAN'T KEEP THE GOD-MAN DOWN

✘

"Father, into Your hands I commit My spirit."

—LUKE 23:46, NIV

THE SAYING GOES, "You can't keep a good man down." I don't know about that, but I do know for certain you can't keep the God-man down.

Jesus had said, "Destroy this temple [meaning His body], and in three days I will raise it up" (John 2:19), and now He was preparing to do just that. But first things first. Before He could rise again, He had to die. And this final statement represents the way He chose to leave this earth.

"I commit My spirit" could also be translated, "I dismiss My spirit." That is, "It's finished. It's completed. It's accomplished. Now I dismiss My spirit to the care of the Father."

This statement reminds us of what He had said on so many occasions: "I lay down My life that I may take it again. No one takes it from Me, but I lay it down of Myself" (John 10:17-18). It's so silly to think that any number of soldiers were going to capture Jesus and take Him to the cross, as though He couldn't escape at any moment. *He laid down His life.* It was a decision He had freely and firmly made. And when He accomplished all He had set out to do, He said, "Into Your hands I commit My spirit."

Jesus was already gone when the soldiers came to break His

bones. They intended to take a heavy mallet and smash Jesus' legs so that He would collapse and quickly suffocate. But by the time they arrived, He had already died. Therefore they didn't break His bones, and so unwittingly fulfilled Psalm 34:20: "He guards all his bones; not one of them is broken."

We have already considered much of what Jesus accomplished on the cross for us. But let's look at one more thing mentioned in Hebrews 10:19-22: "Therefore, brethren, having boldness to enter the Holiest by the blood of Jesus, by a new and living way which He consecrated for us, through the veil, that is, His flesh, and having a High Priest over the house of God, let us draw near with a true heart in full assurance of faith, having our hearts sprinkled from an evil conscience and our bodies washed with pure water."

It was impossible to enter into the Holy of holies until the death of Jesus, but now the veil was ripped and we can enter in. Because of that, the writer of Hebrews encourages us, "let us draw near with a true heart in full assurance of faith." The blood of Jesus has sprinkled and cleansed our hearts and freed us from an evil conscience!

We often make a big mistake at this point. We think we don't deserve to approach God. "I haven't done well this week," we say. "I didn't read my Bible. I had an impure thought. I lost my temper. I said something I shouldn't have. I did something else I'm ashamed of. So I can't pray—it's hypocritical."

But when we think that way, we're thinking as though we're living in the old covenant. That kind of thinking suggests that through our good living we obtain the approval of God.

The writer of Hebrews reminds us that we already *have* God's approval. We have His approval when we're doing well; we have His approval when we fail. He loves us as much when we sin as when we don't. His love for us has nothing to do with what we have done. There's nothing we could ever accomplish that would earn us the right to approach Him.

So when such devilish thoughts attack you, set them aside. You never *will* deserve God, so don't ever say you're not worthy.

You never *were* worthy in and of yourself. You never could be. The very thought is ridiculous.

But you *can* approach Christ. You can approach the throne of God because of what Jesus did for you at the cross. Don't let the devil cheat you out of access to His throne, which is the only place you can find the grace to help you in time of need. You can enter in at any time. Even when you sin—all the more reason to enter in and confess your sin.

The devil wants to keep you away from the cross. He hates the cross. He hates what the cross has accomplished. He hates the preaching of the cross. The Bible says it's through the preaching of the cross that people come to faith. Paul said, "I determined not to know anything among you except Jesus Christ and Him crucified" (1 Corinthians 2:2). The cross is the true power of God.

Satan wants to keep you away because he knows you can approach God day and night, no matter what you've done, and find the forgiveness that will allow you to live in victory over him. He tries to keep you away or lie to you about it.

Don't let this incredible privilege of approaching the throne of God go unused in your life. Remember what the writer of Hebrews said: "Let us therefore come boldly to the throne of grace, that we may obtain mercy and find grace to help in time of need" (4:16). Jesus gained this access for us, so let's take hold of it!

And please, don't wait for a better invitation. There just isn't one.

"Sin had no sooner come into the world than God came in grace, seeking the sinner, and so from the first question, 'Adam, where art thou?' on to the incarnation, God has been speaking to man."

—*Harry A. Ironside*

24

SURPRISE!

✍

"Peter therefore went out, and the other disciple, and were going to the tomb. So they both ran together, and the other disciple outran Peter and came to the tomb first."

—JOHN 20:3-4

EVEN THOUGH THE DISCIPLES forsook their master, He never forsook them.

Early one morning Mary Magdalene came to the tomb. Let's not forget that this was the woman out of whom Jesus cast seven demons; she was one of the faithful few at the foot of the cross. She loved Jesus very deeply. Jesus had said, "To whom much is forgiven, that one loves the more," and Mary had been forgiven of a lot.

She had come to anoint His dead body—that's all she wanted to do. But the tomb was empty. In her despair, perhaps she thought, *I'd better go tell those two great spiritual leaders, Peter and John.* She delivered her news and the men immediately ran to the tomb, John arriving first.

When John looked in, he didn't see what many paintings of the death and resurrection of Jesus would have us believe. He didn't see linen clothes just lying there. The original Greek text makes it clear the clothes were lying in a cocoon-like shape, empty. The Lord's body had passed right through those bandages. The Bible says John looked in, perceived, understood, and left. He always was a perceptive disciple.

Not so Peter. He came to the same scene, probably huffing and puffing, chest heaving. He also looked in, saw the identical scene John encountered . . . and the Bible says he went on his way wondering what had happened (*see* Luke 24:12).

Both men saw the same thing but reacted in two different ways, just as the two crucified thieves heard the same message but had opposite reactions. Peter didn't yet believe, and he left.

A little later Mary returned to the empty tomb. "At least this is where He was," she might have said to herself. She wanted to be as close to Him as she could, even if she couldn't be near His dead body. Hers wasn't some kind of morbid fascination; she knew His body wasn't in the tomb. She simply had an overpowering desire to be close to Jesus. How she missed Him! She couldn't bear the thought of life without Him. Her persistence certainly paid off, as we will soon see.

Soon she spied a man standing nearby whom she mistook for the gardener. She said, "Sir, if You have carried Him away, tell me where You have laid Him, and I will take Him away" (John 20:15).

The man replied with only one word, but it was enough to blow away the fog and lift her gloom and confusion. With tenderness and perhaps even laughter in His voice, Jesus said, "Mary!" (John 20:16).

Instantly, Mary understood. *I've heard that voice before*, she must have thought. Hadn't Jesus Himself said, "My sheep know My voice"? Mary knew His, and she was certain she had just heard it. Quickly brushing away her tears, she recognized her beloved Jesus. "Rabboni!" she cried out, addressing her Master and Teacher. Then she grabbed hold of Him for all she was worth.

"Touch me not," He gently commanded (John 20:17, KJV).

Don't touch Him? Why not? Some people think it's because He was in His mystical, glorified body, and this was not allowed. But I doubt it. If that were true, He would not later have said to Thomas, "Reach your finger here, and look at My hands; and reach your hand here, and put it into My side. Do not be unbelieving, but believing" (John 20:27).

I think it's more likely He gave the command because she was grabbing Him so tightly she was cutting off His circulation: "I've got You, Lord, and this time You're not getting away. Don't even think about it! If You ascend, I'm going up there with You." I'm joking, of course.

Actually, I think there was a much broader significance to His statement. I believe He was saying, "Mary, it's a new covenant. It's not like it used to be. I'm no longer going to be with you physically, walking from place to place. It's different now. I'm going to enter into your life and into your heart. You can't cling to Me like you used to; you need to change in that way. But I'll be closer to you than I ever was."

Mary left that encounter greatly encouraged, and several others got their turn at Jesus' encouragement in the ensuing few days. First He visited His discouraged band of disciples and gave them new hope. He appeared to 500 disciples on another occasion. He again appeared to Peter at the Sea of Galilee after he had gone fishing. About three days after His crucifixion He appeared on the Emmaus Road to two disciples who were terribly downhearted and discouraged. He didn't stay long physically with any of these people, but He reignited all their hearts.

Maybe you're discouraged. Maybe you feel as if God has let you down. Perhaps, like the disciples at the moment of His crucifixion, you're thinking He has forsaken you. He has failed. He didn't do what He promised.

Just hold on! The resurrection changed everything. It turned the disciples' doubt to faith and their hopelessness to hope. It can do the same for you. Because of the resurrection, Jesus now lives inside of His followers. And you can't get any closer than that.

Note how Mary's persistence paid off. She was granted a one-on-one conversation with the risen Lord.

Early-morning meetings with Jesus can bring special blessings; look up Psalm 63:1 and Proverbs 8:17.

25

UP, UP, AND AWAY!

"I will come again and receive you to Myself;
that where I am, there you may be also."

—JOHN 14:3

WHAT'S THE BEST TRIP you've ever taken? To Europe? Hong Kong? Hawaii? The Holy Land? Or are you someone who gets excited every time you hear a celebrity say, "I'm going to Disneyland"?

Whatever your current favorite vacation spot, I know of an upcoming trip that—if you're a Christian—will blow the socks off any journey you've ever made. It's the trip to heaven.

Jesus promised that He would be back for us someday. Notice He said, "I will come again and receive you to Myself." The Lord is not merely going to send for us; He's going to personally escort us to the Father's house. First Thessalonians 4:16-18 says, "The Lord Himself will descend from heaven with a shout, with the voice of an archangel, and with the trumpet of God. And the dead in Christ will rise first. Then we who are alive and remain shall be caught up together with them in the clouds to meet the Lord in the air. And thus we shall always be with the Lord. Therefore comfort one another with these words."

It's important to note that He didn't say, "I'm going to take you." He said, "I'm going to receive you." He's not going to force you into heaven, somehow tearing you from this earth. He will take those who want to go. Yet it's interesting that the word "receive" in the Greek text means "take away by force." I see a picture of a parent reaching out to a child in danger, pulling that child out of the predicament.

Many years ago my son, who was then about three or four, was playing by a large mirror tilted up against the wall. I looked up and saw him making his way toward it. Suddenly everything went into slow motion. He reached up and grabbed that mirror, which was broken, and it started to fall on him. I ran over, snatched him up, and pulled him away. Thankfully, he was all right. There was no way I would have left him in danger. I wanted to get him out of harm's way as quickly as possible.

That's what the Rapture is all about. In the Rapture, the Lord is coming to get us out of harm's way on an earth going from bad to worse. Jesus will reach out to receive us from an earth hurtling toward judgment. But He's coming only for those who want to be received. If you don't want to go, you can stay.

The book of Genesis tells us that when the angels arrived to deliver Lot out of Sodom and Gomorrah, Lot went (*see* Genesis 19:15-29). But his wife was reluctant. Hesitant. She looked back, and guess what? She didn't make it. That is why in Luke 17:32 Jesus said, "Remember Lot's wife." It was a warning to not look back.

If you're in love with this earth and this world system and you want to stay here, then stay here. God's not going to force you to go with Him. He's not going to force you to go to heaven. He's given you free will. If you want to stay, you can stay. It would be the worst decision you could possibly make, but He's given you that option.

Jesus is coming for those who will be watching and waiting. Sadly, many will be left. Jesus also said, "In that night there will be two men in one bed: the one will be taken and the other will be left. Two women will be grinding together: the one will be taken and the other left. Two men will be in the field: the one will be taken and the other left" (Luke 17:34-36). Where are you going to be?

I was in bed with my wife one night and we were talking about the return of the Lord. My wife was saying, "Imagine, Greg, it's going to be so great! The Lord is going to come and we're going to be raptured and be with Him!" As she continued talking, I quietly slipped out of bed and laid down on the floor. Then she said, "Won't it be wonderful?" and reached over to grab my hand . . . and I wasn't there. I was snickering on the floor. She said, "You know, Greg . . . Greg? Ahhhhhhhhhhh!"

It was a horrible trick.

That may be a silly illustration, but the tragic truth is, it's going to fit many people someday. They *will* be left. You may be reading this right now and you're married to a Christian woman or a Christian man, yet you yourself have never made that commitment. When the Lord comes back, your spouse, who is a believer, will be taken—and you'll be left. It will be too late for you. "Well," you say, "I'll just grab onto her leg and hitch a ride."

You will have to be quick! Scripture tells us that event will happen "in a moment, in the twinkling of an eye" (1 Corinthians 15:52). I've been told that the "twinkling of an eye," which is much faster than the blinking of one, lasts about one-thousandth of a second.

The only people Jesus will take with Him to heaven are those who are ready, and the only people who will be ready are those who have Jesus living inside of them. If you don't have Jesus living inside of you when He returns for His church, you won't be living with Jesus in heaven after the Rapture takes place. You'll be left here. Stranded. On a planet that soon thereafter will be engulfed in worldwide horrors worse than anything Hollywood can conjure up—a planet reeling to and fro like a drunken man, according to Isaiah 24:20.

Are you ready? Does Jesus live inside you? If He does, you're in for a treat. Get ready for the trip of your life! But if He doesn't,

I wouldn't get too excited if I were you. The only trip you can expect to make is to a location I wouldn't care to visit.

Read 1 Thessalonians 4:13–5:11 concerning the return of Christ for His church. Are you encouraging others with the news?

26

A DIVINE BLOCKBUSTER

✠

"Then the sign of the Son of Man will appear in heaven, and then all
the tribes of the earth will mourn, and they will see the Son of Man coming
on the clouds of heaven with power and great glory."

—MATTHEW 24:30-31

AT ONE TIME, newspapermen had an interesting name for the huge, bold letters used only for the most important headlines. They called it "Second-Coming type." When a typesetter was told to set a headline in Second-Coming type, he didn't have to know what the story was about—he just knew it was a blockbuster.

According to recent surveys, though, most journalists today don't believe in the resurrection of Christ, let alone in His Second Coming. But that doesn't change the rock-solid fact that there is coming a day when Christ will come again to establish His kingdom. And what a blockbuster that will be!

Bible students describe this event as His Second Coming. It's going to interrupt the battle of Armageddon, which will be the final brawl at the end of the Great Tribulation. John described the scene in Revelation 19:11-12, where he wrote, "I saw heaven opened, and behold, a white horse. And He who sat on him was called Faithful and True, and in righteousness He judges and makes war. His eyes were like a flame of fire, and on His head were many crowns." Matthew says that every eye will see Him coming on the clouds of heaven with power and great glory (24:30). That day is yet in the future.

Though many labor for world peace, doing their best to bring it about, there will be no peace until Jesus returns. I read a statement recently that says, "Visualize world peace." You can visualize all you want, you can teach peace all you want, you can work for peace all you want. But real and lasting peace will not come until Jesus Christ returns.

I've visited an area in Jerusalem they call the Garden of Gethsemane. It features ancient olive trees that date back some 2,000 years. Some think it's possible that this is the very area where Jesus prayed before He was taken into custody.

I don't know if it is or not, but when I visited that particular site and stood on that spot—when I looked at those gnarled, old olive trees and thought they might have been around when Jesus prayed some 2,000 years ago—I was greatly moved. If you look up from that place you see Jerusalem elevated on a hill, and you can't help but wonder if Jesus actually stood right where you're standing and gazed upon the city not far away. It's an unforgettable experience.

But I noticed something else when I visited the Garden of Gethsemane. Within eyeshot of this place stands the ancient Eastern Gate of Jerusalem. The Eastern Gate today is sealed. It is no longer in use. But Ezekiel 44:2 says this is the very gate the Messiah will use to enter the city when He returns to the earth.

History says the gate was sealed in the early sixteenth century by the Turkish conqueror Suleiman the Magnificent. No one knows for sure why he closed it, but one report says he sealed the gate when a rumor swept Jerusalem that Messiah was coming. Suleiman summoned some rabbis, who told him Messiah would be a great military ruler who would enter the Eastern Gate and liberate the city. This paranoid ruler decided to crush such hopes by sealing the gate and placing a Muslim cemetery in front of it, believing that no Jewish holy man would defile himself by walking over a Muslim cemetery. The gate has been sealed ever since.

That almost changed during the Six-Day War of 1967, when Israel regained control of Jerusalem for the first time in nearly 1,900 years. Several members of one Jewish commando group involved in the assault on the city had hoped to catch its Jordanian defenders off guard by blowing a hole in the gate. But the group's leader, an Orthodox Jew, nixed the idea when he fiercely insisted that the Eastern Gate can be opened only when the Messiah comes. The gate remained closed.

It's possible that from Gethsemane, Jesus looked up and saw the Eastern Gate. It would have reminded Him that a day was coming when He would return to the earth, not with a crown of thorns, but with a crown of gold. Many crowns, in fact. What He did in both Gethsemane and later at Calvary would set the stage for Him to come back and rule in glory.

But His Second Coming will not be much like the first.

His first entry into Jerusalem led to His rejection; His second entry will end in His coronation.

His first entry led to a cross; His second entry will bestow upon Him a throne worthy of the King of the universe.

His first entry left Him horribly alone; His second entry will be a time of rejoicing, when every knee will bow and every tongue will confess that Jesus Christ is Lord, to the glory of God the Father.

Jesus is coming again! First in the air for His church at the Rapture, and then at the end of the Great Tribulation to stop the battle of Armageddon and begin His 1,000-year rule of perfect peace and justice on a rejuvenated earth.

Jesus is coming again! Jesus is coming again! Jesus is coming again! And when He does, I guarantee that there won't be Second-Coming type big enough to do it justice.

"There are two ways of looking at the Lord's coming: a looking *for* it and a looking *at* it. It is possible to look at it with keen intellect and profound interest, and yet have it mean nothing to us personally. It is also possible to know but little of the theology of the subject, and yet have a deep and holy longing for our Lord to appear. May this theme be not only our study but also our personal hope; for 'unto them that look for him shall he appear a second time without sin unto salvation.'"

—*A.B. Simpson*

27

HOME SWEET HOME

✠

"In My Father's house are many mansions; if it were not so,
I would have told you. I go to prepare a place for you."

—JOHN 14:2

THERE'S NO COMFORT LIKE ETERNAL COMFORT.
Remember this the next time you lose a job or you have a fight with your parents or your spouse: We are going to spend eternity in heaven. Remember it the next time you're sick. Or an investment goes south. Or someone at church criticizes you. Or you face some other kind of difficulty. Remember this: You are going to heaven to live with Jesus forever. You may be having a hard time now, but it's temporary. It's not going to last forever. You are going to heaven!

Jesus says heaven has many mansions. When He said "mansions," He didn't mean you'd receive a neatly mowed lawn with either an upscale, middle-class, or lower-income housing unit, depending upon how godly a life you lived while on earth. That is, if you lived a really godly life, you would have a mansion similar to those in, say, Beverly Hills; if you lived a fairly godly life, you would get a nice tract home; and if you didn't do so well, you would live in a condo or small apartment.

He didn't mean that at all. In fact, it's virtually impossible for us even in our wildest dreams to imagine the splendor, beauty, and sheer awesomeness of heaven.

When Jesus said "mansions," He was probably referring to the new bodies that God is going to give us. It's not so much that we're going to live in little homes and we'll visit each others' homes for dinner. He was speaking of a new state of existence, a supernatural state without the boundaries of earth or the limitations of sin. God will give us new bodies.

Paul wrote in 2 Corinthians 5:1, "For we know that if our earthly house, this tent, is destroyed, we have a building from God, a house not made with hands, eternal in the heavens."

Then we're told in Philippians 3:21 that when Jesus comes back, He will take these dying bodies of ours and change them into glorious bodies like His own.

What else can we learn about heaven? It will be a place without darkness. Revelation 22:5 tells us, "There shall be no night there: They need no lamp nor light of the sun, for the Lord God gives them light."

Heaven will be a place free from fear. It seems as though our society is becoming increasingly dangerous, more and more violent. But in heaven you won't need bars on your windows. You won't have to put locks on your doors. You won't need any of that when you get to heaven. You'll be safe. You will walk the streets and not have to look over your shoulder. You won't be afraid for your safety.

In heaven, all your questions will be answered. In this life there are certain things I have learned to file away. I have a special folder in my brain labeled, "Wait for further information." I just file those things away. There are many things I don't understand. I don't know why God allows certain things. I don't know why He does certain things. I don't know why He doesn't do other things.

But I've come to realize that God is sovereign. He knows what He's doing; He's in control. I'm confident one day that when I see Him face to face, my questions will be answered.

Quite honestly, however, I don't see us standing around with God for a couple of decades and running our questions by Him. I think that one single look into His face and into His eyes, seeing Him in His holiness, will either answer all our questions or cause them to fade into insignificance.

And the best thing of all? Far more than the promise of streets of gold or answered questions is the knowledge that we will spend eternity with Jesus.

The Bible says that God has loved us in order "that in the ages to come He might show the exceeding riches of His grace in His kindness toward us in Christ Jesus" (Ephesians 2:7). Imagine that! God can't wait to make it clear to you how much He has loved you from eternity past. The Lord is looking forward to giving you a guided tour of heaven and showing you all He's done for you.

When people come to our home for a visit, my little boy Jonathan likes to take them up to his room and show them all of his toys. He proudly displays them. Even more so, God is looking forward to showing you the glories of heaven. He's looking forward to revealing things to you that He has not been able to show you yet because you're not ready for them.

Why aren't you ready? Because right now you're in a physical body with sinful limitations. But God is looking forward to the day when He can give you the grand tour!

Jesus says, "I go to prepare a place for you." What a fantastic promise! It's a little word of comfort that lasts for a long, long time. For eternity, in fact.

The greatest part about going to heaven is being with our Savior. We get a glimpse of heaven in the story of Stephen's death in Acts 7:54-60. As it did for Stephen, the joy of heaven should help us forget about our troubles and suffering on earth.

28

WHAT DO <u>YOU</u> THINK OF JESUS CHRIST?

✠

"But who do you say that I am?"

—LUKE 9:20

IN THE FIRST THIRD OF THIS BOOK, I have shown you, from God's Word, who Jesus Christ is. By now you should have a pretty good idea of what I think of Him. But there's just one question I have to ask you.

What do *you* think of Jesus Christ?

Or, put another way, Who do *you* say He is?

According to the Bible, that is the most important question you or anyone else will ever answer. It's important because it is inescapable; it demands a response.

Like Pontius Pilate, many will try to wash their hands of Jesus and say, "I have no comment. I have nothing to say." But the Bible presents us with inescapable questions that demand our response. We must answer yes or no; we must either follow the One who calls us or turn our backs on Him.

If Jesus was only a man, then we can safely forget about Him and not give Him a second thought. But if He was only a man, He was a *bad* one, not a good one, for liars are not good men.

Jesus claimed to be God, to be equal with the Father. He claimed to be the only One who could forgive our sin and give us the hope of eternal life. To say that He was a good man, but not God, is nonsense. He claimed to be God. Either He is who He claimed to be, or He was an impostor or a liar or worse.

John insists that Jesus was nothing less than God Himself come to earth. That is an essential; you must believe it to be a Christian. To disbelieve it is to dismiss Christ as a fraud, a liar. Jesus was God from the beginning.

In fact, even before the creation of the universe, Jesus was always there as God without beginning or end. Jesus said of Himself, "I am the Alpha and the Omega, the First and the Last" (Revelation 1:11). As God, He never had a beginning, nor does He have an end. In Jesus' prayer to the Father in John 17, the Savior said, "O Father, glorify Me together with Yourself, with the glory which I had with You before the world was" (verse 5).

Don't forget that the Jewish religious leaders wanted to kill Jesus because He equaled Himself with the Father. He said, "Before Abraham was, I AM" (John 8:58) and they took up stones to kill Him. On another occasion He said to a man, "Your sins are forgiven you" (Matthew 9:2), and they said, "This Man blasphemes!" (verse 3)—and they would have been absolutely right if He were not God in human form. Nobody but God can forgive sins. And yet Jesus claimed to do just that. What other conclusion could they make than that He claimed to be God?

Consider one more example. After Jesus' resurrection from the dead, Thomas fell down before Him and said, "My Lord and my God!" (John 20:28). If Jesus had not been God, He would have rushed to correct Thomas for uttering such blasphemy. That's what the angel did with John in Revelation 19:10 and what Paul and Barnabas did with the people of Lystra in Acts 14:13-15. But Jesus accepted the worship and praise of Thomas for one overpowering reason: He is the God-man.

I know this is hard for us to understand, but it's central to everything else. When Jesus came to the earth, in one sense He was born, but in another sense He wasn't. God wasn't born; God is eternal. But Jesus humbled Himself and was born as a man. He came as a human.

Isaiah 9:6 sums it up so well. It gives us heaven's perspective as well as the earth's. It says, "Unto us a Child is born, unto us a Son is given; and the government will be upon His shoulder. And His name will be called Wonderful, Counselor, Mighty God, Everlasting Father, Prince of Peace."

"Unto us a Child is born." That's our perspective. On Christmas we celebrate the birth of Jesus in the manger.

"A Son is given." That's God's perspective. What for us was the arrival of the Messiah to planet earth, was for God the departure of the Son from heaven.

One person put it like this: "Christ was hungry as a man, but He fed the hungry as God. He was thirsty as man, but yet He said, 'Let him that is athirst come to me and drink.' He was weary, but yet He says He is our rest. He paid taxes, but yet He is a king. He prays, but yet He hears prayer. He weeps, but yet He dries our tears. He was sold for thirty pieces of silver, but yet He redeemed the world. He was led as a lamb to the slaughter, but yet He was the good shepherd. He dies, and yet He gives life and by dying destroys death. There has never been a person like Jesus. God and man walking this earth."

The Bible insists that Jesus was the God-man, the only One who could make possible our salvation. As God, He provided an infinitely worthy sacrifice capable of *atoning* for the sins of all mankind. As a perfect man, He provided an infinitely worthy sacrifice capable of *dying* for the sins of all mankind.

That's what the Bible says about Jesus, and I believe it. But I'm sure you already knew that. The only real unanswered question in this chapter is, Who do *you* say Jesus is? Who is He to *you*?

That's not only the $64,000 question, it's the Priceless Question, because the answer you give will determine your place in eternity.

Who do *you* say Jesus is?

An unknown author gave this rendition of John 14:6:

> I am the Way, the Truth, and the Life.
> Without the Way there is no going,
> Without the Truth there is no knowing,
> Without the Life there is no living.

Do you know where your life is going?

PART TWO

WORKING OUT WHAT GOD HAS WORKED IN

"Let nothing be done through selfish ambition or conceit, but in lowliness of mind let each esteem others better than himself. Let each of you look out not only for his own interests, but also for the interests of others. . . . Therefore, my beloved, as you have always obeyed, not as in my presence only, but now much more in my absence, work out your own salvation with fear and trembling; for it is God who works in you both to will and to do for His good pleasure."

—PHILIPPIANS 2:3-4, 12-13

When Jesus calls us into a living relationship with Himself, everything changes. As the apostle Paul wrote in 2 Corinthians 5:17, "Therefore, if anyone is in Christ, he is a new creation; old things have passed away; behold, all things have become new." ✄ The way we look at life changes. The way we do things changes. The way we respond to people changes. In fact, *the way we live changes.* ✄ That's what Paul meant in Philippians 2:12 when he wrote, "Work out your own salvation with fear and trembling." He didn't mean that Jesus helped you reach the first rung on the salvation ladder, and now you've got to climb the rest of the way to heaven on your own. You could never do it! No, Jesus brings His children all the way to the Father—otherwise, none of us would ever make it. ✄ Paul also tells us, "It is God who works in you both to will and to do for His good pleasure" (Philippians 2:13). Verses 12 and 13 demonstrate the balance in Scripture: God has a part and we have a part. ✄ Did you know that there are certain things that only God can do and certain things that only you can do? For instance, only God can convict you of your sins. Only

God can forgive you of your sins. Only God can convert you. On the other hand, only you can obey Him. Only you can repent. The Bible says God wants to work through you—the question is, will you cooperate? He will not force you against your will. If you desire to be a true follower of Jesus Christ, your "walk" must match your "talk." Let's take a journey now with the first followers of Jesus as they learned the practical lessons of spending every day with Jesus.

1

GROWING GOD'S WAY

✄

"Abide in Me, and I in you. As the branch cannot bear fruit of itself,
unless it abides in the vine, neither can you, unless you abide in Me."

—JOHN 15:4

HOW DO WE GROW SPIRITUALLY? What is the secret? According to Jesus, it's simple and straightforward: "Abide in Me."

The word "abide" implies permanence of position. It means that we sink our roots deeply into our relationship with God. Jesus said, "If anyone desires to come after Me, let him deny himself, and take up his cross daily, and follow Me" (Luke 9:23).

Following the Lord is a daily lifestyle. The psalmist spoke of this when he wrote, "I will extol You, my God, O King; and I will bless Your name forever and ever. *Every day* I will bless You, and I will praise Your name forever and ever.... The LORD is near to all who call upon Him, to all who call upon Him in truth. He will fulfill the desire of those who fear Him; He also will hear their cry and save them" (Psalm 145:1-2, 18-19). The psalmist's relationship with the Lord was marked by a regular, continuous commitment.

That's hard for us. We live in a culture that prizes speed. We don't like to wait for anything. We're always on the lookout for shortcuts. In the old days, if you wanted to send a letter, you had to write it, put a stamp on it, and wait for the postman to pick it up. Nowadays, you just fax it. Once we had to look for pay phones when we were away from home. Not anymore. Now we have portable cellular phones. I saw a guy in the store the other day with two cellular phones, talking on both of them at once.

These days you can send messages across the world at the speed of light. You can cross the Atlantic in under three hours. You can microwave a whole meal in minutes. You can even get your dry cleaning back the same day!

We move in a fast-paced society where everything is *now*. We don't want to wait. We ask for it and it's there. Sometimes we try to carry over that attitude to our relationship with God. We wonder, *What are the shortcuts? What are the easy angles? What's the inside track?*

I'm sorry, but there aren't any shortcuts, there are no easy angles. The only way to spiritual growth is to abide. Sink your roots deeply into Jesus Christ and continually walk with Him, and *in time* you will see fruit.

Are you abiding in Jesus? It's interesting that 1 John 2:6 says, "He who says he abides in Him ought himself also to walk just as He walked." Walking is a steady motion. You put one foot in front of the other. It's a regular, continuous gait. The only way to bring forth fruit is to stick with it.

A lot of people don't stick with it. Oh, maybe they go to church and even get excited about Jesus Christ. Perhaps they go forward at an invitation or pray a prayer. Things go well for a couple of weeks, but as soon as a little difficulty or hardship comes their way, they say, "Forget this. I tried Jesus Christ and it didn't work for me." The problem for these people is that they never learned how to abide. They never got their roots into Jesus. They never learned what it was to discipline themselves to stick with it.

Do you want to grow in your relationship with Jesus? If so, you have to put forth some effort. There has to be a commitment. That is why David prayed in Psalm 51:10, "Create in me a clean heart, O God, and renew a *steadfast* spirit within me." The word translated "steadfast" means "a constant spirit." It means "stick with it."

But how does this work out in day-to-day living? How do we abide in Jesus in a practical sense?

One aspect of abiding is to take time for God and His Word every day. Notice, I said *take* time. I didn't say to wait for time to materialize. If you wait for a convenient moment to read the Bible, you'll rarely find it. *Take time.* Make time for the Word of God—it's an indispensable discipline for growing in grace.

Second, make time to communicate with God in prayer. John wrote, "This is the confidence that we have in Him, that if we ask anything according to His will, He hears us. And if we know that He hears us, whatever we ask, we know that we have the petitions that we have asked of Him" (1 John 5:14-15). Prayer is your lifeline. You can no more grow in your faith without prayer than a branch can grow without being attached to the vine.

Third, those who want to grow must continually confess their sin. Jesus says He will clean us through His Word—we're made clean through the Word He has spoken to us (*see* John 15:3). If we're abiding in Him, we're not going to live in continual sin. First John 3:6 literally says, "Whoever abides in Him does not habitually and continually sin."

Fourth, to abide means to take time to be with God's people. Hebrews 10:24-25 says, "And let us consider one another in order to stir up love and good works, not forsaking the assembling of ourselves together, as is the manner of some, but exhorting one another, and so much the more as you see the Day approaching."

Abiding makes all the difference. In Acts 2 we read of an early church that was thriving and powerful and impacting its world. Acts 2:47 says, "The Lord added to the church daily those who were being saved." Abiding is not something we do only on

Sunday morning or Sunday night. All through the week we must seek opportunities to get together with God's people, to get into the Word, to pray, to grow spiritually.

No, abiding is not a quick process. There are no short courses and we can't skip a grade or two. But that's no problem if we're abiding with *Him*. Because, after all, that's exactly what we were made for!

"God's training is for *right now*, not for some mist-shrouded future. His purpose is for this minute, not for something better down the road. His power and His presence are available to you as you draw your next breath, not for some great impending struggle. This moment is the future for which you've been preparing!"

—Joni Eareckson Tada

2

THE SECRET OF CONTENTMENT

"But seek the kingdom of God, and all these things shall be added to you."

—LUKE 12:31

ALL OF US ARE SEEKING something in life. We're all living for something; there's something we desire. Our ambition is directed in a certain way.

Some people are seeking to be loved. Others are seeking success. Some are seeking wealth. Some are seeking fame. Others are seeking power. Still others are seeking inner peace or happiness or contentment. But according to Jesus, the only possible result of seeking these things *in and of themselves* is frustration and failure.

The Bible tells us to seek the kingdom of God above all else. What is this kingdom? It is simply the rule and reign of Christ. That's what it means to seek first His kingdom. I'm going to trust in, follow after, and live in the will of God. When we seek first the reign and the will of God in our lives, everything else will come into balance.

This is a foundational truth in the Christian life. Allowing other pursuits or possessions or people to take the place of God's kingdom in our lives will only guarantee confusion, failure, emptiness, and dissatisfaction.

It is impossible to overstate the importance of seeking first the kingdom of God. Even the word "seek" that Jesus used in Luke 12:31 means "to pursue earnestly." We must live for the kingdom of God. If you want to find contentment, seek the kingdom before all other pursuits.

Every day we make a series of decisions as to what kingdom we're going to seek. Are we going to seek our own kingdom or are we going to seek God's kingdom? Are we going to take time for His Word? Are we going to take time for prayer? Are we going to take time to consider the will of God?

You must decide if you are going to honor God and His Word and do what is honest and truthful and live a life of integrity—even if it means you don't reach a little higher on the career ladder or bank a few more dollars in your savings account. If you make that choice, God will honor you for it. God says, "Those who honor Me I will honor" (1 Samuel 2:30). Best of all, you'll have a clean conscience. You won't have to worry about getting caught. You will know you have done what is right before God because you sought first His kingdom.

First Kings 3 tells the story of Solomon, to whom God said, "Ask! What shall I give you?" (verse 5). Imagine! He was given carte blanche. What if tonight God woke you up from your sleep and said, "I will give you whatever you want"? What would you ask for? To become rich? To be made powerful? What would be the real passion of your heart if God were to give you a blank check and say, "You write in what you want. Write in the amount. What is it I can give you?"

Solomon demonstrated that he was seeking first God's kingdom when he said, "I need wisdom to rule Your people." God was enormously pleased by his request and not only gave the young king great wisdom, but also riches and honor and a long life. Because Solomon sought first the kingdom of God, God gave him those other things. David's son had his priorities straight.

It's when we forget God's will, when we become obsessively oriented toward our own lives, when we put our will and our desires and our kingdom first, that we grow confused and worried and anxious and agitated. You cannot pray, "Thy kingdom come" until you first pray, "My kingdom go."

Seek first His kingdom! So often we seek first success or personal happiness or financial prosperity. But if we seek first the kingdom, God will bring us the success we need—maybe not as much as we want, maybe more! But He will give us what we need.

When you seek first His kingdom, He will bless your marriage. When you seek first His kingdom, He will bless your ministry. When you seek first His kingdom, He will take care of your needs. Concentrate your energies and channel your ambitions into seeking above everything else the rule and reign of Jesus Christ. Let Him be Lord of your business, Lord of your personal life, Lord of your finances, Lord of your imagination. Let Him be Lord of everything. If you do that, everything in life will come into its proper balance.

You and I *must* seek Him first. That's our part. God will take care of the rest. Seek Him earnestly. Seek Him continually. Live for His kingdom and His rule and reign in your life. Failure to do this will ensure a life full of worry, fear, uncertainty, and a world falling apart at the seams.

Maybe you have been choked out by worry. Maybe you are on a troubled sea of anxiety. Maybe something is really frightening you right now. Maybe you have been diverted into other things and God's Word is being choked out in your life. If so, you need to refocus your priorities and get back to the balanced life. Seek first the kingdom! Put Him first! Follow Him! And *then* all these things will be added to you.

Read the first chapter of Joshua. There you will find God's prescription for success and happiness, as told to Joshua, the new leader of the Israelites. How can you apply the principles God gave Joshua to your own life as you seek His kingdom?

3

GOD'S ANSWER TO BURNOUT

✄

"And she had a sister called Mary, who also sat at Jesus' feet and heard His word. But Martha was distracted with much serving."

—LUKE 10:39-40

YOU CAN'T GIVE OUT what you don't possess. You cannot take a person any further than you yourself have first gone. You must make time to take in before you can give out. If you don't believe me, consider the story of Martha in Luke 10.

When Jesus arrived at Martha's for a visit, she hoped to make a great impression by busying herself with meal preparation and housecleaning. Mary, meanwhile, decided to spend some time at Jesus' feet, listening to His teaching. Finally, in exasperation, Martha reprimanded her sister and asked Jesus to use His executive privilege to tell Mary to get up and come into the kitchen to help. But to Martha's surprise, the Lord commended Mary and told Martha to follow her example.

You might say Martha was a doer. She wasn't the type who sat around and just talked. You could count on her to say, "Let's get in there and get our hands dirty." Yes, she wanted to please the Lord, but she made the common mistake of offering work for worship, activity instead of adoration, perspiration in place of inspiration. Jesus wanted her attention, but she offered Him a flurry of activity. As a result, she wore herself out.

106

Mary, on the other hand, found the balance. She recognized there was a time to work and a time to worship, a time to stand and a time to sit, a time to move and a time to pray.

The irony of Martha's dilemma is that she received Jesus into her house and then neglected Jesus in the process. She apparently prepared an elaborate meal that He really did not need. Then afterward she was so busy cleaning up that she didn't take time to enjoy His presence. Certainly a meal was in order—but what we do *with* Christ is far more important than what we do *for* Christ. It's not an either/or situation. It is a matter of balance.

While Martha was bustling in the kitchen, Mary sat at Jesus' feet and heard His word. Now, don't get the idea that Mary was lazy. Of course, there are lazy people out there. They look for an opportunity to get out of work—any excuse. Mary was no such person. The term used here implies that Mary, like Martha, had worked to prepare the meal, but knew when it was time to take off the apron and sit at the feet of her most honored guest. Here in her living room was the Creator of the universe, the almighty God who made heaven and earth. And He wanted to talk to them!

All Martha could think about, in a manner of speaking, was doing the dishes. It's crazy, really. It was as if Mary was saying, "Martha, let's seize this opportunity, this wonderful moment to sit at the feet of Jesus." But Martha just had to get those dishes done.

Perhaps another translation will help us to get a better handle on the situation. The text could be translated this way: "Martha was going around in circles, overoccupied with preparing the meal. And bursting in upon Jesus, she assumed a stance over Him and said, 'Lord, is it a concern to You that my sister has let me down to be preparing the meal alone? Speak therefore to her at once that she take hold and do her part with me.' And answering, the Lord said to her, 'Martha, Martha, you are worried and excited about many things, but one thing is needed and Mary has chosen for herself the good portion which is of such a nature that it shall not be hastily snatched away from her.'"

My favorite part of that translation is, "Martha was going around in circles, overoccupied," and then "assumed a stance over" the Lord. That's classic! I can just see it. She has her hands on her hips and is demanding, "Lord, will You tell this lazy sister of mine to get in the kitchen and help me clean up?"

That really sums up a lot of our lives, doesn't it? "Going around in circles" while we "assume a stance" over the Lord. We're engaged in a flurry of activity. Sometimes we just need to stop and say, "Exactly what am I accomplishing? Is this all necessary?"

I've noticed that when people suffer some kind of a physical breakdown, they tend to reevaluate their lives. Someone has a heart attack and he is told it occurred because he is stressed out and not eating properly and not exercising. He is doing too much and he needs to slow down. Many times I have heard people say on their hospital beds, "Boy, I just realized I've been wasting my time. I've been too busy working and doing all these things that aren't that important. Now I'm going to spend more time in the Word and in prayer and more time with my family." Unfortunately, as they begin to get better, often the old habits reappear.

If you are growing weary and tired, it may be because you are acting like Martha, running around in circles in the kitchen, when you should be following the example of Mary by sitting at Jesus' feet. You can't give out more than you take in. You can't give out more than you possess. Any ministry of any lasting value will be the overflow of a Christ-filled life.

Paul wrote to young Timothy, "The hard-working farmer must be first to partake of the crops" (2 Timothy 2:6). In other words, in all of Timothy's activity for the Lord, he was to remember to take time to feed himself. He couldn't feed others effectively until he himself had been fed first.

You know, things haven't changed one bit since New Testament times. We all need to take in before we can give out. Just ask Martha.

"The measure of the worth of our public activity for God is the private communion we have with Him."
—*Oswald Chambers*

4

A CHANGED LIFE

✄

"Lord, I give half of my goods to the poor; and if I have taken anything from anyone by false accusation, I restore fourfold."

—LUKE 19:8

THE ONLY WAY YOU CAN KNOW if someone has truly been converted is to note a change in his outward actions and lifestyle.

Zacchaeus showed he had really met Christ by the radical change in his life—drastic, dramatic, and instantaneous. Up to this point his motto had been, "I get." Now his motto was, "I give." Up to this point it could have been said of his past, "I robbed." Now he was saying, "I restore."

If a man or a woman's character and lifestyle do not change, it is doubtful his or her heart was ever touched by God. The great preacher Charles Spurgeon once said, "Of what value is the grace I profess to receive if it does not dramatically change the way that I live? If it doesn't change the way that I live, it will never change my eternal destiny." If your life isn't changed, your eternal destiny probably isn't, either. You must become a different person. You will stop doing certain things and start doing others.

In Acts 26:18 the apostle Paul described what happens when people meet Christ. God opens the eyes of unbelievers so they turn from darkness to light and from the power of Satan to God. Notice the steps. First our eyes are opened. Then we turn from darkness to light and from the power of Satan to God. And then we are forgiven.

Some people have their eyes opened. They see that they need God. They see there is a heaven and a hell beyond the grave and they want to live in heaven. They see their life is empty. They realize that Jesus died on the cross for them—but they do nothing about it. Until we turn from darkness to light and from the power of Satan to God, however, we've only taken the first step. We have to follow through. We have to go all the way.

Suppose you are drowning. It is good that you recognize your danger. Now you need to cry out for help. Knowing you are drowning isn't good enough. You had better make your needs known and cry out for help.

Faith without works is dead, according to James. He wrote, "What does it profit, my brethren, if someone says he has faith but does not have works? Can faith save him?" (James 2:14). And then he adds, "You believe that there is one God. You do well. Even the demons believe—and tremble!" (verse 19).

It's great to acknowledge the existence of God. But you must receive Him as your own and then turn from known sins. Some people claim to be Christians, but they're still involved in drinking or drugs or sexual immorality or lying or stealing. If you live that way continually, it's doubtful you are a Christian. If there has been no marked change from the day you supposedly gave your life to Christ, it's questionable that you are saved. If there isn't a change in the way you live on earth, there will be no change in where you will spend eternity.

Galatians 5:21 says, "Those who practice such things will not inherit the kingdom of God." Take this as a warning. If you are living a dual life, putting on a good face in church and being the first to say, "Praise the Lord!"—but are involved in an affair, dishonesty, stealing, lying, or in any other willful sin, you're in grave danger! Every day that you continue in that sin and refuse to repent, your heart is getting harder and you are one step closer to judgment.

God's Spirit doesn't convict you to ruin your life. He convicts you because He loves you and He wants you to come to your senses. He doesn't want you to face judgment. Repent! Your Father loves you. Come out of that lifestyle! Be a new person in Christ! Old things have passed away; all things have become new.

The day Zacchaeus was converted, Jesus told him that He had to dine with him. He wasn't saying, as they do in Hollywood, "Let's do lunch." He was looking for a much longer-term commitment than that.

In that time, having a meal was not like getting into a car and driving through a take-out restaurant. A meal in this culture was a long, drawn out, relaxed affair. You didn't sit in straight-backed chairs around a table with linen and fine silverware. You sat on pillows in a reclining position at a low table. Mealtime was an enjoyable, relaxed atmosphere perfect for talk and interaction.

Jesus used this picture to describe the kind of relationship He wants with you. In essence, He says to you, "Relax. Let your hair down. Be yourself with Me. Don't put on an act. Don't try to pretend you are something you're not. Be honest with Me. Bare your heart to Me. Tell Me of your failures, of your shortcomings, and I'll tell you how to correct them. I'm going to show you which way to live. I'm going to be there with you. I want to be your Lord and I want you to be surrendered to Me. As long as you run and try to do it in your own strength, you are going to be miserable. But if you get in alignment with Me, things will go as they ought to and your life will be rich and full of joy."

That doesn't mean life will go smoothly with no problems. Not at all! But you will have the assurance that when you encounter difficulties, He will be there with you, guiding you through the storms to make you more like Him. And that, after all, is what true salvation is all about—becoming more like Him.

It's time to check your own reflection. Does the face staring back at you look more like Jesus than it did yesterday?

What kind of changed life is Jesus looking for? Read Ephesians 4:17–5:21. Can people identify you as a child of God?

5

POWER UNDER CONSTRAINT

✦

"Blessed are the meek, for they shall inherit the earth."

—MATTHEW 5:5

I ONCE WENT HORSEBACK RIDING with my 6′4″ friend, Dennis. He had a beautiful quarter-horse which he graciously allowed me to ride for the afternoon, while he borrowed a considerably smaller steed. Dennis was so much bigger than this horse that his feet nearly touched the ground as he sat in the saddle!

Understandably, the horse was not pleased with his rider and tried desperately to buck him off. But Dennis was in charge, and at last the horse submitted to his fate and carried his determined rider. Dennis was in control.

It wasn't that the horse no longer had a mind or strength or will of its own, but the animal realized it had to surrender its will and strength and mind to its stronger rider.

In other words, that horse became *meek*. A person (or a horse) who is meek simply recognizes who he is. He comes to an accurate and honest assessment of himself, resulting in a new way in which he approaches others. When we see ourselves as we really are, we come to a true state of meekness. We are emptied of selfish ambition and arrogance.

"Blessed are the meek," Jesus said. But don't equate meekness with a lack of strength. Jesus didn't say, "Blessed are the weak." By meek He meant that we are to willingly surrender our will and strength to God.

Some people are shy and softspoken and we call them meek, but they may not be meek at all. They might just be shy and softspoken.

The word "meek" means "power under constraint." It was a word used to describe the taming of a wild stallion. If you are a horseback rider and you have tamed or broken horses, you know what it is like to try to get a horse under your control.

Meekness is strength under control, and it doesn't come naturally. It needs to be worked into our lives by the power of the Holy Spirit.

Suppose someone were bothering you and you knew that with one punch you could level him, yet you did not do so. That would be meekness. On the other hand, let's say someone much stronger than you hit you and you knew he would pulverize you if you dared to retaliate, therefore you chose not to hit back. That's not meekness; it's common sense. It is an admission that your adversary is powerful and that you don't want to tangle with him.

What a contrast Jesus' words are to this world's way of thinking! The world says, "If you want to get ahead in life, you've got to assert yourself." Our culture is obsessed with personal rights. Everybody is demanding their rights and they stand up for them. It seems as if many people today believe there is nothing more important than their personal rights. We must assert ourselves and get our piece of the pie. Yet Jesus insists, "Blessed are the meek."

Such a statement was as much a shock in Jesus' day as it is in ours. His listeners expected Him to establish an earthly kingdom immediately. They thought He was going to overthrow the tyranny of Rome and reign as their Messiah right then and there. But He had no intention of complying with their expectations. One day He would reign—but before that day would come, He would subject Himself to the humiliation of the cross.

To be meek is not to be weak! Jesus Himself said, "I am meek and lowly in heart" (Matthew 11:29, KJV). It is the only autobiographical description He ever gave of His personality.

Jesus was anything but feeble. He was power incarnate. There was never a more powerful individual who walked the face of this earth. Yet He kept that power under control. He never performed a miracle for His own benefit. He never used His power to vanquish His enemies as He could have, even when He was arrested on trumped-up charges in the Garden of Gethsemane or when He hung on the cross and the crowd mocked Him. He could have dealt with them; He could have used His power. But He operated in meekness. He exemplified power under constraint.

Philippians 2:6-8 gives us a good definition of what the Master did for us. Paul writes, "Who, being in the form of God, did not consider it robbery to be equal with God, but made Himself of no reputation, taking the form of a servant, and coming in the likeness of men. And being found in appearance as a man, He humbled Himself and became obedient to the point of death, even the death of the cross." Now, *that* was meekness!

What does this mean for us? Paul answers that very question in the verses immediately preceding the passage just quoted: "Let nothing be done through selfish ambition or conceit, but in lowliness of mind let each esteem others better than himself. Let each of you look out not only for his own interests, but also for the interests of others. Let this mind be in you which was also in Christ Jesus" (Philippians 2:3-5).

God wants you and me to be meek persons. He wants us to stop asserting our own will and to look out for others. He calls us to be concerned for the welfare of those around us, not focused merely on our own desires.

Meekness is not weakness! We must all choose to be meek—and if we don't, we should expect some divine spurs in our ribs.

Read 1 Peter 2:20-23 to see how important meekness is to God. Remember Jesus' example the next time you feel like exerting your own will when you should keep it under restraint.

6

A CRAVING FOR HOLINESS

⚔

"Blessed are those who hunger and thirst for
righteousness, for they shall be filled."

—MATTHEW 5:6

HAVE YOU EVER BEEN SO HUNGRY that you felt as though you could eat almost anything? It went beyond a casual hunger. It was a ravenous craving in which eating was all you could think about.

Perhaps you have visited a foreign country and you couldn't wait until you could get back to eating the food you're used to—a pepperoni pizza, a burger with the works, or a good, old-fashioned ballpark hot dog.

Imagine feeling this same kind of hunger for the Word of God. Think about how different your life would be if you had an insatiable craving for holiness!

That's exactly the kind of hunger Jesus was talking about when He spoke of those who hunger and thirst for righteousness. It's a hunger and thirst for God Himself. As the psalmist said, "As the deer pants for the water brooks, so pants my soul for You, O God. My soul thirsts for God, for the living God" (Psalm 42:1).

We can come to this point in our spiritual walk only if we

have seen ourselves as we really are (sinful and dependent upon God), become emptied of our selfish ambitions, and seek solely the things that God wants for us. Otherwise, we will never develop a real hunger and thirst for righteousness. We have to taste it before we develop a craving for it.

Paul writes about this pursuit of righteousness in 2 Timothy 2:22. He admonishes Timothy, "Flee also youthful lusts; but pursue righteousness, faith, love, peace with those who call on the Lord out of a pure heart."

Have you noticed that when you snack between meals during the day, you lose your appetite for dinner? If you eat junk food, you lose your appetite for the good foods that provide you with the nutrition you need. In the same way, we can fill ourselves with so much mental junk food that we lose our interest in God's Word.

Think about it. How interested are you in spending an hour in prayer and Bible reading after watching two hours of television? After 120 minutes in front of the tube, you probably don't feel like doing much of anything! We have to beware of overexposing ourselves to anything that would cause us to lose our appetite for God.

The question we all need to ask ourselves is not whether a particular action or activity is allowable, but whether it is helping us or hurting us. G. Campbell Morgan put it well when he said, "Anything that dims the vision of the ultimate, that kills the passion in our life, is a waste."

Morgan was commenting on Hebrews 12:1, which instructs us to "lay aside every weight, and the sin which so easily ensnares us." That weight is anything that would slow down our spiritual progress, dull our conscience, or choke out the spirit of prayer. Like Paul told Timothy, we need to flee youthful passions.

But maybe that's not your problem. You have already removed yourself from a sinful situation or a compromising matter, but you still don't have that passion for God you read about in Scripture. The second part of 2 Timothy 2:22 provides you with the keys to developing a deep hunger for God. You need to discover where to find righteousness, and then spend time with others who want to join you in this pursuit.

Find godly people who will influence you, thus helping you to become godly yourself so that you, likewise, can influence others. When you spend a lot of time around a godly person, you might say it "rubs off." Just try spending a couple of evenings a week with someone who loves to share his faith. You will find that you'll suddenly have more courage and opportunities to witness. Try getting together with someone who loves to pray, and then see if your prayer life begins to change. Something happens when you run the race of life with people who are sold out to Jesus.

Show me someone who is constantly being trapped by sin and stumbling in his walk, and I'll show you someone who is not fleeing youthful passions. I'll show you someone who is filling up on mental junk food, leaving no appetite for God and His Word. I'll show you someone who is hanging out with people who have no interest in spiritual things.

But show me someone who has been spending time in God's Word and with His people, someone who craves to learn more about God and to be in His presence, and I'll show you someone who is, as Jesus promised, "filled"—someone who is spiritually blessed in all aspects of life.

May God help us to become people who are hungry and thirsty for righteousness! And may we be satisfied with nothing less than God Himself.

"Many of us would love to have sin taken away. Who loves to have a hasty temper? Who loves to have a proud disposition? Who loves to have a worldly heart? No one. You ask Christ to take it away, and He does not do it. Why does He not do it? It is because you wanted Him to take away the ugly fruits while the poisonous roots remained in you. You did not ask that henceforth you might give up self entirely to the power of

His Spirit. Do you suppose that a painter would want to work out a beautiful picture on a canvas which did not belong to him? No. Yet people want Jesus Christ to take away this temper or that other sin while as yet they have not yielded themselves utterly to His command."

—*Andrew Murray*

7

MATTERS OF THE HEART

✦

"Blessed are the pure in heart, for they shall see God."

—MATTHEW 5:8

SOMETHING IS SORELY LACKING in our culture today: Purity. I'm shocked by what some little children say, at the vile things that come out of their mouths. Of course, it should come as no surprise. The most wicked things are being aimed all the time at younger and younger audiences by producers of many TV programs, movies, and music.

It has come to the point where innocence and purity are almost lost virtues. It even seems as though anyone seeking such virtues is an oddball in today's confused culture. None of that changes God's opinion, however. He wants us to be pure in heart.

Consider Romans 16:19: "I want you to be wise in what is good, and simple concerning evil." This could be translated, "I would have you to be well versed and wise as to what is good and innocent and guileless as to what is evil."

But does this describe most people today? It seems as though most people are well versed in evil and ignorant of what is good. They know more about Hollywood celebrities than they do about the holy God. They are more familiar with rock stars than with the Rock of Ages and they are better versed on the latest gossip from afternoon TV talk shows than on the gospel!

We are well versed on perverse things, but how many of us are ignorant about what is good? We need to know far more about holiness and far less about evil. Purity of heart is obtainable. Otherwise, Jesus would not have commanded it.

In Matthew 5:8, Jesus was exposing the false teaching of the Pharisees, who outwardly observed the teachings of the Mosaic law but who inwardly violated them. They might not commit adultery, but their hearts were filled with lust. They might not commit murder, but their hearts boiled over with hatred. They gave offerings, but only to be seen by men. They prayed, but only to call attention to their piety. Their motives were wrong, and God passionately cares about what motivates us.

God said, "These people draw near to Me with their mouth, and honor Me with their lips, but their heart is far from Me" (Matthew 15:8). Jesus asks us, "Why do you call Me 'Lord, Lord,' and do not do the things which I say?" (Luke 6:46).

God is very interested in our motives, as Paul so clearly pointed out in 1 Corinthians 13:3: "Though I bestow all my goods to feed the poor, and though I give my body to be burned, but have not love, it profits me nothing." If my motives aren't right, my actions are worthless, meaningless. They are even self-deceptive, because I say, "This must be pleasing to God," when in fact God is offended. God wants your heart. He wants your motives to be right.

Suppose that I told my youngest son Jonathan, "Come over here and give me a hug or I'll spank you." He would hug me, but it wouldn't come from his heart. On the other hand, imagine that he came over voluntarily and said, "Dad, I love you so much." Usually he is buttering me up for something when he says things like that; he is planning to ask me for some money, for candy, or a new toy. But when it's genuine and comes from the heart, it touches me deeply because I know he did it just because he wanted to.

God wants the same. He wants our motives to be right. He wants our heart to be right. He wants us to be pure.

What exactly does it mean to be pure of heart? A literal definition might be "without hypocrisy." It means to be committed to doing good, veering neither to the left nor the right.

But this isn't easy. We want to do what is right; we want to be pure. But the old nature pulls us in the other direction. We all know what it's like to face this struggle. Paul summed it up well when he described his personal struggle: "For what I am doing, I do not understand. For what I will to do, that I do not practice; but what I hate, that I do. . . . For I delight in the law of God according to the inward man. But I see another law in my members, warring against the law of my mind, and bringing me into captivity to the law of sin which is in my members" (Romans 7:15, 22-23). Paul was being candid. He was saying, "Hey, this can be tough. It can be a real struggle."

So what is the answer to this double-minded dilemma? It's twofold: First, realize you are in it; and second, turn from it. James 4:8 says, "Cleanse your hands, you sinners; and purify your hearts, you double-minded." It is possible to solve the dilemma when we submit ourselves to the control of God's Holy Spirit. Jesus would not command us to be pure if it were an impossibility.

For those who seek such purity, Jesus promises a reward: "They shall see God." One day all of us will stand before God. We will see Him face to face, no longer through a glass darkly. But I also think purity of heart enables us to see God actively at work in our life *right now*. As we live a singular life, as we get our priorities right, we remove the barriers that separate us from God so we can see His hand more clearly and hear His voice more effectively.

May God help us to avoid being double-minded! And may He help us to have a singular devotion in which we love Jesus Christ more than anyone or anything else. When our hearts become that pure, we will truly know what it means to be blessed.

Read 1 Samuel 15:22-23 to see what kind of worship the Lord expects of us. Have you been truly pleasing the Lord in your life?

8

THE CHRISTIAN'S BADGE OF HONOR

✄

"Blessed are those who are persecuted for righteousness' sake,
for theirs is the kingdom of heaven."

—MATTHEW 5:10

WE ARE QUICK to claim promises of God's protection, but when was the last time you claimed a promise of persecution? How thankful are you that the apostle Paul wrote, "All who desire to live godly in Christ Jesus will suffer persecution" (2 Timothy 3:12)? When did you last say, "Lord, I claim that promise today"? I'll bet you never have. And to be honest, I don't necessarily want to claim it, either.

Yet the Bible does not present persecution as a circumstance to be dreaded. It presents it as a privilege, a great honor. As Paul wrote, "For to you it has been granted on behalf of Christ, not only to believe in Him, but also to suffer for His sake" (Philippians 1:29). You say, "If it's an honor, God can honor someone else." Or as Tevya prayed in *Fiddler on the Roof* as he reflected on the suffering of his people, the Jews: "Lord, if we are the chosen people, why don't You choose someone *else* for awhile?" Maybe you would say, "Lord, if this is a privilege, give it to someone else. In fact, I'll give You the name of who You can 'bless.'"

Consider what Jesus said in John 15:18-20: "If the world

hates you, you know that it hated Me before it hated you. If you were of the world, the world would love its own. Yet because you are not of the world, but I chose you out of the world, therefore the world hates you. Remember the word that I said to you, 'A servant is not greater than his master.' If they persecuted Me, they will also persecute you."

If you are living a life like Jesus Christ, you are going to receive the same kind of treatment He received. Oh, not all the time—even Jesus had His moments of popularity when He was the toast of the town. But there will be times when you will be let down, when you will be mocked and ridiculed...or even worse.

Persecution will come. The question is, Are you going to hide? Are you going to try to avoid it? Or are you going to stand up for Jesus Christ and be counted? God promises a blessing to every believer who stands up for Him. My deep hope is that we will be persecuted for the right reasons.

I fear too often we Christians are persecuted for the wrong reasons. Far too often we're not being persecuted for righteousness' sake, but because we're acting in a "holier than thou" manner. Too often we're persecuted for being obnoxious, tactless, condemning, moronic, idiotic, or for acting like a Pharisee.

If I'm going to be persecuted, I want to suffer for the right reasons. First Peter 4:15 says, "Let none of you suffer as a murderer, a thief, an evildoer, or as a busybody in other people's matters."

But why would we be persecuted for living a righteous life? Because righteousness is confrontational. When you live a godly life, even though you don't necessarily say anything, you are an open rebuke to the ungodly. It's like being in a pitch-dark room when someone flicks on the light. "Turn that light off! It's blinding," they scream.

You are shining as a light in a dark place. You may not be openly condemning people or accusing them, but they know what you stand for. Either they are going to receive what you stand for or they may harass and oppose you, because light does not mix with darkness any more than righteousness mixes with unrighteousness.

As you live a godly life, Jesus Christ will overflow from you and you will naturally develop a desire to talk about your Lord with others. But as you proclaim your faith, you can bank on the persecution that's coming, and brace yourself for it.

When was the last time you were persecuted? Persecution needn't imply a physical beating. Jesus identified one aspect of it when He said, "Blessed are you when [men] *revile* you" (Matthew 5:11). The word "revile" means "to insult, to be mocked." When was the last time you were mocked for being a Christian? When was the last time you were insulted for your faith? If you are living a godly life, it is inevitable.

The great evangelist John Wesley was persecuted regularly during his ministry. It was common for bricks and eggs and vegetable projectiles to come flying his way when he was preaching. One day Wesley was riding along on his horse and it dawned on him that three whole days had passed during which he had suffered no persecution. Not a brick or an egg had been thrown at him. Greatly alarmed, he halted his horse, fell on his knees and cried out, "God, have I backslidden? Have I sinned, causing me to suffer no persecution?"

A good pagan on the other side of a hedge where Wesley was praying overheard this, picked up a brick, and said, "I'm going to get that crazy preacher!" He heaved the brick over the hedge, just missing Wesley as he prayed. The evangelist jumped up joyfully and exclaimed, "Thank God, it's all right. I still have His presence!"

Would that be your attitude? Or would you cry out, "God, why did You let this happen? If You loved me You wouldn't allow it!"

Persecution is not something to avoid or to be ashamed of. It's something to be proud of. Wear it as a badge of honor, Christian, that Jesus would count you worthy to be His representative and to face the same kind of treatment He received. Don't go looking for it or seeking it, but rejoice when it comes your way. It means you still have His presence.

Read 2 Timothy 2:8-13 for Paul's powerful words about suffering for the sake of Christ. May this be an encouragement to you in times of testing!

9

WHEN THE WORLD DOESN'T LIKE YOU

✄

"Blessed are you when they revile and persecute you, and say all kinds of evil against you falsely for My sake. Rejoice and be exceedingly glad, for great is your reward in heaven."

—MATTHEW 5:11-12

MOST OF US are a lot more like Nathanael than we realize. Remember him? He's the one who initially responded to Jesus the Nazarene with a sarcastic, "Can anything good come out of Nazareth?" (John 1:46).

Of course, we might rephrase his question a little. We're good Christians and we would never challenge the Master, but we're not above challenging His wisdom. So we ask, "Can anything good come out of persecution?" The answer is a resounding yes!

For one, did you know that persecution is often the first step a person takes toward conversion? We all know unbelievers who are passive and easygoing toward us as Christians. They may say, "I'm glad you're a Christian. I am glad that *you* have found peace with God. I am glad *you're* a happy person. I really admire you." When you ask, "Will you come to church with me?" they respond, "No, I won't. But I think it's wonderful for *you*." They are exceptionally pleasant to you and you think, *Isn't that great, this person is so close to the kingdom.* But they may not be as close as you think; appearances can be deceiving.

On the other hand, there is that obnoxious person whom you dread seeing. It's as if he spends his weekends thinking up hard questions to ask you. He waits until a room fills with people and then says, "Hey Christian, I have a question for you." And he lays some monster puzzle on you. He antagonizes you. He harasses you. He makes fun of you and you think, *He is so far from the kingdom.*

Did you ever stop to think that your antagonistic friend might be the one with an arrow of conviction sticking out of his chest? He's antagonistic because he is in pain, but he asks those questions because he is searching. He wants to see how you will react to the disagreeable way he asks his tough questions.

I know a little about this because I used to be quite the mocker. I made fun of Christians. I thought they were fools. I laughed at the way they lived.

But even when I mocked Christians, I respected them. I admired something in them—the way they bore up under the abuse, the way they stood up for their faith even when they were ridiculed. That caused my admiration to grow. So if there's a mocker in your life, don't write off that person too quickly. He might be much closer to the kingdom than is your gracious friend.

This isn't the only benefit of persecution, however. Notice in Matthew 5 that Jesus twice used the word "blessed" when He spoke of persecution. God promises a double blessing to the persecuted Christian.

Persecution confirms that you are a child of God, for Jesus says, "Blessed are those who are persecuted . . . *for theirs is the kingdom of heaven*" (emphasis added). Persecution becomes a tangible evidence of your salvation, a confirmation that you indeed are a child of God.

Then consider Matthew 5:12. The phrase "rejoice and be exceedingly glad" could be translated "jump and skip with happy excitement." By the way, in the original language, it's in the imperative. Jesus is commanding us to be glad, not sad. He is saying, "Rejoice!"

Persecution draws us closer to Jesus and further away from a world system hostile to Him. Beyond that, it guarantees us a reward—and not just any reward, but a "great" one. God knows something about "great"; He's the one who created the immensity of our vast universe. So when He uses a word like "great" to describe our reward for patiently enduring persecution, we would do well to sit up and take notice.

Last, persecution has a way of reminding us about which side we are on. It makes us realize that we're on the winning side. Paul tells us not to be "in any way terrified by your adversaries, which is to them a proof of perdition, but to you of salvation" (Philippians 1:28).

"Stop, stop!" you say. "This is not the kind of thing I want to hear. I don't want to be persecuted. I don't want to face any difficulties. I don't want friction in my life. I want to get along with everyone." If that's what you really want, here is how to get it:

- Don't tell others about Jesus.
- Mix in with the ungodly.
- Don't take a stand for righteousness.

But if you choose this route, remember what Jesus said: "Woe to you when all men speak well of you" (Luke 6:26). Remember that He declared, "Whoever is ashamed of Me and My words, of him the Son of Man will be ashamed when He comes in His own glory" (Luke 9:26). And realize that 2 Timothy 2:12 says, "If we endure, we shall also reign with Him. If we deny Him, He also will deny us." Jesus stands up for you when you stand up for Him.

But enough of the negative. Look to the reward! It's yours for the taking, and it's well worth the small price of persecution.

A young man once asked F.B. Meyer to help him find a new

job because he was the only Christian in the entire establish-ment and he found it terribly lonely to stand by himself. "But," said Meyer, "is it not that one reason to hold your ground? Surely the loneliness of a light is the more reason why it should shine. If there were more than one, it might with some grace re-tire, but not if it is alone."

10

COUNT YOUR BLESSINGS

"Therefore I say to you, do not worry about your life, what you will eat or what you will drink; nor about your body, what you will put on. Is not life more than food and the body more than clothing?"

—MATTHEW 6:25

A COUPLE FROM OUR CHURCH once visited a family in Beirut, Lebanon, while that country was in the midst of a shaky cease-fire. At one point a Christian family invited the couple over for dinner. The family had no electricity and no running water. Makeshift trenches surrounded their apartment building and their balcony had been hit by a bomb fragment just days earlier. Yet, before saying the blessing for the meal, the man asked everyone to sing the old, familiar hymn "Count Your Blessings."

What an example! This family demonstrates that happiness is not dependent on our circumstances. We need to remind ourselves of God's goodness to us, even when things are difficult.

David did this often in his psalms. When overwhelmed by adversity, he would remind himself of God's promises and faithfulness and then thank and praise God. Psalm 63:3-4 is a wonderful, God-inspired poem that can become our song and prayer as well: "Because Your lovingkindness is better than life, my lips shall praise You. Thus I will bless You while I live; I will lift up my hands in Your name."

You may say, "Yes, that's a wonderful psalm to sing if I'm in the mood, but I'm not right now. I'm not feeling well . . . I just had a fight with my spouse . . . someone just sideswiped my car."

Yet if David had waited to "feel better," he never would have written this psalm. Conditions were much less than ideal when he took pen in hand to write down these words. David, as an old man, was now running for his life. His son Absalom was out to kill him and take his throne. The bottom had dropped out for him.

David could have said, "When my circumstances are going perfectly, my lips shall praise You" or, "When I'm in the right mood, my lips shall praise You." Instead, he said, "Because Your lovingkindness is better than life, my lips shall praise You."

Those words didn't lift David out of his circumstances, but they caused him to put his problems in perspective. He was not praising God because of what had happened; he praised God despite what had happened and reminded himself that God was still on the throne. Instead of being gripped by fear and worry, he was filled with trust and hope.

That is how we can give thanks in all things. Not *for* all things—there are certain things for which I will not say, "Thank God that happened." Still, I can say, "Lord, I don't know why that happened. I don't understand why You allowed that, but I thank You that You are still in control."

Think of Paul and Silas when they were thrown in prison for preaching the gospel (*see* Acts 16). First their backs were beaten with a Roman whip. Then their ankles were fastened into iron stocks that spread their legs as far apart as possible, causing excruciating pain. There in that dark, damp dungeon, Paul and Silas, in terrible pain and hopeless circumstances, began to sing and praise God.

That's remarkable. They were able to look beyond their hardships and thank God—not because of what had happened, but because God was in control.

Amazingly, as they continued praising God in the midst of

those dire circumstances, God brought an earthquake that destroyed the prison, freed Paul and Silas, and enabled them to lead the prison guard to Christ. Talk about bringing the house down! When Paul and Silas had a concert, they really shook a place up.

But notice: They gave thanks *before* something good happened. Sometimes we think, *I'll give thanks only when things work out.* But we need to learn to give thanks ahead of time, because God is in control. The word "oops" is not in God's vocabulary. At times that's hard for us to see.

When I was a young pastor, I thought I had to understand everything about God and have an answer for everyone's problems. Since then I've realized that is not necessary, nor is it possible. I cannot explain certain things to you. I wish I could give you all the answers, but I don't know them. Maybe one day you will look back in your life and say, as did Joseph to his evil brothers, "You meant evil against me; but God meant it for good" (Genesis 50:20).

We must remember that God is wiser than us and He is looking out for our eternal good. Sometimes that is tough to swallow. What will benefit me in the heavenly realm will not always benefit me in the earthly. It helps to remember that God's ultimate goal is to make us like Jesus. Romans 8:29 says, "Whom He foreknew, He also predestined to be conformed to the image of His Son."

Everything God does in your life is filtered through love—not through anger, not through hostility, not through vengeance—but through love.

If you're going through a tough time today, sit back for a moment and "count your blessings." I promise that you will find a happiness the world does not know. Try worshiping instead of worrying!

Read all of Psalm 63. Meditate on verses 3 and 4 and try to memorize them. These verses will help strengthen your faith when you go through tough times.

11

IT'S NOT EASY

"To him who strikes you on the one cheek, offer the other also."

—LUKE 6:29a

WHEN WAS THE LAST TIME someone took advantage of your kindness? When was the last time a coworker belittled your faith? When was the last time someone accused you of something you didn't do? When was the last time you were assaulted in any way for your beliefs?

Such questions bring unpleasant memories, don't they? I'm sure you can identify with one of these scenarios. The question is, how did you respond?

Some of us read Luke 6:29 and say, "Hold on. Is that what Jesus really said? That doesn't come easy to me."

I've got news for you. It doesn't come easy to me, either. It's one of the hardest teachings Jesus ever gave. Easy to say; hard to do.

I have to admit that I don't have the kind of nature that easily turns the other cheek. If someone treats me cruelly for no good reason, I don't merely want to get even—I want to get them worse. In my eyes, the person's action demands a stiff response.

Such an attitude comes out most often when I'm behind the wheel. If someone tailgates me, I want to tailgate him. If someone cuts me off, I want to cut him off. I want to teach that person a lesson. It's the old, "Don't get mad, get even" principle. I know this is the wrong attitude, but I think most of us struggle in varying degrees. We all have a deep-seated desire to defend ourselves. But Jesus tells us to turn the other cheek.

If you wrestle with this teaching, you are in good company. Even the apostle Paul battled with it on at least one occasion. In Acts chapter 23, we read that the high priest, Ananias, had Paul slapped across the face. Instead of turning the other cheek and taking it, the apostle responded, "God will strike you, you white-washed wall! For you sit to judge me according to the law, and do you command me to be struck contrary to the law?" (*see* verse 3).

What kind of reaction is that for a follower of the One who told us to turn the other cheek? I think it was an honest one. This teaching did not come easy for Paul, as it does not for many others.

Don't think, however, that just because this is a difficult standard to live by, we can disregard it. We simply need to realize we need supernatural assistance to live it out.

In Paul's case, one of the men in the room turned to the apostle and asked, "Do you revile God's high priest?" Paul quickly confessed he didn't know Ananias was the high priest, or else he wouldn't have responded the way he had. Paul apologized for his outburst in court and eventually turned the other cheek as far as possible when he died for his faith.

I'm sure this command to turn the other cheek was even harder for the people listening to Jesus. Among the Jews, a slap in the face was one of the most demeaning and contemptuous acts possible. It was the ultimate insult, a deliberate gesture of disrespect. Perhaps a more contemporary version of that would be if someone were to spit in your face.

Luke 6:29 doesn't only speak of cheek slapping, however; Jesus intended to teach us about how we should react to mistreatment in general.

First Peter 2:20-23 says, "If you suffer for doing good and

you endure it, this is commendable before God. To this you were called, because Christ suffered for you, leaving you an example, that you should follow in his steps. 'He committed no sin, and no deceit was found in his mouth.' When they hurled their insults at him, he did not retaliate; when he suffered, he made no threats. Instead, he entrusted himself to him who judges justly" (NIV).

Jesus was describing an inner disposition, not a legal duty. He was explaining how we should respond to others. We need to be positive when others are negative, generous when others are selfish. We need to be more like Jesus.

In some cases, you may have to turn your cheek more than once. And it may even turn out that as your persecutor sees how you respond, he may turn from insulting you to asking you about what makes you tick.

Do you feel like a failure in this area already? Don't worry. God still used the apostle Paul, even though he seemed to struggle with turning the other cheek. Just ask God to forgive you and help you with your responses toward others.

Galatians tells us that self-control is a fruit of the Spirit (see 5:23). May God, by the power of His Spirit, teach us to live out this principle today as we seek to represent Jesus in this indifferent world. May our example get other people's attention and earn us the right to give them His Word.

That is, may we follow in His steps.

For an idea of what God wants you to do when people wrong you, read Romans 12:17-21.

12

YOU CAN'T OUTGIVE GOD

✠

*"Give to everyone who asks of you. And from him who takes away
your goods do not ask them back. And just as you want men
to do to you, you also do to them likewise."*

—LUKE 6:30-31

SOME PEOPLE ARE VERY GENEROUS. You come up a couple of bucks short when you go out to lunch, and they cover it without any problem. The next day you're out to lunch with them again and this time they're the ones a couple bucks short, so you cover it. You don't keep a tally, you don't write it down in a book. They're friends. They come through for you and you come through for them. You help them, they help you.

There are other people who are willing enough to help when you're short, but the conversation goes something like this:

"How much do you need?"

"I need $1.64."

"I believe I have that precise amount."

This friend has one of those little change dispensers on his belt and a calculator nearby. He gives you the money and writes down the amount in a little notebook. The next day he says, "By the way, you owe me $1.64 and I've added four cents for interest."

You're grateful for his help, but when *he* is in need, how do you want to treat *him*? In exactly the way he treated you.

This is what Jesus is describing in Luke 6:31. The way you put it out is the way you will get it back. If you're caring, considerate, loving, and generous, you will find one day that when you're down, you will receive the same treatment. If you're a tightwad, uptight, and judgmental toward others, don't be surprised if you reap the same sort of diseased crop.

The basic, biblical principle is that you reap what you sow, and I have found that God will never be my debtor. I firmly believe that as you give to God, you will receive back.

But don't misunderstand. Some false teachers claim that if you give to their ministries, God is bound to give back to you a hundredfold. The more you give to them, the more God is required to give to you. They take a beautiful teaching of the Bible and distort it into a lie. In essence, they teach that you give to get. If you give, they say God is required to give back to you.

One of the problems with this distorted doctrine is that it corrupts our motive for giving. We begin to give to get, which perverts our motives and forfeits the reward we would have received otherwise.

So what is the true biblical emphasis? As you give to God, He will give to you—*but you give because you have received.* You don't give to get.

God says through Malachi, "Bring all the tithes into the storehouse, that there may be food in My house, and prove Me now in this . . . if I will not open for you the windows of heaven and pour out for you such blessing that there will not be room enough to receive it. And I will rebuke the devourer for your sakes" (Malachi 3:10-11). God is saying, "Try Me on this one. If you will give to Me, if you will be faithful in your tithing, you will always be taken care of and I will meet your needs."

You cannot outgive God. I have found this to be true. I have found that if you honor this principle with the right motives, God will bless you.

The greatest investment you can make is in the kingdom of God. Not only does God promise to meet your temporal needs as you seek Him first and His righteousness, but He has promised eternal rewards as well. What else could Jesus have meant when He said, "Do not lay up for yourselves treasures on earth, where moth and rust destroy and where thieves break in and steal; but lay up for yourselves treasures in heaven" (Matthew 6:19-20)?

Some people have financial problems. I would venture to say that 19 out of 20 Christians with severe financial difficulties don't give to the Lord on a regular basis. If you were to ask them, "Do you tithe?" they would respond, "Do I what? Well, ah, I just don't have enough money to do that sort of thing. I can't afford to tithe."

Truthfully, I can't afford *not* to tithe. I don't say that to impress you, but because God's Word tells me that if I will bring to Him the firstfruits of my income every month, thereby honoring Him and recognizing that everything I have comes from His hands, He will provide for all my needs. God tells me He will open up the windows of heaven and pour out a blessing that I will not have room enough to receive.

I have found that as I give to God, He always gives back to me. "Give, and it will be given to you: good measure, pressed down, shaken together, and running over will be put into your bosom. For with the same measure that you use, it will be measured back to you" (Luke 6:38).

If you get cheap, you are going to find the resources drying up. If you have an open hand to pass on what God has given to you, just watch how He will bless you and how He will provide for you. You won't have to worry about material things. You won't even have to think about them. Everything you have belongs to the Lord anyway, so it's just smart to honor Him with the discipline of regular giving.

You can't outgive God. Why not try it and see for yourself?

Read 2 Corinthians 8:1-7 and see what Paul means when he talks about "the grace of giving." Is God leading you to share in this service to other believers?

13

SPECKS AND PLANKS

✥

"Why do you look at the speck in your brother's eye,
but do not consider the plank in your own eye?"

—MATTHEW 7:3

HAVE YOU EVER NOTICED that a certain sin in your own
life always seems more pronounced in the life of someone else?
Jesus reminded us of this when He told a story about the man
with a plank in his eye. It's comical to picture a guy trying to pick
a sliver or a speck out of someone's eye while he's got a plank
lodged in his own.

This simple analogy contains a profound truth. The words
Jesus used in the original language imply that the speck and the
plank are made up of the same substance. In other words, the
only difference between the speck and the plank was their varied
sizes. That explains why we can spot certain sins in other people
so easily—we are familiar with them because they are our own.

Isn't it interesting how ugly our sins look on someone else?
Somehow we find a way to rationalize thoughts or behavior in
our own lives that we condemn in others. Our problem is that we
often have a plank of some sin while the other person has only a
speck.

As a young Christian I used to think that people who easily

noticed spiritual problems in others must be very holy and godly. I thought that if they were in a position to put everybody else down, they obviously must be living a very holy life.

But one by one, I would find out that those nitpickers and sin-sniffers—who always had a critical word to say about every-one else—were guilty of a far worse sin than the one they accused others of committing. If you're a picky person, I suspect you are struggling with a far greater sin in your own life than that in the lives of those you harass. And I have to wonder what you are try-ing to hide.

Jesus said we will be judged by the same standard we apply to others. That is worth thinking about before we start pointing out the flaws in someone else's life.

A good illustration of this point may be found in the life of David. As you may recall, David committed several terrible sins as a result of his adulterous relationship with Bathsheba. First, he lusted after her. Then he misused his authority as king and brought Bathsheba into his chambers and had sexual relations with her. When she became pregnant and David was unable to make it appear that the child belonged to her husband, David conceived a plot in which Uriah would be murdered. So went the chain of sin in David's life. It began with lust and ended with cold-blooded murder.

Amazing as it may seem, David found a way to rationalize those sins. Maybe he even thought he had gotten away with it. For almost a year nothing had happened. No one said anything. Perhaps he even thought, *Well, I've pulled it off.*

But one day the prophet Nathan paid a visit to David and told him a story (*see* 2 Samuel 12). He recounted the wicked deeds of a wealthy man who had many sheep—more sheep than a man could ever need. This man had a neighbor who had only one sheep. In fact, it wasn't just a sheep, it was the family pet. The family loved it very much.

One evening a hungry visitor came into town to visit the rich man. The wealthy man didn't want to kill one of his many sheep, so he took his neighbor's only sheep and butchered it. Nathan then turned to David and asked, "Now what should we do with such a man?" David, filled with rage, answered immediately, "He should be put to death!"

Put to death? Isn't that a bit harsh? Without question the wealthy man had acted wrongfully, but even the strictest punishment in the Mosaic law called for the man only to restore what he had taken fourfold. It didn't impose the death penalty for killing someone's sheep. But David says, "Kill the guy." Do you suppose someone had a guilty conscience?

After David passed his harsh judgment on the man, Nathan pointed his finger into David's face and said, "You are the man!" How quickly things came into focus in David's mind! *He* was the man with the many sheep. He had many wives; Uriah had only one. Yet David took her for himself.

Isn't it interesting that the king was willing to condemn another person for a crime much less serious than his own? He thought it was fine for him to steal another man's wife, but he would have someone executed for stealing a sheep. It's strange. But that's the crazy pattern of sin. You rationalize what you do and condemn others for the same thing.

Maybe after reading this, something has come into focus in your own mind. Like David, have you been quick to see the speck in someone else's eye while neglecting to see the plank in your own?

If so, take some time to deal with that plank today, asking the Master Optometrist, Jesus Christ, to clear your vision. You will be amazed at what a difference 20/20 vision makes.

"The ultimate proof of the sinner is that he does not recognize his own sin."

—*Martin Luther*

14

CAUGHT IN THE ACT

✄

"They said to Him, 'Teacher, this woman was caught in adultery, in the very act. Now Moses, in the law, commanded us that such should be stoned. But what do You say?' This they said, testing Him."

—JOHN 8:4-6a

I ONCE READ an interesting anecdote about Sir Arthur Conan Doyle, author of the famous Sherlock Holmes stories. One day Doyle decided to play a practical joke on twelve of his friends. So he dispatched a telegram to each of them, saying, "Flee at once. All is discovered." It was just a joke, but within 24 hours, all twelve of his friends had left the country! That's what you call having a guilty conscience.

What if you received a letter that said, "Flee at once. All is discovered"? Would you flee? Do you have a secret sin? If so, you're probably thinking about it right now—that thing you pretend isn't a problem. It just popped back in your mind. It keeps coming back to haunt you. You're afraid that one day you will be caught in the act.

In John 8, we read the story of a woman caught in the act of adultery. Under the Mosaic law, she could have been put to death by stoning. But on this day, she would be spared. Instead of coming face to face with death, she would come face to face with Jesus. And her life would never be the same.

This woman had been brought to Jesus by some religious leaders who were trying to trap Him. If Jesus told them not to stone her, He would have broken the holy law; if He said to stone her, some people might say, "He may be just and righteous, but I'm never going to Him with a problem." The Pharisees were putting Jesus in a difficult situation. But Jesus went around all that and got to the heart of the matter: how to deal with sin.

The Bible says Jesus then wrote something in the sand. We don't know what He wrote, but perhaps He scribbled each religious leader's secret sin. After all, Romans 2:16 tells us there will be a day when "God will judge the secrets of men by Jesus Christ."

Many people have "secret sins," but they are no secret with God. It may be unknown among people, but secret sin on earth is open scandal in heaven. The Scripture says, "All things are naked and open to the eyes of Him to whom we must give account" (Hebrews 4:13).

Some people in the church live double lives. They appear to be spiritual and holy, but in reality they are living a different kind of life altogether—almost like a Jekyll and Hyde. But God knows what is going on. They are not fooling Him.

The Pharisees thought they had Jesus trapped, but they had only succeeded in trapping themselves. They were looking at the sin in another's life while neglecting the sin in their own. Jesus went beyond the law to look at the condition of the heart. After the religious leaders realized that Jesus had seen through their facade of holiness, they could no longer condemn the woman.

Why did Jesus forgive this woman from a blatant violation of God's law? In short, it's because He is much more merciful than we often are. Second Peter 3:9 says, "The Lord is not slack concerning His promise, as some count slackness, but is longsuffering toward us, not willing that any should perish but that all should come to repentance."

Does that mean we can disregard God's law and live as we please? Far from it! We should never confuse leniency with

God's loving patience and willingness to forgive. Yet, the Bible tells us that it is only because of the Lord's mercies that we are not consumed (*see* Lamentations 3:22).

Some think that because nothing happens to them when they sin, God must not really care. The Bible says, "When the sentence for a crime is not quickly carried out, the hearts of the people are filled with schemes to do wrong" (Ecclesiastes 8:11, NIV).

You may think, *I can go ahead and do this. Nothing has happened. I'm getting away with it.* Then one day your sin comes to the surface. It would be like planting a crop and thinking that because nothing has broken ground immediately, it never will. Then one day that seed bursts out from the soil all around you.

The same is true with that "seed of sin" we sow. We think that because it produced no immediate repercussions, we somehow got away with it. Even though the Bible tells us we will reap what we sow, we think we are the exception. Then, surprise! Those seeds start breaking ground. That white lie you told your boss has grown out of proportion. The juicy bit of gossip has ruined the reputation of someone in your church. That seemingly innocent friendship with one of your coworkers has turned into something it shouldn't have.

People forget that their actions carry consequences. If you keep playing with sin, sooner or later it's going to catch up with you and you will be caught in the act. You can't sow your wild seed all week long, and then on Sunday pray that none of it takes root. Sooner or later it's going to get you. The Bible says, "Your sin will find you out" (Numbers 32:23).

Perhaps you are involved in some kind of sin right now. Maybe you are engaged in a lifestyle that displeases God. The words Jesus spoke to the adulterous woman still speak to you and me today. God has given you a warning for your sin, but He has also offered you His forgiveness. Take it, then "go and sin no more" (John 8:11).

For an example of what can happen if you leave sin unchecked, read the story of Samson in Judges 13–16.

15

WHERE ARE YOUR ACCUSERS?

❧

"Neither do I condemn you; go and sin no more."

—JOHN 8:11

MANY PEOPLE HAVE THE WRONG IDEA about following Jesus. "I need to live a good life," they say. "I need to do certain things. I need to clean up my life and follow certain standards. Then, just maybe, God will forgive me."

That's not the way it is. Jesus said to the woman in John 8, "Neither do I condemn you; go and sin no more." Had He reversed His two sentences, the meaning would have changed altogether. But He did not say, "Go out and live a good life, get your act together, don't sin again—and maybe, just maybe, I won't condemn you."

Don't misunderstand: This woman *was* guilty. Under the law, she deserved the punishment suggested by her accusers. But Jesus did not give her what she deserved. He forgave her on the spot.

That is what God has done for you, if through faith in the risen Christ you have committed your life to God. He has wiped your slate clean. He has forgiven you. Now He says to you, "In recognition of that, go and sin no more."

When some Christians fail they think, *God doesn't approve of me; God can't love me. I've failed this week.* And when they do well they think, *Oh, I've done great this week. Now God must really love and approve of me.*

I've got news for you. He approves of you when you fail as much as He does when you succeed. He approves of you when you sin and He approves when you walk closely with Him. His approval and His love for you are not based on what you have done. They are based on what Christ did for you on the cross. He took the sin that should have been upon you and me and took it upon Himself. It's because of Jesus that God can love us unconditionally regardless of how lovable or good we are.

If you can get hold of that, it will cause you to realize, *God loves me so much! God will forgive me for all that I've done. Then I want to serve Him. I want to please Him. Not to merit it, not to earn it, but just because I'm so thankful.* We're not bound by rules and regulations, but are constrained by His love.

Some Christians shuffle around saying, "I can't do this, I can't do that. Oh, the Christian life is so hard!" They've got it confused. Our attitude should be, "I love Jesus so much that I don't want to commit this sin. I love Jesus so much I don't want to do what will displease Him. I don't want to dishonor Him. Because I love Him so deeply, I'm going to be faithful to Him." That's the kind of love we need to keep us walking close with God.

I love the phrase Jesus used in this incident: "Woman, where are those accusers of yours? Has no one condemned you?" (John 8:10). The word "woman" is a term of respect. It would almost be like calling someone "lady" or "madam." He saw her for what she could become. He didn't merely see her for what she was.

She replied to His question by saying, "No one, Lord" (verse 11). In a moment, in a flash, belief blossomed in her once-hardened heart. While the convicting power of God's Spirit drove her accusers away, this woman came closer. Just one look into His eyes answered all of her questions, melted all of her doubts, and drove away all of her fears.

Belief is like that. It happens in a flash, instantaneously. Stop and think about your own conversion. What was it that brought you around? If you were converted during a sermon, I doubt you can remember every point mentioned in that sermon. Most people are attracted by one single statement. It varies from person to person, but one statement causes something to jell, to put things into focus. Something clicks.

I remember what the statement was for me. I heard, "Jesus said, 'You're for Me or against Me. With Me or opposed to Me.'" I looked around and I realized the Christians around me in the meeting I was at were for Him—and I looked at myself and realized I wasn't one of them. The thought that I must be against Him made me horribly uncomfortable. I desperately wanted to be *for* Jesus. I really wanted to know Jesus, but I didn't know it was possible. That one statement turned me around.

Having forgiven this woman, Jesus promised her three things. First, her sins would be forgotten. If you come to Jesus Christ and ask Him to forgive you, He will wipe the slate clean. Have you done something you deeply regret? Are you terribly sorry for something you've done? If only you could rewrite history, if only you could go back in time! Well, God *can* forgive and He *can* forget and He *will* make things just as if you had never sinned.

Second, the woman did not have to fear judgment day. Jesus did not condemn her and neither does He condemn us. Romans 8:1 says, "There is therefore now no condemnation to those who are in Christ Jesus."

Third, she gained new power to face her problems. Jesus would be with her. That is why she could "go and sin no more." The same hope is given to us. Galatians 5:16 says, "Walk in the Spirit, and you shall not fulfill the lust of the flesh."

When you evaluate your own spiritual experience, what do you see? Do you try to earn God's approval by being good, or do you do good because of what God has done for you? The first way leads inevitably to misery and failure, the second to joy and glorious victory . . . and if you have any question about which way you choose, allow me to suggest that you read this vignette again.

The late Bishop Taylor Smith, a well-known evangelical of the Anglican church, never lost an opportunity to share his faith with ordinary people. One day he began telling his barber about the message of salvation. "I do my best," snapped the barber, "and that's enough for me." When the barber was through shaving the bishop, the bishop asked, "May I shave this man?" "No, I'm afraid not," replied the barber with a grin. "But I would do my best," answered the bishop. "So you might," said the barber, "but your best would not be good enough for this man." "No," replied the bishop quietly, "and neither is your best good enough for God."

16

THE PROBLEM OF WORRY

✄

*"Therefore I say to you, do not worry about your life,
what you will eat; nor about the body, what you will put on."*

—LUKE 12:22

A SONG POPULAR A FEW YEARS AGO advised us, "Don't Worry, Be Happy." That's easy enough to say, but it's not so easy to do when unpaid bills stack up or a crisis looms or the future looks shaky at best. Worry can overwhelm us and brutalize us. It's a hard emotion to suppress.

Even the disciples worried about not having enough. They worried about where their next meal was coming from and what they were going to wear. They had left everything to follow Jesus and they were anxious about the future.

Worry is a powerful emotion that grips us tightly in times of crisis. What about tomorrow? What if this happens? What if that happens? Worry cripples us. It chokes us. It strangles us. If we don't have enough, we worry about getting more. If we have a lot, we worry that it might be stolen or that it will get scratched or damaged.

Some people are terribly worried about getting old. They don't want to accept the aging process. They are worried about death and eternity. Certainly, you should be concerned about old age, but worrying about it won't help you.

And in any event, haven't you noticed that most of what we worry about never takes place? We worry about events that never transpire. Let me ask you this: Has worry ever made your situation get any better? I doubt it. It just makes it get worse.

Medical science tells us that worry can actually shorten our lives. Often when people are worried, they turn to drugs or alcohol or other chemicals that cause them physical harm. They overeat or smoke or otherwise wreak havoc upon their bodies. Worry can indeed shorten your life, but it certainly won't lengthen it.

Dr. Charles Mayo of the famed Mayo Clinic said that "worry affects the circulation, the heart, the glands and the whole nervous system. I have never met a man or known a man to die of overwork, but I have known a lot who die from worry."

The word "worry" used in Luke 12:22 also appears in verse 29, where it is translated "don't have an anxious mind." It means literally "to be held in suspense." The word pictures a ship stuck in a storm-tossed sea because the captain failed to take advantage of an available safe harbor. The ship could have been in that safe harbor, but it never made it. It's in a predicament it never needed to experience.

Worry is unnecessary. We bring it upon ourselves. It chokes us and strangles us.

In the parable of the sower in Matthew 13, Jesus talked about the seed that was choked out by the worries of this world and the deceitfulness of riches. The seed of the Word of God never brought forth fruit because it was strangled by worry. It isn't only those who are well off or those who have a lot of money who are plagued with this problem; it also bedevils those who have very little but who are always worrying about what they don't have. The effect is the same: It chokes you out and strangles you spiritually.

Dr. Martin Lloyd-Jones once said, "The result of worrying about the future is that you are crippling yourself in the present." And Corrie ten Boom added, "Worry does not empty tomorrow of its sorrow. It empties today of its strength."

Philippians 4:6-7 tells us we are to channel the emotion that generates worry. It says, "Be anxious for nothing, but in everything by prayer and supplication, with thanksgiving, let your requests be made known to God; and the peace of God, which surpasses all understanding, will guard your hearts and minds through Christ Jesus."

That's an interesting phrase in the original language, because it literally means that God's peace will mount a garrison around our heart. It might be translated, "God's peace will stand guard at your heart." The idea is of a soldier standing sentry over our emotions. God's peace will protect our heart against the invasion of worry and anxiety and fear.

The next time you are gripped with worry and you begin to panic, take your situation before the throne of God. Jehoshaphat prayed to God in the Old Testament, "Nor do we know what to do, but our eyes are upon You" (2 Chronicles 20:12). Say to the Lord, "Lord, I cast this on You. You said for me to cast all my care upon You, for You care for me. So that's what I'm doing. I'm casting my care on You. I'm casting my problems on You. Instead of worrying, I'm waiting. Instead of panicking, I'm praying. Here it is, Lord. I look to You."

The best defense against worry is to be walking with God, living in close relationship with Him through Jesus Christ. When you do that, you won't have to fear the future. God has your future in His hand. You won't have to fear death, because to live is Christ and to die is gain (*see* Philippians 1:21); when you leave this earth, you go directly to be with the Lord!

So don't worry. Trust instead. When you walk hand in hand with Jesus, you can walk into the future without anxiety or worry.

And that's the only real way to not worry and be happy.

Psalm 37:1-11 tells us what we should do instead of worrying and fretting about situations out of our control. Read it, then commit to Him today whatever you may be concerned about.

17

EVEN SEA GULLS GO TO WORK

"Consider the ravens, for they neither sow nor reap,
which have neither storehouse nor barn; and God feeds them.
Of how much more value are you than the birds?"

—LUKE 12:24

SOME TIME AGO I VISITED the Sea World aquatic park with my wife and two sons. First off, we went to feed the dolphins. My son Christopher was holding a fish out for one of the dolphins when a sea gull swooped down, grabbed the fish right out of his hand, and flew off with it. Christopher was hopping mad.

A little while later we left to have a meal. Christopher ordered chicken and when he got up to get a straw, another sea gull dove down from the sky and stole his entire chicken dinner! Now my son was steaming. I had never seen a sea gull quite this aggressive; this was a new one for me.

An hour or so later we were feeding the dolphins again and a third sea gull snatched another fish right out of my son's hands (or maybe it was the same thieving sea gull the entire time!). He nearly fell apart. And if that weren't bad enough, just as we were leaving, one last sea gull committed one final act of insult against my son's shirt. You can imagine what that was.

I really don't care for sea gulls anymore. I think they're culprits. They're thieves. I have seen them steal people's lunches at the beach. They huddle together, waiting for you to leave your towel for a moment, then they swoop in and make off with your sandwich.

Nevertheless, as impolite as sea gulls are, they help to illustrate Jesus' point in Luke 12:24. The Lord doesn't mean that birds just sit around and wait for food to drop in their laps (if they had laps). Birds go out and get their food. I've seen pelicans dive-bomb into the ocean to scoop up fish. I've seen little sparrows pick up seed or scavenge around for other kinds of food.

Jesus does not use the example of birds to encourage us to remain passive and not work. In fact, the Bible teaches the opposite. It insists that we must work. Like it or not, in the curse God told us, "In the sweat of your face you shall eat bread till you return to the ground" (Genesis 3:19). And in Proverbs 6:6-8, God says, "Go to the ant, you sluggard! Consider her ways and be wise, which, having no captain, overseer or ruler, provides her supplies in the summer, and gathers her food in the harvest." In other words, the ant prepares for the future. The ant works—and so should we.

The point of Luke 12:24 is that birds don't spend all their time worrying about where their next meal will come from. Why should they? Many of them just wait around until you plan your next picnic.

Some Christians use Scripture as a cloak for laziness. They say, "The Lord will provide. God will take care of me." But we're told in 2 Thessalonians 3:10, "If anyone will not work, neither shall he eat." We are commanded to get out there and work. Find a job, make some money, and provide for yourself and your family. Failure to do so prompts some of the harshest words in the entire Bible. Paul wrote, "If anyone does not provide for his own, and especially for those of his household, he has denied the faith and is worse than an unbeliever" (1 Timothy 5:8).

We hear a lot these days about the homeless. We are told

we've got to do something for them, and I agree. In fact, the church I pastor has been helping homeless people for many years and we will continue to do so. But I think we need to understand what "the homeless" really means.

This phrase has been used to describe many people from many walks of life who end up on the streets for many reasons. Some of the homeless have chosen to be on the streets. They don't want to be in shelters and they don't want to be rehabilitated. They don't want to work at a job; they like life just as it is.

Certainly there are some who have landed on the streets through a series of unfortunate circumstances. They need our help and we should do everything we can to help them get back on their feet and become productive members of society. But people who have chosen to live on the streets because they don't want responsibilities or pressures shouldn't simply have money given to them. Many of these people use the money they beg off of passersby to buy booze or drugs.

I don't think we should indiscriminately give our money to anyone who asks us for it. We must be careful. If someone is hungry, take him out to eat. Feed him and share the gospel of Jesus Christ in the process. But often that's not what he wants.

People come into Harvest Christian Fellowship all the time because they know our church has a reputation for helping hurting people. It's a good reputation, but that doesn't mean we just throw money at anyone who walks through the door! If they're able-bodied, physically capable of working and simply need some money, we give them work to do and then pay them for the job. But if they are capable of working yet don't want to work because they would prefer a handout, we tell them, "No, we're not going to give cash to you. If a man doesn't work, neither should he eat."

The general rule for Christians is summed up well in 1 Thessalonians 4:11-12: "Aspire to lead a quiet life, to mind your own business, and to work with your own hands, as we commanded you, that you may walk properly toward those who are outside, and that you may lack nothing." Do that, and the Lord will be very pleased.

My only regret is that it doesn't apply to sea gulls!

"Do not pray for easy lives. Pray to be stronger men. Do not pray for tasks equal to your powers. Pray for powers equal to your tasks."

—Phillips Brooks

18

THAT SINKING FEELING

✦

"When Peter had come down out of the boat, he walked on the water to go to Jesus. But when he saw that the wind was boisterous, he was afraid; and beginning to sink he cried out, saying, 'Lord, save me!'"

—MATTHEW 14:29-30

IT IS ALL TOO EASY to get discouraged when you are serving the Lord. People won't always listen to you. They put you down and criticize you. Sometimes you'll patch up three problems and six more will take their place. You begin to wonder if you're making any progress at all. You can almost decide to give up.

It's at times like these that I have to ask myself, "For whom am I doing this? Am I serving man or God?"

There is nothing wrong with becoming weary *in* service. But we must never become weary *of* it. The Bible says, "Let us not grow weary while doing good, for in due season we shall reap if we do not lose heart" (Galatians 6:9).

The strength you and I need to keep going comes from spending time in God's presence. We will be able to do what He calls us to do only by remembering that we labor *through* Him and *for* Him.

Sometimes people ask, "How do you handle all the problems of the pastorate? How do you carry all those burdens?" I say,

"I don't." If I personally tried to carry the problems of all the people in our congregation, I would be a basket case. I have enough trouble with my own problems. My shoulders weren't designed to carry others' burdens; they're not even designed to carry my own. I have been told to cast all my cares upon Jesus, for He cares for me.

Now of course, Scripture tells us to "bear one another's burdens" (Galatians 6:2). That does not mean we single-handedly carry them, but rather, we help and encourage one another and take our problems to God in prayer.

When someone asks me, "Here's my problem, Greg. What am I going to do?" I like to say, "Let's pray right now and put it in perspective by looking to God."

I can't answer everyone's questions nor can I carry their burdens. This is *His* church and we are *His* people. All the problems we face are His problems. All the problems I face are to be given to Him, because He has asked me to do that.

The author of Hebrews realized that the individuals to whom he was writing were discouraged. They were feeling sorry for themselves and saw life as hard. So he gave them a message fit for their condition: "Therefore strengthen the hands which hang down, and the feeble knees, and make straight paths for your feet" (Hebrews 12:12-13).

But before Hebrews 12 was written, the author wrote Hebrews 11, which is often called "the hall of faith." It contains the stories of faithful men and women who stood firm by trusting God's Word. There we find Noah, who obeyed God even when the request seemed ridiculous. He built an ark that saved his family and so became an heir of righteousness. We also find Abraham, who followed God's instruction to go to an unknown land in order to receive an unseen inheritance. Then there is Moses, who left a life of prominence and privilege to lead an often complaining, ungrateful people to the land God had promised them.

After showing all that these faithful people had endured, the writer then comes to the secret of their faith and perseverance: They "[looked] unto Jesus, the author and finisher of [their] faith" (Hebrews 12:2).

Are you weary in ministry? If so, there is only one cure: You need to take your eyes off of yourself and your own problems, off of other people, and fix them on the Lord. He will give you the strength to run.

The writer of Hebrews, alluding to the Greek games of that time, knew that when an athlete ran in a great race he could look up at any moment, at any place on the track, and see the stand where the judge was: the Bema Seat. Perhaps the judge was holding out the laurel leaves to be awarded to the winner, and when the runner looked up at the reward, it gave him the strength to finish the race.

In essence, the writer tells us, "You have been looking down too much. Look up! Keep moving forward."

That was Peter's problem as he walked on the Sea of Galilee. When he looked to Jesus, he walked on water—but when he took his eyes off of the Lord, he began to sink. If anyone ever experienced a "sinking feeling," Peter did!

But do you remember Jesus' response to Peter when the disciple began to sink? He said, "O you of little faith, why did you doubt?" (Matthew 14:31). There was never any need for Peter's feet to slip beneath the waves. Had he kept his gaze locked onto his Master's eyes, he would have known the thrill of Galilean surfing at its finest—no board, no wave, no problem.

Peter's episode reminds us that the calling of God is the enabling of God. When God calls you to do something, you can do it—if you keep your eyes on Jesus. In your own strength, you will fail. Every time.

Are you frustrated serving the Lord? Do you feel as though you have let God down? Maybe you have lost your perspective and forgotten who you are serving.

Give your frustrations and disappointments to God, then let Him take care of your problems. Remember, your work for the

Lord may not be appreciated on earth, but it will be richly rewarded in heaven. And His is the only opinion that counts.

Recall Peter's words in 1 Peter 5:7: "Casting all your care upon Him, for He cares for you." Perhaps as the Spirit directed Peter to record those words, the apostle remembered that day on the Sea of Galilee when he thought he was going to drown. But Peter *did* cast all his care upon Jesus and was not disappointed! Meditate on the wise words of Corrie ten Boom:

Look without and be distressed;
Look within and be depressed;
Look at Jesus and be at rest.

19

THE GRASS ISN'T ALWAYS GREENER

✄

"But when he had spent all . . . he began to be in want."

—LUKE 15:14

AS A FATHER, I've come to realize that telling my young son not to do something only makes the forbidden activity more appealing. This became especially apparent when my children were younger. When I told my son not to touch some fragile object, for example, he would just wait for the opportunity to play with it when I wasn't looking.

Unfortunately, we never seem to grow out of this fascination with the forbidden—and if we allow it to get the best of us, we can make some devastating decisions.

Some people take this rebellious attitude into their relationship with God. They see the boundaries God lays out in His Word as restrictive instead of protective. Some look at the Christian life and the teachings of the Bible and say, "That's too narrow and confining. I can't live that way."

But I don't find the Christian life restrictive at all. In fact, I can do anything I want to do. It's like Augustine said, "Love God and do as you please."

You may be saying, "I don't know if I like the sound of that." But hold on. If you really love God with your whole heart, soul, and mind, you will want to do what He wants you to do. Your desire will be to please Him. So you can love God and do as you please. I do whatever I want to.

Of course, there are certain things I no longer want to do because I have received a new nature. As a result, those things that displease God have become displeasing to me. And how do I know what displeases God? He tells me in His Word. I believe God has given me the teachings of the Bible for my own protection.

Jesus' parable of the prodigal son addresses the problems that come with living by your own rules. In that familiar story, we see what happens when we stray from God.

In the parable, the prodigal son asks his father for his portion of the father's estate. When the father grants the boy's request, the son decides to take all he has and leave home.

It's clear this young boy wasn't thinking clearly. According to the text, it appears the boy had a happy home. Yet, he somehow believed his father was holding something back from him and he wanted to go out and discover what life was all about. You might say he struggled with the old the-grass-looks-greener-on-the-other-side dilemma. The bright lights of the big city were calling, and the son hit the road. Once outside of his father's house, he found out what life was really like.

I've met some Christians who suffer with an attitude much like the prodigal's. I remember one young woman from a fine Christian home who told me, "You know, I go to church and listen to all these people who have these dramatic testimonies of being delivered from drugs or a life of crime, but I don't really have a testimony. I've loved the Lord since I was a little child. I'm going to go out there and live a little so I can have a testimony." Tragically, that woman went out and never came back.

The prodigal thought his father knew nothing, so he went out and wasted all of his goods on wild living. I'm sure when he first hit the road, the money hanging out of his pockets attracted a lot of friends who wanted to help him spend the cash.

But as soon as his resources dried up, he was left all alone. His time and energy went down the drain.

When the son hit bottom, however, he didn't want to go back to his father. It would be too humiliating. Instead, he took a job feeding a man's pigs—a humiliating task for a Jew. You might think that such dreadful circumstances would cause the young man to come to his senses and return home. Yet he prolonged his miserable situation and sank even deeper.

That's just the way the devil works. He will use whatever he has to get you where he wants you. But once he has you, all he will give you is misery.

Perhaps you've thought, *I wonder what it would be like to go back and do some of those things I used to do?*

If you're thinking something like that, put the brakes on! Life outside of your Father's house is crazy. The prodigal discovered that sin would rip him up one side and down the other—and it will do the same to you.

Remember, God has given you guidelines to live by because He is thinking of your own good. The prodigal did finally return to his father and found forgiveness. But at what a price!

Interestingly enough, when the son returned to his father, he found everything at home he had hoped to find in the far country. He found forgiveness, love, and assurance for the future.

Those same things are available to you from the heavenly Father. Take a moment to think about the many blessings you have in Christ. I promise that any thoughts you ever had about tasting what the world has to offer will disappear quickly.

Sometimes we may think that if we walk closely with God, our lives will be restricted and miserable. Take a few minutes to read Jeremiah 29:11 and see what God has promised you concerning your life and future.

20

HOPE FOR THE PRODIGAL

✄

"'Bring the fatted calf here and kill it, and let us eat and be merry; for this my son was dead and is alive again; he was lost and is found.' And they began to be merry."

—LUKE 15:23-24

WHO SUFFERS MORE when a child is spiritually lost, the parents or the child? You might say the child. But wait till you've been a parent. There's no greater suffering than fearing for your child's eternal safety. It rips you like nothing else.

The famous story of the prodigal son suggests that it was the father who suffered the most during his son's journey into the seamy side of life. The father was in anguish.

That gives us a very different picture of God than many of us are used to. Often we think of God as angry with us, as saying, "Wait until you come back. We'll settle the score."

Thoughts like that are way off the mark. There is great truth in the children's song that says, "Jesus loves me when I'm bad, though it makes Him very sad." God grieves over our sin. He is in anguish. He wants fellowship with us. He misses us. He's not eager to judge us. He's already poured out His wrath on His Son at Calvary and what He has for us is kisses, hugs, and forgiveness.

Luke 15:20 says that when the prodigal was nearly home, his

father saw him a great way off and ran and fell on his neck and kissed him. The phrase could be translated, "he smothered him with kisses."

Understand that in this culture it was undignified for an old man to run—running would require that his long tunic be pulled up way above his knees. That would have been scandalous enough, but then to throw his arms around some smelly prodigal who had taken the family name and dragged it through the gutter and to kiss him and kiss him and kiss him! Yet Jesus portrays God as an older man losing His dignity as He runs to greet us and smother us with kisses.

Now, I would not have suggested such a thing if Jesus had not. I would not dare on my own to suggest such a portrait of God because it might sound almost blasphemous or sacrilegious. But remember, it was Jesus Himself who suggested this. It was the Lord who used this illustration to demonstrate how God feels about us.

Before the prodigal could receive such undeserved treatment, however, he had to swallow his pride. The three hardest words for a man or woman to utter are found in verse 18: "I have sinned." Those words are hard to say. We tend to admit, "I have been inconsistent in some ways. I have strayed from the path to a certain degree. I have failed somewhat." But if you don't call it what it is, you won't be forgiven for it. You need to say, "I have sinned" and cut all the malarkey. Get down to what it is. If you confess your sin, He is faithful and just to forgive and cleanse you from all unrighteousness (see 1 John 1:9). But if you make excuses for your sin or refuse to call it sin or blame someone else, you'll still be stuck with it.

The prodigal made one other important statement in this story. In verse 19 he said to his father, "I am no longer worthy to be called your son. Make me like one of your hired servants." How different from his departure speech! At that time he said, "Give me the portion of goods that falls to me" (verse 12). How his vocabulary had changed! Before he thought of himself as somebody and something who could demand rights; now he feels he is nobody and nothing and realizes his first need is to be made into something. That's our first need, as well.

Perhaps you have been a prodigal. Maybe you have strayed. Perhaps you have left your Father's house. Maybe there was a moment in your life when you made a commitment to Jesus Christ, but you've gone astray. Maybe you've wandered off and done some things you are ashamed of.

It's time for you to come back again. It's time for you to be forgiven. Perhaps you have been wondering, "Will God forgive me? Will God receive me?" He will treat you just as Abraham Lincoln treated the rebellious Southerners who had been defeated and had returned to the union of the United States. Lincoln said, "I will treat them as if they had never been away." God will treat you as if you had never been away. But you must come back.

He is waiting for you. He has been looking for you. When He sees you come, He is going to run and greet you and smother you with kisses.

Are you a prodigal son or daughter? Have you strayed? Have you tasted the bitter fruit of sin? Have you landed in that place of emptiness and frustration and realized that life outside of fellowship with God is both meaningless and desolate? Perhaps there was a glamour and an attraction and an excitement when you first began to dabble in sin. But that's all worn off. Now you're in the pit and you are embarrassed. You say, "I can't come back now." *But you can and you must.* Don't put it off another day. "You've given me something to think about," you say. "I'll consider it."

Do it now! You can talk about it over and over, but until you return to the Father, you will sink deeper and your heart will grow harder. Don't put it off.

If God has spoken to you and you realize you've been a prodigal who needs to come back, come back! You might not remember, but kisses and hugs are a whole lot better than tears and regret.

"If I am not enjoying this place of maintained fellowship with the Father and with Jesus Christ, when did I depart therefrom? To that point let me return, whether it be but an hour ago or years ago, and there let me surrender at whatever cost, and do whatever God requires, however irksome it appears to be."

—*G. Campbell Morgan*

21

A NEW PEOPLE

"As Jesus passed on from there, He saw a man named Matthew sitting at the tax office. And He said to him, 'Follow Me.' And he arose and followed Him."

—MATTHEW 9:9

ISN'T IT INTERESTING how God calls people of different backgrounds and puts them together? That's really what the church is—people of unique backgrounds, of various races, of differing ages, who come together and become a new people.

Try to picture how the disciples might have reacted when Jesus called Matthew the tax collector to join their numbers. I can see them looking at each other, saying, "What? *He's* going to join us?" They had to deal with some heavy-duty prejudices.

We know that at least one, and possibly two, of the disciples were Zealots. A Zealot was passionately dedicated to the violent overthrow of Rome. A Zealot dreamed of the day when Rome would be driven from the land. He hated the Romans and rebelled against their government.

Consider for a moment the feelings aroused by the arrival of Matthew. In the Zealots' eyes, he was a traitor to Israel who had traded in his heritage for a few bucks. And now Jesus says to all of them, "Hey, meet Matthew, your new brother. Come on in, Mr. Tax Collector."

Then think of the fishermen. Peter, James, and John had to pay taxes on every fish they caught. They had to pay taxes on the place where they moored their boat. Matthew, a tax collector, was going to be one of them now. It made for a volatile mix of personalities.

The disciples represented a diverse group of people. And to all of them, Jesus said in essence, "I want all of you to be of one mind, of one accord, and walk together with Me."

He gives us the same charge today. When we enter into His church and become a part of His body, He asks us to lay aside the differences that divide us. He asks us to lay aside racial divisions, economic divisions, divisions brought about by varied educational backgrounds. The Bible describes those of us in the church as living stones. First Peter 2:5 says, "You also, as living stones, are being built up a spiritual house."

It's fascinating to consider how buildings were constructed in ancient Israel. Whatever they did, they did it right, because some of their buildings have been standing now for hundreds of years. They would take large rocks and join them together so each rock would conform to the adjacent rock. They made the rocks fit by grinding them together, thereby making a perfect fit.

We in the church are living stones, and sometimes God will put opposites together. Often God puts someone in your life who grates on you, who irritates you. Alan Redpath used to say, "Difficult people are the nails that God uses to drive us to Calvary's cross."

You may agree and say, "Yes, I know some difficult people." But did you ever stop to think *you* might be a difficult person to someone else? God may be using you to grate on another person—but in the process He is teaching all of us patience and love and forgiveness. We are living stones brought together.

This is not always easy to take. It's easy to love people to whom we're naturally attracted. But there are always people who rub us the wrong way. They are peculiar, odd. We think, *I don't want to deal with them. They irritate me. I don't normally hang out with them.* Yet they are a part of the body of Christ and God has put us together with them.

Maybe God has brought a difficult person into your life. Perhaps you work with a difficult person. Maybe you are married to a difficult person. But God has called you to lay aside your prejudice, lay aside your hang-ups, and learn to love that person with the love of God.

It's true, Christians will let you down. At times they may disappoint you. But the church is not a museum for saints; it's a hospital for sinners. After we go out into the world and are wounded and hurt, we can find restoration in the church. Galatians 6:1 says, "If a man is overtaken in any trespass, you who are spiritual restore such a one in a spirit of gentleness, considering yourself lest you also be tempted." That is, if you see someone else who is fallen, pick him up, because next time it might be you. The next time around you might be the one with the fiery arrows of the devil lodged in your chest. That's why we need to help out and pick up one another.

Perhaps you have been disillusioned with a church or a preacher. Maybe you had an experience early in life where something unpleasant happened to you in church. You were treated badly or someone was harsh with you and you withdrew from the church.

Or perhaps there was someone who was supposed to be an example to you—a Christian friend or someone who turned out to be a hypocrite. So you decided they're all hypocrites, and because of that you have written off the church.

Understand this: Even though people fail, Jesus does not. Jesus is consistent. Jesus is no hypocrite. And He is the One who created the church in the first place, who "loved the church and gave Himself for it" (Ephesians 5:25). It makes no sense to despise the very thing for which Christ gave His life. If you love Him, you will love her. You will be active in church. It's just that simple.

"The Church is not a human society of people united by their natural affinities but the Body of Christ, in which all members, however different (and He rejoices in their differences and by no means wishes to iron them out) must share the common life, complementing and helping one another precisely by their differences."

—C.S. *Lewis*

22

HOW TO BE A KINGDOM BUILDER

⤢

"The kingdom of God does not come with your careful
observation, nor will people say, 'Here it is,' or 'There it is,'
because the kingdom of God is within you."

—LUKE 17:20-21, NIV

IF YOU WERE TO ASK the average, unbelieving person on the street to describe a Christian, you would probably get some interesting—and badly distorted—answers. Many would probably describe a person who lives by the "golden rule" and goes to church all the time. An increasing number of other voices would say that a Christian is a narrow-minded bigot who always has something to complain about.

On one hand, I take some of these descriptions as compliments—we *are* supposed to be distinctly different from the world-at-large, and we *do* have specific moral guidelines to live by. On the other hand, I think we need to take a closer look at some of those descriptions.

Far too often, Christians are perceived as negative. Many times it's a caricature or a misrepresentation, but in some ways we have brought it upon ourselves. Sometimes it seems as if all we Christians are known for is what we oppose. If we don't approve of a certain movie, we'll boycott it. If we don't like what a certain store is selling, we'll picket it.

Of course, not all these things are wrong; in fact, they can even be effective in some cases, for we do need to exercise our rights as Americans and seek to stop the spread of corruption in our society. But we must balance trying to make an outward change in our world with trying to bring about an inward, spiritual change.

Many Jews misunderstood what Jesus intended to do at the beginning of His ministry. Many expected Him to be a military leader who would deliver them from the yoke of Rome and establish a new kingdom on earth. When Jesus miraculously fed the multitude by the Sea of Galilee, the people wanted to make Him king by force (*see* John 6:11-15). They saw Him as a political and social Messiah.

I fear we have the same problem today. We want to take Him by force and make Him king, or have Him bless our agenda. We think that by doing so we are building His kingdom on earth.

The question is, What did Jesus mean by "the kingdom"? The Bible does teach the day is coming when Christ will return to this earth and establish a perfect kingdom. There will be no scandals, no corruption. It will be perfect. He will rule perfectly as our Shepherd.

The Bible also teaches, however, that the kingdom of God is in our lives today. That simply means the kingdom is in you the moment you surrender your life to Christ and give Him control. When Jesus told us to "take My yoke upon you and learn from Me" (Matthew 11:29), He meant that we are to surrender the direction of our lives to Him, just as a farmer used a yoke to direct his plow animals.

In the same way, when Jesus says we are to seek first the kingdom of God and His righteousness, He means that we are to seek the rule and reign of Jesus Christ above everything else in our lives. His kingdom is a *spiritual* kingdom.

When Jesus appeared before Pontius Pilate, the governor asked Him, "What have You done?" (John 18:35). Jesus replied, "My kingdom is not of this world. If My kingdom were of this world, My servants would fight, so that I should not be delivered to the Jews; but now My kingdom is not from here" (verse 36). God's kingdom is not of this world.

None of us are going to bring about the kingdom of God by force, and if we try it, we're only going to hurt our cause. God's Word tells us the weapons of our warfare are not physical, but mighty through God to the pulling down of strongholds (*see* 2 Corinthians 10:4).

God has given us weapons far more effective than guns or swords or even boycotts or protests. One of them is prayer. When is the last time you prayed about the problems plaguing our society?

Acts chapter 12 opens with James being put to death, Peter in prison, and Herod on the throne. Talk about a bleak scenario! So what did the church do? They could have had a sit-in. They could have picketed Caesar's palace. They could have boycotted all products made by Rome. Instead, they gathered at a believer's house to pray. And—here's the best part—when the story ends, Peter is out of prison, Herod is off the throne, and things have changed dramatically. We need that kind of strategy today!

Another weapon in our arsenal is the gospel. We should share the good news of Christ with the young girl who wants to get an abortion. We need to give the gospel message to the person trapped in a homosexual lifestyle. We should share Christ with the gang member. We must preach the gospel to the people who are hurting our society. As people learn there is another kingdom, it will change the way they live in this one.

I agree with a recent statement by Cal Thomas: "Let us resolve to know Him better, present Him and nothing else to a despairing world, pray as never before and, when we do, anticipate the rumble of revival across America, without which this nation cannot much longer prevail under the blessings of God."*

Yes, we are in a spiritual battle, but we're also in a building

---

*Cal Thomas, Christian syndicated columnist, "Why Is Thy Soul Cast Down?" *Religious Broadcasting*, April 1993, p. 52.

campaign. We must remember that building the kingdom of God does not mean changing the ways of the world, but changing the hearts of people. Can you be called a kingdom builder?

Read Acts 12 and see the power of prayer at work!

23

A LIFE OF PRAYER

"And it came to pass, as He was praying in a certain place, when He ceased, that one of His disciples said to Him, 'Lord, teach us to pray.'"

—LUKE 11:1

THE *GOSPEL HERALD* once printed an interesting story about a British soldier who was caught creeping back to his quarters from the nearby woods. Taken before his commanding officer, he was charged with holding communications with the enemy. The man pleaded he had gone into the woods to pray by himself. That was his only defense.

"Down on your knees and pray now!" roared the officer. "You never needed it so much!"

Expecting immediate death, the soldier knelt and poured out his soul in prayer. After he had finished praying, the officer simply said, "You may go." As the soldier stood there in utter amazement, the officer explained, "I believe your story. If you hadn't drilled so often, you could not do so well at review."

How is *your* prayer life? If someone were to listen in while you prayed, would he or she be able to tell how often you speak with the Lord? Would you, like the soldier, do well "at review"?

Jesus' disciples had observed the profound effect prayer had in the life and ministry of their Lord. They had seen Him withdraw from the multitude, and even leave them, so that He could spend time alone in prayer with His heavenly Father. And they noticed the power, peace, and tranquility that emanated from His life, enabling Him to stay calm in troubled circumstances. This lifestyle of prayer so moved the disciples that one day they asked Jesus, "Lord, teach us to pray."

When Jesus instructed His disciples to "pray and not lose heart" (Luke 18:1), He was not merely advocating that they break for prayer at specified times during the day. Rather, He was encouraging His men to develop a prayerful lifestyle permeated by a trust in and dependence upon God. The Bible tells us to "pray without ceasing . . . for this is the will of God in Christ Jesus for you" (1 Thessalonians 5:17-18).

A literal definition of the word "pray" in Luke 11:1 is "to wish forward." In other words, prayer should not be mere lip service, or a grocery list of requests, but a genuine expression of our desire to seek God's will for our lives. Our prayer should reflect our desire to move forward in our walk with Christ.

Certainly, if Jesus, the perfect Son of God, had to depend upon prayer during His life on earth, how much more do you and I need to pray?

In order to have a dynamic and effective prayer life, we must make prayer a vital part of our day. Our time with God in prayer should be indispensable.

And I'm not talking about simply keeping a legalistic prayer scorecard. It's possible to offer little prayers to God and never really pray. The rabbis during Jesus' day often told their followers to pray a certain prayer in a given situation. You might equate those prayers with a prewritten prayer today. But unless such prayers express what is really on your heart, they don't have much to do with real communion with God.

More than anything else, God wants to hear from *you*. Jesus has instructed us to worship God in spirit and truth (*see* John 4:23). Don't worry if your grammar is not perfect or if you have trouble saying things in an orderly fashion. Just be honest and open with God. He's more concerned with the sincerity of your heart than the eloquence of your speech.

All of us have a choice before us. We can decide either to pray or to lose heart. Those are the only options.

Look at the example of the apostle Paul. He knew what it was to suffer. He was beaten, stoned, often thrown into prison, ship-wrecked, and abandoned by his friends. He knew what it was to be discouraged—yet he was able to keep going. How? He tells us in 2 Corinthians 3:18–4:1, "We all, with unveiled face, beholding as in a mirror the glory of the Lord, are being transformed into the same image from glory to glory, just as by the Spirit of the Lord. Therefore, since we have this ministry, as we have received mercy, we do not lose heart."

Paul realized that he needed to take time to bask in God's presence and, like a well-used and dried-out sponge, be replen-ished. He needed to be in an attitude of prayer. You, too, must recognize that wherever you are, no matter how difficult your circumstances, God is right there with you. He's only a prayer away! When you pray, you draw strength from His presence and He will give you the grace and resources you need.

Take a minute to review your own prayer life. The British of-ficer could tell that his young soldier was a man of prayer; can others tell that you have a prayer life which reflects a close rela-tionship with God? Prayer is a privilege, not an afterthought.

I urge you to take your problems to God before you take them to your spouse, your friend, or your relatives. Pour out your heart to God and let Him minister to you. Remember, when prayer be-comes a natural part of your daily life, life itself becomes much eas-ier to cope with as you lay hold of God and His resources.

I know of at least one British soldier who can vouch for that!

"Prayer is more than verbally filling in some requisition blank. It's fellowship with God! It's communion with the Lord through praising Him, rehearsing His promises, and then sharing our needs."   —*Billy Graham*

24

FATHER KNOWS BEST

✄

"If you abide in Me, and My words abide in you, you will ask what you desire, and it shall be done for you."

—JOHN 15:7

DO YOU EVER quote verses to God in prayer? I do. But it's not because I'm trying to remind God of His Word. It's not as if God says, "Oh, I've forgotten that. Thanks for bringing that to My attention, Greg."

I quote those verses to remind myself. First, I'm laying hold of a promise. Second, it builds my faith to realize this promise has been made available to me.

John 15:7 is one of the most incredible promises Jesus ever made. A broader translation of this verse might read like this: "If you maintain a living communion with Me, and My words are at home with you, I command you to ask at once for yourselves whatever you desire, and it is yours."

Most of us gravitate immediately toward the latter part of that verse: "I command you to ask at once for yourselves whatever you desire, and it is yours." We think of all the things we would like to have. But the key is to get into alignment with the will of God. Only then will I want what God wants. Only then will I desire what God desires. This verse is really saying that if I maintain a living communion with God and His Word is at home in my heart, I will start to change.

First John 3:22 says, "[We] receive from him anything we ask, because we obey his commands and do what pleases him" (NIV). If we give a listening ear to all of God's commands, He will give a listening ear to all of our prayers.

How are we going to know God's will? From searching the Bible and knowing what it says. When we do that, we will get a better understanding and a better grasp of God's will and purpose for us.

Charles Spurgeon said, "When you have great desires for heavenly things, when your desires are such as God approves of, when you will what God wills, then you will have what you like."

Do you want anything? What is burning most on your heart? The salvation of your child? The salvation of your husband or your wife or your friend? Or even of an enemy? Then maintain a living communion with Him and keep praying.

Do you really want to see revival in America? Do you really want to see a spiritual awakening? Then abide in Him and don't give up asking—even when you pick up the newspaper and read of out-of-control violence and rampant sexual immorality and a culture on the brink. Even when you think there is no hope. Keep praying. Persist. Remember that what may initially appear to be indifference on the part of God is actually a barrier He puts up that He wants us to overcome by persistent faith. He doesn't put up those barriers to drive us away, but to draw us closer. Any genuine faith can hurdle such a barrier. So keep praying. Keep seeking. Keep knocking. And the door will be opened.

Many times as fathers and mothers and even grandparents, we don't know how to pray for our children. We always want to pray that our children will be healthy and safe and that everything will go well for them. But that's not necessarily what they need.

Suppose you had been Joseph's mother. Surely you would have prayed that God would keep him safe, not realizing that it was part of God's plan for this young man to suffer some extremely hard times. It was those hardships that equipped him to rise to second in command of all Egypt and to save the lives of his whole family.

Had you been Daniel's mother, surely you would have prayed that Israel would never fall captive to the Babylonians. But God used Daniel as a mighty prophet in the courts of Nebuchadnezzar, Darius, and Belshazzar.

Had you been Mary, the mother of Jesus, don't you think you would have prayed, "Don't let Him be crucified, Lord. Anything but that!" Imagine her anguish as she looked up to see the beaten, bloodied body of her son hanging on the cross. Yet it was all part of God's plan.

Sometimes we pray a certain way and something else happens, and we conclude God isn't answering our prayers. Don't be too quick to conclude that God is wrong, however, because you haven't seen the big picture. It wasn't until many years had passed that Joseph could say to his brothers, "You meant evil against me; but God meant it for good" (Genesis 50:20). I don't know if he could have said that when he was in prison or when he was carried away into slavery—but he definitely said it later.

So, trust that God is in control! The key is to get our will in alignment with His. True prayer is not overcoming God's reluctance, but taking hold of His willingness. It's not getting my will in heaven, but His will on earth.

You might say, "Do you mean to tell me that if I have my own desires and I pray for them, that God will not respond unless I pray only for what He really wants?" That's right, that's exactly what I am telling you. Our desires are not necessarily the best things for us, but God's desires always are. When we come to realize that God knows more than we do, life will go a whole lot better for us. Because the truth is, Father knows best.

Martin Luther said, "By our praying, we are instructing ourselves more than Him." What kind of instruction have you been giving yourself lately? For a look at the power of prayer and the changes it can make in even the bleakest situation, take a look at 1 Samuel 1.

25

HINDRANCES TO ANSWERED PRAYER

✣

"Then He spoke a parable to them, that men always
ought to pray and not lose heart."

—LUKE 18:1

HAVE YOU EVER BEEN TEMPTED to give up praying because the answer to your prayer didn't arrive when you hoped it would? I doubt any believer has been spared this trial. I know I haven't. But it's always too early to give up on God. There may be several reasons why our prayers aren't answered.

First, be sure your prayer is a scriptural one and not merely self-indulgent. James 4:3 says, "You ask and do not receive, because you ask amiss." He says that sometimes we ask with an evil intent so that we may use God's provision for self-gratification. Make sure your prayer is scriptural.

Second, make sure there is no unconfessed sin in your life. If you have failed to deal with some sin, it could put a dead stop to anything God wants to do for you. The psalmist said, "If I regard iniquity in my heart, the Lord will not hear [me]" (Psalm 66:18). I cannot emphasize this enough. The word "regard" means "hold on to" or "cling to." If there is a sin in my life—if I hold on to it and fail to confess it—God will simply not hear me. If I'm hanging on to some sin that I know I should let go of, my prayer life will come to a screeching halt. A barrier is erected between God and myself.

It's as if I have hung up on God. I was having a conversation and I've hung up the phone. I've severed the communication. God says in Isaiah 59:1-2, "The LORD's hand is not shortened, that it cannot save; nor His ear heavy, that it cannot hear. But your iniquities have separated you from your God; and your sins have hidden His face from you, so that He will not hear." We erect such a barrier by unconfessed sin in our lives.

If there is some "little sin" you're dabbling with and it seems as though God isn't answering your prayers, realize that it was you who shut the door and only you can open it again by confessing your sin and repenting of it.

Yet another reason why our prayers are not answered right away has little to do with us. Some prayers are delayed because there is satanic interference. Did you know that? We don't realize that there is a spiritual battle going on in prayer. We keep praying, but nothing seems to happen.

Remember that Daniel prayed a specific request for three weeks before he got the answer (see Daniel 9). The answer was delayed by satanic forces. It was easier for Daniel's prayer to reach heaven than it was for the answer to reach earth. But he didn't give up, for he knew that what he was praying for was right. That encourages us to keep praying.

Last, if everything else is in order, keep asking, keep seeking, and keep knocking. Be persistent. Don't give up praying for that loved one who is not yet a believer. Keep praying. You know God is not willing that any should perish but that all should come to repentance (see 2 Peter 3:9). He may be in his final days. He may be on his deathbed. He may pass away tomorrow. But don't give up praying. Someone prayed for you, and that person's prayer was answered in God's timing.

If you are single, don't give up praying for God to provide you with a mate. Maybe you get impatient at times. "Why haven't You provided, Lord?" you demand. Please don't run ahead of the will of God and take things into your own hands! You'll regret it for the rest of your life. Wait. When God brings that person into your life, he or she will be just what you need. You can start praying for that person right now even though you don't know who it will be. When the time is right, he or she will come.

I don't know about you, but I get impatient. I get impatient when I cook my food. I want to eat it. *Now*. The very fact that I'm cooking means I'm desperate because I'm such a lousy cook. My older son Christopher makes brownies and pancakes and they all turn out great. I said to him the other day, "It's amazing, those brownies were delicious. How did you do it?" He said, "Dad, it's so easy. Just follow the directions." When I bake them, they don't come out nearly so well. I don't take time to read the directions.

Have you ever been so hungry for a pizza that when it was ready you couldn't wait for it to cool off to take a bite? The hot, melted cheese sticks to the roof of your mouth and you're forced to gulp down some water. You've just burned the top of your mouth. So what do you do? You take another bite. It's hard to wait. You get impatient. You want it *now*.

Sometimes we approach prayer in the same way. We start praying and say, "Lord, I need this now. Please provide me with a husband." The Lord says, "Eventually, but not yet. You're not ready for him. He's not ready for you. You just wait." "Well, I'll just go help myself then," you say. Go ahead—but you'll be sorry.

Or maybe there is a loved one you're praying for. You want him to come to faith. You want him to know Jesus Christ. You so want him to know Jesus like you do. You grow tired of waiting for the Holy Spirit to work. So you try some pressure tactics. Maybe a little guilt. You think you're helping God when in reality you do more harm than good.

Sometimes we run ahead of the Lord. We try to make things happen that aren't meant to happen. Wait for God's perfect timing! If you believe that what you want is scriptural and that there is no unconfessed sin in your life, keep praying and don't give up. Waiting is hard, but it's a lot easier than picking up the pieces of a shattered dream.

The apostle Paul knew what it was like to have God refuse one of his prayer requests. Yet, he sought to understand why God did not answer his prayer, and then he was able to glorify God. Read 2 Corinthians 12:7-10 to see Paul's response. What has God allowed or not allowed in your life that can be used for His glory?

26

CARTE BLANCHE

⚞

"Then Jesus answered and said to her, 'O woman, great is your faith!
Let it be to you as you desire.' And her daughter was
healed from that very hour."

—MATTHEW 15:28

HOW THE CHURCH needs intercessors today! The woman described in Matthew 15 fits this description. Her daughter was "severely demon-possessed" and she pleaded with Jesus to heal her. This woman, like any loving mother, cared for her daughter. She loved her more than life itself. She wanted Jesus to take action—but on her initial approach, the Lord appeared almost heartless and uncaring. The text simply says He "answered her not a word" (verse 23).

Why did He respond this way? First, it would be helpful to understand the woman's background. The Bible says she was a Canaanite. The Canaanites, you'll remember, were idol worshipers, the ancient enemies of Israel whom God ordered destroyed.

Here was a descendant of the avowed enemies of Israel. It's entirely possible that this woman (whom Mark identifies as a Syro-Phoenician) was a worshiper of the false goddess Ashtoreth. Yet she comes to Jesus, seeking help. Apparently, her idols had been unable to assist her—in fact, they had contributed to the problem.

They no doubt helped to bring her daughter under the control of demons.

When Jesus "answered her not a word," it appeared He was rejecting her. But He was not trying to destroy her faith; He wanted to develop it. He was not playing games with her, nor was He trying to make the situation more difficult. He was seeking to draw out her faith. He could see how strong her faith was and how she was aligning herself with His will—so He set her apart as an example of true faith. He put up barriers so she might step over them and show her true commitment. Jesus knew what she wanted and He knew what He was going to do.

The Master had grown tired of phoniness and superficiality. He had spent considerable time exposing the sham religion of the Pharisees and repeatedly emphasized the critical importance of the heart. Finally, He encountered someone with a true heart. He discovered an honest person, someone who wanted Him for the right reason.

How did the woman react to His silence? No sooner had Jesus put up this barrier than the woman stepped over it. She was absolutely undeterred. She pleaded with Him a second time, "Lord, help me!" (verse 25).

At that point Jesus moved to level two. Listen to His response: "It is not good to take the children's bread and throw it to the little dogs" (verse 26). What strong words to say to a woman with a demon-possessed daughter!

His words sound insulting, but they're not as harsh as they first seem. In those days people used two different words to talk about dogs. One was a phrase that described mangy, dirty mongrels which roamed the streets and lived off of garbage. The second was used for the family pet, the dog you really loved. The latter is the word Jesus used here. He was saying, "It is not right to take food from the master's table and give it to the family pet."

But not even this response could deter this woman. Her faith was so strong that she realized even a tiny leftover of Jesus' power would be enough to heal her daughter. She first scaled the barrier of silence and now she hurdled the barrier of seeming rejection. She replied, "True, Lord, yet even the little dogs eat the crumbs which fall from their masters' table" (verse 27).

This is what Jesus had been waiting to hear; here was a woman who would not let go. At that moment the heavens opened and Jesus gave her carte blanche: "O woman, great is your faith! Let it be to you as you desire" (verse 28). And her daughter was healed that instant.

What earned this woman such an incredible privilege? Persistence and commitment. When the door was shut in her face, she kept knocking. When Christ portrayed her as a dog, she simply picked up His words—just like a good little dog would pick up his master's stick—and dropped them at His feet. She would not give up. She would not go home without the touch of the Master on her daughter's life. If at first she did not succeed, she would keep asking, keep seeking, keep knocking.

This woman was a true intercessor. Intercessory prayer means that you stand in the gap for someone and you will not give up. You are going to keep praying for that person till you see something happen.

People can reject your influence and escape your presence, but they can never escape your prayers. Sidlow Baxter said, "Men may spurn our appeals, reject our message, oppose our arguments, despise our persons, but they are helpless against our prayers."

So take a tip from this Syro-Phoenician woman. Don't give up! Hang in there! Keep praying! Keep seeking! Keep knocking! If an obstacle lies in front of you, go over it. If a door is shut, knock harder. Don't give up!

The hurdle in front of you may be the last one before the finish line.

Look at the words of Jesus in the Sermon on the Mount, where He speaks about the value and reward of persistent prayer (Matthew 7:7-12).

27

WHERE ARE THE OTHER NINE?

✠

*"Were there not any found who returned to give glory
to God except this foreigner?"*

—LUKE 17:18

IF YOU HAVE EVER SPENT any time with toddlers, you know their vocabulary rarely includes words such as, "Thank you" or, "I appreciate your thoughtfulness." Instead, their sentences often begin with, "I want" or, "Gimme." They believe the world revolves around their needs.

Thank goodness that we mature as we get older . . . or do we? When was the last time you thanked God for answering your prayers? When was the last time you thanked Him for meeting your needs (beyond the usual prayer before mealtime)? Sometimes I think we revert to a toddler mentality when it comes to spiritual matters. Our prayer life contains 98 percent requests and just 2 percent thanksgivings.

You may be familiar with the story of the ten lepers in Luke. As the story goes, all ten asked Jesus for healing, but only one returned to thank Him.

Sadly, many follow this pattern today. They are "foxhole believers" in times of crisis, but practical atheists otherwise. I call them practical atheists because they acknowledge the existence of God, but show no indication that God is part of their day-to-day living. Most of the time they live as they please; but when a crisis hits, they fall to their knees and cry out, "God, help me!" As soon as He gets them out of that jam, they return to their old lifestyle.

It may surprise you, but God wants to bless you more than you want to be blessed. He wants to speak to you more than you want to be spoken to. He's interested in you. He wants to work in your life. The tragedy is that many of us are in danger of being among the nine lepers in this story. We are so quick to pray for help, yet so slow to give thanks. In a sense, Jesus is still asking the question today: "Where are the other nine?"

Philippians 4:6 instructs us, "Be anxious for nothing, but in everything by prayer and supplication, *with thanksgiving*, let your requests be made known to God" (emphasis added).

God wants us to make thanksgiving an essential part of our prayers. Why is that? First, as we give thanks, it bolsters our faith. By giving thanks, we are reminded of God's power and faithfulness to us over the years. As our faith in God grows stronger, we come to realize that nothing is too hard for the Lord.

Have you come to the Lord for help, then forgotten to thank Him for what He has done for you? Do you thank God for the blessings He gives you each day?

You may say, "But I have nothing to be thankful for!" Let's consider some of the many blessings we have as believers.

Are you in relatively good health? You can thank God for that. We don't realize how valuable good health is until we begin to lose it. When I visit hospital wards, I am reminded how fragile life is. I always walk out thanking God for the ability to do just that: Walk out. Your health is a blessing you should never take for granted.

Then think about your personal freedoms and privileges. Here in the United States, you don't have to fear being arrested for carrying a Bible and going to church, or fear being tortured for your faith in Jesus Christ. And if you had a meal today and were able to get dressed in a different set of clothes than what you wore yesterday, you're better off than many people in this world.

Most importantly, you can be thankful that your sin is forgiven and that you have an inheritance waiting for you in heaven. That alone is more than enough to be thankful for! You can be thankful you have a relationship with the living God and that you have open access to Him 24 hours a day. You can be thankful He has filled that emptiness in your life and given you hope in a hopeless world.

When you come before the Lord to pray and pour out all your problems before His throne, preface your requests with some praise and thanksgiving. Thanking God not only strengthens your faith, but also puts your life in perspective.

Second, thanksgiving enhances our worship. When we give thanks to God, we're acknowledging that He is in control and is worthy of our praise. It does not matter how we feel at that moment or what problems we are facing, because He has already done so much for us.

Sometimes we can begin to take our walk with Jesus Christ for granted. We forget that the peace we wake up with every morning, the serenity and hope we possess, is something we did not always have.

Unfortunately, some people do not realize this until they fall away and begin missing those gifts. First they lose their joy. That's why David, after his sin with Bathsheba, wrote in Psalm 51, "Restore to me the joy of Your salvation" (verse 12). Thanksgiving reminds us what a privilege it is to be a child of God.

So don't be like the nine who were too preoccupied with themselves to come back and give thanks. Be like the one who came back to the Lord and worshiped and glorified God for being so good to him. Take some time to thank Him today.

> "Thou hast given so much to me,
> Give one thing more—a grateful heart,
> Not thankful when it pleases me,
> As if Thy blessings had spare days,
> But such a heart, whose pulse may be Thy praise."
> —*George Herbert*

28
MAKING OUR HEART HIS HOME

✠

"Today I must stay at your house."

—LUKE 19:5

HAVE YOU EVER VISITED someone's home and felt really uncomfortable? Perhaps the people you were visiting had some things in their home that bothered you as a Christian. For some reason you just weren't comfortable, and you wanted to leave.

Sometimes I wonder if Jesus feels comfortable in our hearts. Of course, He entered our hearts when we accepted Him into our lives—but does He really feel at home?

Paul offers an interesting prayer for his friends in Ephesians 3:17. He prays that "Christ may dwell in [their] hearts through faith." But if Christ already entered their hearts at the time of their conversion, why should the apostle pray that Jesus would dwell in their hearts? Didn't Christ already dwell there?

To understand what Paul meant when he used the word "dwell," let's look at the original Greek term. The word "dwell" is actually made up of two words. One means "to live in a home." The other means "to be comfortable" in that home. Yet another shade of meaning implies "staying with permanency." So Paul is really saying, "My prayer is that Christ may finally settle down and feel completely at home and comfortable in your hearts."

This verse suggests that Jesus isn't necessarily comfortable in every heart in which He has taken up residence. You may be doing some things that make Him ill at ease. You may be hiding little areas of compromise, attempting to keep them out of the Lord's sight. You may say, "All right, Lord, You can walk around in the front room. You can come into the dining room. But don't come upstairs! It's off-limits. Stay out of the closets! I have a few skeletons locked up there that I would rather You not see."

Instead of giving Him the freedom to roam around, you've given Him only a tiny section of your heart. You say, "Okay, Lord. You can do whatever You want in my life while I'm at church on Sunday—but let me deal with the rest of the week. That's my business."

Perhaps you are worried about giving Him your leisure time because you intend to go to certain movies and you don't want God to bother your conscience. You might be reluctant to give God your future because you are afraid He might send you to some remote, uncivilized part of the world, filled with bugs and rodents.

We do that a lot, don't we? We tell God to stay out of certain areas of our lives. Why do we do that? Are we afraid that God is going to spoil all of our fun and make our lives miserable? Let me tell you this: To be in the perfect will of God is the most joyful and fulfilling place you can be. On the other hand, to be out of God's will is the most miserable, unhappy place you can be.

Let Him be Lord of every area of your life. Let Him be Lord of your relationships. Let Him be Lord of your leisure time. Let Him be Lord of your finances. Let Him be Lord of all. Because if He is not Lord *of* all, He is not Lord *at* all.

To say, "No, Lord!" is a contradiction. If He is Lord, then you must say yes. If you are trying to push Jesus away from certain areas of your life, then He is not really at home in your heart. But He wants to be!

It's time to give Jesus the master key. I'm not talking about a key that opens only this door or that door; I'm talking about the master key that opens every door.

I'll be honest with you. If you do that, He will definitely do some spring cleaning. But keep this in mind: He only takes something out in order to replace it with something better. Don't be afraid! Paul wrote, "I also count all things loss for the excellence of the knowledge of Christ Jesus my Lord . . . and count them as rubbish, that I may gain Christ" (Philippians 3:8). There is no comparison between what you trade in and what you get back. What God gives us is so much greater.

What happened in Luke 19 when Jesus visited the home of Zacchaeus is not recorded, but the ultimate result is clear. Zacchaeus became a fully committed believer. He had an encounter with God in which he was instantaneously made into a different person.

Jesus' invitation to Zacchaeus—"I must stay at your house"—is also given to you and me today. Our hearts can become the home of Jesus Christ, where He will feel completely comfortable.

Before that wonderful day, the heart of Zacchaeus was cluttered with all sorts of useless junk that only clogged the hallways and made the rooms dark. But then Jesus changed all of that. He threw out the ratty furniture and replaced it with elegant, hand-made originals guaranteed for life. He repainted the black walls in dazzling white and illuminated every square inch of his heart with divine light.

He wants to do that in your heart, too. He is waiting for the invitation. Why not hand over the master key today? You won't regret it—Jesus is one Interior Decorator who really knows how to make property values skyrocket.

For a look at the futility of saying no to Jesus, read the story of Peter and his vision in Acts 11.

PART THREE

MAINTAINING AND SHINING

"Do all things without murmuring and disputing, that you may become blameless and harmless, children of God without fault in the midst of a crooked and perverse generation, among whom you shine as lights in the world, holding fast the word of life."

—PHILIPPIANS 2:14-16

*Y*ou are the only Bible many people will ever read. You are the only sermon they will ever hear, the only advertisement they will ever see. If many of your friends and family who don't know the Lord are ever to grasp the wonder of what God wants to do in a person's life, they may have only one example open to them: you. ✄

It is a mystery to me that God has chosen to use frail, flawed humans to communicate His message. It seems that angels would have done a far more effective job than us. But make no mistake about it: God works through people. ✄

People just like you. ✄ Our world is becoming an increasingly dark place spiritually. How we believers need to shine our lights! As Jesus shines through us, men and women will begin to leave behind their lives of sin and darkness and will instead stream toward heaven's glorious, blazing light. ✄

But if that is to happen—if men and women are to be drawn into the loving arms of the Savior—you and I must take care to do two things: maintain and shine. We must continue to live according to the level of spiritual maturity we have already attained (*see* Philippians 3:16) and we must hold out the hope of the gospel for others to see. We will find our witness becoming ever stronger as we choose to walk every day with Jesus.

✄

1

DO YOU LOVE THE LORD?

*"'You shall love the LORD your God with all your heart, with all your soul,
and with all your mind.' This is the first and great commandment."*

—MATTHEW 22:37-38

SO MANY PEOPLE claim to love the Lord today. But do they? Do you? Do I? How can we know for sure?

I would like to lay out a little five-part test—a litmus test, if you will—of how to determine whether you really love the Lord. It's an important question, for the apostle Paul wrote, "If anyone does not love the Lord Jesus Christ, let him be accursed" (1 Corinthians 16:22). What are some of the earmarks of a person who truly loves God and is growing in that love for Him?

First, a person who loves the Lord will long for personal communion with God. Prayer will not be a duty to such a person. Bible study will not be a drudgery. Getting together with God's people will be a delight and a joy. As the psalmist said, "As the deer pants for the water brooks, so pants my soul for You, O God. My soul thirsts for God, for the living God" (Psalm 42:1-2). And as he wrote a little later, "O God, You are my God; early will I seek You; my soul thirsts for You; my flesh longs for You in a dry and thirsty land where there is no water. So I have looked for You in the sanctuary, to see Your power and Your glory. Because Your lovingkindness is better than life, my lips shall praise You. Thus I will bless You while I live; I will lift up my hands in Your name" (Psalm 63:1-4).

Worship is a delight for those who love the Lord; it isn't something they have to force themselves to do. They are excited about it, thrilled to do it, because they know that in worship they commune with the very God of the universe.

Second, a person who loves the Lord will love the things that He loves. And how do we know what He loves? He tells us in the Scripture. Therefore, whoever claims to love the Lord will love His Word. Psalm 119:97 declares, "Oh, how I love Your law! It is my meditation all the day." As you are being made more like Jesus, you will start loving what God loves. You will love righteousness. You will love what is good. In other words, you will love what He loves.

Third, a person who loves the Lord will hate what God hates. As His nature becomes our nature, we will begin to recoil from everything that displeases God. Psalm 97:10 says, "You who love the LORD, hate evil!" Proverbs 8:13 says, "The fear of the LORD is to hate evil." We are to hate what He hates—and He tells us to hate evil. The Bible commands us in Romans 12:9, "Abhor what is evil. Cling to what is good." If you love the Lord, you will hate what He hates.

Fourth, those who love the Lord will long for the return of Christ. The Bible teaches that Jesus is going to return for His people and we're going to be caught up together to be with Him in the air. The Bible says, "We shall all be changed—in a moment, in the twinkling of an eye" (1 Corinthians 15:51-52).

What comes to mind when you hear a truth like that? Does it excite you? What if Jesus were to come back tonight? Would that thrill you or fill you with dread? Those who love the Lord should look forward to His return. Paul wrote, "There is laid up for me the crown of righteousness, which the Lord, the righteous Judge, will give to me on that Day, and not to me only but also to all who have loved His appearing" (2 Timothy 4:8).

Fifth, if you love the Lord, you will keep His commandments.

It's so easy to lift our hands in worship and sing of our deep love to Him. It's so easy to profess our love for Him. But John wrote, "For this is the love of God, that we keep His commandments. And His commandments are not burdensome" (1 John 5:3). He also said, "He who says, 'I know Him,' and does not keep His commandments, is a liar" (1 John 2:4).

Jesus Himself says, "If you love Me, keep My commandments" (John 14:15). He also said, "He who has My commandments and keeps them, it is he who loves Me. And he who loves Me will be loved by My Father, and I will love him and manifest Myself to him" (John 14:21).

A cathedral in Germany displays an engraving which says, "Thus speaketh Christ our Lord to us: 'You call me Master and obey me not. You call me light and see me not. You call me the way and walk with me not. You call me life and don't live with me. You call me wise and follow me not. You call me fair and love me not. You call me rich and ask me not. You call me eternal and seek me not. If I condemn thee, blame me not.'"

It's so easy to say, "I love the Lord. He's so good!" But how does your love affect the way you live? That's what it boils down to.

Maybe we need to examine these things again and say, "Do I really love Him?" There may be some of us who, like Peter, have fallen away from Him. There was a time when we walked with the Lord, but other things somehow got in the way.

Could it be that you have denied Him or turned your back on Him? If so, this would be a great day to come back to Jesus! God longs to throw a great homecoming party for you, just like the one arranged by the father in the story of the prodigal son (*see* Luke 15:11-32). God wants to greet you in a full sprint, throw His arms around you, smother you with kisses, and say, "Welcome home, son or daughter! I've missed you. I love you. Welcome home!"

The Father loves you that much. Do you love Him?

Read for yourself in Luke 15:11-32 the dramatic account Jesus personally gave us to illustrate the magnitude of God's love.

2

THE CHRISTIAN'S STRATEGIC ROLE

≼

"You are the salt of the earth."

—MATTHEW 5:13

IT'S HARD FOR US TODAY to appreciate the significance of Jesus' statement in Matthew 5:13. Salt had great importance in biblical times. So valuable was salt that the Romans considered it the most precious thing on earth, next to the sun. Salt was so valuable that it was actually used to pay Roman soldiers. That's where the expression, "He's not worth his salt" came from. In some cultures, salt was considered even more valuable than gold.

Jesus' phrase in Matthew 5:13 could be translated, "You and you alone are the salt of the earth." He emphasized the word "you." Jesus intended to single out certain people in His audience. In this case, He was speaking to His own disciples. But in a broader sense He was speaking to all disciples throughout history, including us.

Those whom Jesus addressed would recognize immediately that He was speaking about something of value. He meant, "You are precious. You are important. You are salt." Then He said, "You and you alone are that."

Jesus was telling us that we as committed Christians play a vital and strategic role in the world. Wherever you live, wherever you work, wherever you are, Jesus calls you "salt." Don't underestimate how great your impact can be!

People in Bible times knew nothing of refrigeration, canning, or chemical preservatives. It's amazing today how long we can preserve food. But back in those days they did not have such capabilities, specifically in the keeping of meat.

Instead, they would rub salt into the meat to prevent putrefaction. Without the use of salt, meat would quickly rot. That helps us to understand a little more clearly what Jesus meant when He called us "salt." He expected certain things from us.

Christians have been called and equipped to stop the spread of corruption in society. This world is rotten to the core as a result of the Fall, and life in this world tends to degenerate toward a rotting, putrefied state. It's the presence of godly people living godly lives which is stopping this world from decaying into its natural, corrupt state.

If you don't think this is true, just note what the Bible says will happen after the church is taken from the earth. Observe what this world will look like after Christians are removed at the Rapture. We're told in 2 Thessalonians 2:7-9, "For the mystery of lawlessness is already at work; only He who now restrains will do so until He is taken out of the way [referring to the working of the Holy Spirit through the church]. And then the lawless one [the Antichrist] will be revealed, whom the Lord will consume with the breath of His mouth and destroy with the brightness of His coming. The coming of the lawless one is according to the working of Satan, with all power, signs, and lying wonders."

When the Lord comes for His church, the preserving influence which now keeps the world from completely putrefying will be removed. That explains the rapid spread of wickedness during the tribulation period. If you think everything is bad now, it will become worse during the tribulation. Violent crime will explode throughout the world. Drug use will soar, becoming even more widespread than it is today. Sexual perversion will mushroom all over the globe. And why will evil spread so quickly? Because God will remove His church; the Christians who now are keeping a lid on things will be gone. And Satan will have his heyday.

One way Christians preserve society can be illustrated through another characteristic of salt. Salt stings a little, especially if it's applied to a cut or wound. Although salt can function as an antiseptic, it isn't pleasant to apply it to your own sores.

In one sense, we Christians sting people. If those around us are disobeying God and living a lifestyle contrary to Scripture, our very presence stings them as though they had an open wound. We bother them. It may not so much be what we say at any given moment, but because of what we are and what we believe.

Suppose someone is in the middle of telling a dirty joke and you walk in. The joke teller knows you're a Christian. Your presence ruins everything. Has that ever happened to you? You walked into a room and everyone became real quiet. People looked over at you and you thought, *It's so tough being a Christian.* Don't hang your head—rejoice! It means you're making a difference, that you impact what happens around you.

How important can our presence be? It is believed by many historians that the revival which broke out in eighteenth-century England is what saved it from the kind of bloody revolution that overtook France. As France suffered revolution, England enjoyed revival. Christians helped preserve the nation.

It's that kind of role that we're called to fill even today. We're still salt. We're still called to preserve society. And judging from the moral malaise that's rapidly overtaking this country, I think it's about time we Christians started acting like salt.

"Men and women involved in ministry full-time may regularly be leading people to Christ. But almost never are they able to do this apart from someone who has lived the life before these people, which is then the reason they sought out 'professional ministers' for further help. It's individuals like you who make the difference in work settings far more often than people in professional ministry."

—*David Mains*

3

SHINING HEARTS

"You are the light of the world. A city that is set on a hill cannot be hidden."

—MATTHEW 5:14

CAN YOU IMAGINE A WORLD WITHOUT LIGHT? No colors. No sunrises. Nothing to see, only perpetual darkness. May I tell you a secret? Jesus says our world is just like that if we refuse to let His light shine through us.

How does this light shine? It shines when He who is the light of the world has taken up residence in our hearts. It just naturally overflows. It's not something that we do: "Now I'm going to make my light shine—there it is! And now I'm going to turn it out—you have to reserve your energy, you know." No, it's not like that at all. If you're a Christian, it just happens.

The only light you have is the overflow of Christ living in you. The Scripture says in 2 Corinthians 4:6, "For it is the God who commanded light to shine out of darkness who has shone in our hearts to give the light of the knowledge of the glory of God in the face of Jesus Christ."

The time we spend in Jesus' presence will naturally reflect in our attitudes and actions. People are going to see a difference in us. That's why Paul wrote in 2 Corinthians 3:18, "But we all, with unveiled face, beholding as in a mirror the glory of the Lord, are being transformed into the same image from glory to glory."

Light such as that will be noticed because it will stand out against the darkness of this world. A black background makes a shaft of light all the more conspicuous.

The holiest moment in any church service is when God's people go out the doors and into the world. People on the outside ought to be noticing your light and saying, "What is it about you? What makes you different?" When we allow our light to shine, people can't help but notice.

That's why Jesus was so concerned that we don't permit anything to obscure that light. "A city that is set on a hill cannot be hidden," Jesus said (Matthew 5:14). "Nor do they light a lamp and put it under a basket" (verse 15). The Master challenges the person who would try to hide his light. He targets the compromising Christian.

The compromising Christian does not want to offend anyone and would like to blend in with the woodwork. When a dirty joke is told, he laughs along with everyone else. When it's time to go out and get a drink with the girls, she goes out with everyone else. He or she does everything just like everybody else because they don't want to offend. They want to blend in.

The problem with this is that a compromiser reaches no one. She thinks she's doing the gospel a favor, but she's not. He's likely to say something like, "You have to let people know you're a normal person, that you're just like them. Only then can you really preach the gospel." Excuse me? If you merely show them you are just like them, why would they want to change and become like you? You have nothing to offer.

Of course, we shouldn't act odd or strange for the sake of strangeness. But we do have to realize there are certain stands we must make if we call ourselves Christians. Don't be ashamed of your light. Let it blaze!

Think of Lot in the Old Testament. He tried to blend in. He tried to be one of the people. He didn't want to offend anyone. Then one day two angels came to this compromiser and told him that judgment was coming on the city. Lot tried to warn his sons-in-law, but the Bible says they thought he was joking. When he tried to tell them angels had brought him this solemn warning, his sons-in-law must have said, "You're kidding, right? Angels came to *you*? The way you live? Why would we want to listen to you?" Lot had hidden his light for so long that no one believed he had any.

Graham Scrogee said of compromise, "It prompts us to be silent for fear of offending when we ought to speak. It prompts us to praise when it's not deserved, to keep people our friends. It prompts us to tolerate sin and not to speak out because to do so might give us enemies."

For the person who wants to blend in, who doesn't want to offend, Jesus says in effect, "What good are you? You're no good to people. And you're no good to God." Jesus insists that compromising Christians are the most useless people in the world. They have betrayed their light. They are cast off by the world and by Christ. A compromiser reaches no one.

How often we as believers shoot ourselves in the foot in our witness by compromise. By inconsistency. A nonbeliever notices we're not practicing what we preach and he hardens his heart to the gospel. *My life is at least as good as that Christian's*, he thinks. *He doesn't have anything I need*. And he moves one step further away from the Savior.

May God help us to see how important our presence and our witness can be! May we let our light shine in a very dark and corrupt society—because if it was ever needed, it is needed now.

David Livingstone, a great pioneer missionary to Africa, wrote, "People talk of the sacrifice I have made in spending so much of my life in Africa. Can that be called a sacrifice which is simply paid back as a small part of a great debt owing to our God, which we can never repay? Is that a sacrifice which brings its own blest reward in healthful activity, the consciousness of doing good, peace of mind, and a bright hope of a glorious destiny hereafter? Away with the word in such a view, and with such a thought! It is emphatically no sacrifice. Say rather it is a privilege."

4

OUR MARCHING ORDERS

✦

"Then He said to them, 'Thus it is written, and thus it was necessary for the Christ to suffer and to rise from the dead the third day, and that repentance and remission of sins should be preached in His name to all nations, beginning at Jerusalem. And you are witnesses of these things.'"

—LUKE 24:46-48

A WITNESS IS SOMEONE who sincerely tells what he has seen and heard. Suppose someone witnesses a traffic accident. He reports it to the police officer, who takes down his name and address. It's possible that man might be called to a courtroom to testify, to describe what he saw. He was there and he witnessed it himself.

In the same way, the disciples were witnesses of the life, death, and resurrection of Jesus, and they were to tell others what God had done. Peter later said, "We cannot but speak the things which we have seen and heard" (Acts 4:20).

Matthew's Gospel tells us that Jesus said something else of great significance just prior to His ascension: "Go therefore and make disciples of all the nations, baptizing them in the name of the Father and of the Son and of the Holy Spirit, teaching them to observe all things that I have commanded you; and lo, I am with you always, even to the end of the age" (Matthew 28:19-20).

Why did the Lord say, "Go *therefore*"? Because just prior to that statement, He had said, "All authority has been given to Me in heaven and on earth" (Matthew 28:18). His disciples were to go because He would be with them. He had all power and authority. He would be taking up residence inside of them. They were witnesses of these things, and *therefore* they were to make disciples of others.

These are the marching orders of the risen Lord for all Christians. They're not addressed only to missionaries or to pastors and evangelists. They are intended for all Christians, to every man or woman who follows Jesus Christ. We've been given not just the responsibility but the privilege of giving out what God has given to us.

I know this isn't easy. That is why the Lord has provided a dimension of power to make it possible. One aspect of that power is found in Luke 24:52. The text says the disciples worshiped Him and returned to Jerusalem with great joy. I think if they had their way, they probably would have gone back to Jerusalem and formed a little holy huddle and never would have left. But those weren't their marching orders.

I agree with the statement of G. Campbell Morgan, who said, "To lie at His feet is a sacred and blessed thing, but to remain there is to miss the meaning of His resurrection. It is a greater thing to tell some soul of our personal knowledge and relationship that is available with Jesus Christ." It's a great thing to worship and to take in, but the message of the resurrection demands that we go and tell others.

Jesus told His followers to go into Jerusalem and wait for power (*see* Luke 24:49). They didn't know exactly what they were waiting for; they simply had a promise that they would receive power after the Holy Spirit came upon them. When it hit, I don't think anyone doubted what had happened. Pentecost was a dramatic, life-changing, empowering move of God's Spirit.

You may ask, "Did these disciples not already have the Holy Spirit in their lives?" Yes, they did. Jesus appeared to them in the upper room, as recorded in John 20:22, and breathed on them the Holy Spirit. The disciples had the Spirit in their lives, just as does every person who comes to Christ. When you ask Jesus to enter your life, His Spirit comes in and He seals you.

But in Luke 24:49, Jesus wasn't talking about the disciples having the Spirit in their lives. He was talking about a dimension of power that would be available to them. The disciples received this power when the Spirit came upon them as recorded in Acts 2. Then they turned their world upside down for Christ.

Maybe that is one reason why we are not turning our world upside down—we don't have the same power the early church enjoyed. That's unfortunate, to say the least. The promise quoted by Peter on Pentecost pertained to "you and to your children, and to all who are afar off, as many as the Lord our God will call" (Acts 2:39). I don't see any limitations there; I see a promise that continues on.

If you have received Christ, this same power is available to you. God gives you a supernatural endowment to be His witness, to stand up for Christ. That power came upon the disciples and their lives were never the same.

A.W. Tozer correctly said some years ago, "If the Holy Spirit were taken away from the early church, 95 percent of what they did would come to a halt. But if the Holy Spirit were taken away from the church today, only 5 percent of what we do would come to a halt." In other words, we're moving far too much in the power of the flesh and programs and gimmicks instead of the power of the Spirit.

That power is still available to you . . . if you want it. If you ask the Lord to give it to you, He will do so. Jesus said that the Father gives the Holy Spirit to everyone who asks (*see* Luke 11:13). It's as simple as that. You don't have to plead. You don't have to do back flips. You don't even have to have an emotional experience. All you have to do is ask.

It seems to me that we need all the help we can get and all the power that is available. If ever a world needed turning upside down, it's ours.

> "I have learned to place myself before God every day as a vessel to be filled with His Holy Spirit. He has filled me with the blessed assurance that He, as the everlasting God, has guaranteed His own work in me."
>
> —*Andrew Murray*

5

HOW TO BE AN EFFECTIVE WITNESS

⚜

"There was a man sent from God, whose name was John. This man came for a witness, to bear witness of the Light, that all through him might believe."

—JOHN 1:6-7

WE CAN LEARN MUCH about being an effective witness for Jesus Christ by looking at the example of John the Baptist. John's whole purpose in life was to point other people to Jesus. His motto was, "He must increase, but I must decrease" (John 3:30).

When John definitely knew Jesus was the Messiah, he said to his disciples, "Behold! The Lamb of God who takes away the sin of the world!" (John 1:29). Having said that, he was ready to fade into obscurity.

It's important to remember John was a major public figure. Prior to the arrival of Jesus, he was the talk of the town, a legend in his own time. Hundreds of people came out to see the man who fearlessly proclaimed the truths of God while baptizing people in the Jordan River. To give you an idea of his significance and fame, it is worth noting that the Jewish historian Josephus wrote more about John than he did even about Jesus. John made a dramatic impact on his culture and society.

John realized, however, that he was to do a work only until

Christ came. Once Christ arrived on the scene, he was to disappear, to fade into obscurity. His job was done. Once he pointed people to the Messiah, his time in the sun was over.

Contrast that perspective with an all-too-common one today. So many people wonder how God can enrich their lives, how He can make them feel better about themselves, how He can help them succeed in business. Their question in life is, "What can God do for me? How can God make me better? How can God make me succeed?"

That wasn't John's attitude. He asked himself what he could do to prepare people for the Messiah. He strategized about how to direct attention the Lord's way. He wanted to decrease as Jesus increased. As a result, John was a great man in the eyes of both God and men—and he shook his nation. He readied his people for the kingdom of God.

Unlike John, we spend so much time looking within. We have a serious case of "I" trouble. It's the "unholy Trinity": me, myself, and I. We're obsessed with our own problems and needs. John focused his life on following the Lord and serving the Lord and honoring the Lord and seeking the glory of the Lord. As a result, he found fulfillment and purpose.

Do you want fulfillment and purpose? Then follow John's example. Point people to Jesus. Just as John prepared people for the Lord's first arrival, we should be preparing them for His next arrival. We should be saying, "Look, there is the Lamb of God. This is the One you should be following."

But how can we point others to Jesus? How can we decrease so God can increase in our lives? How can we take the focus off ourselves?

Let's look briefly at John's life for the answers to those questions.

John was a credible witness. People believed John because he had a certain glow, an unmistakable light. In fact, it was said of him that he was a burning and shining light (*see* John 5:35). He was a powerful and effective witness for Jesus Christ. But where did he get this glow? What set him ablaze?

The Bible says he was filled with the Holy Spirit. Luke 1:15 says he would be "filled with the Holy Spirit, even from his mother's womb." The Spirit's power gave him the boldness to fearlessly proclaim God's Word.

Every effective witness needs to be filled with the Spirit. Ephesians 5:18 says, "Do not be drunk with wine, in which is dissipation; but be filled with the Spirit." The original Greek text makes it clear this applies to all believers: to men as well as women, to the young as well as the old. Everyone needs to be filled with the Holy Spirit.

Notice that it's a command. God is not saying, "If you wouldn't mind, as a personal favor to Me, would you please . . . ?" He commands you to be filled with the Holy Spirit.

It's also an ongoing process. This verse could be translated, "Be constantly filled with the Holy Spirit." It's not merely a one-time experience. God wants you to come in for a refill.

It's somewhat like putting gasoline in your car. Suppose you ran out of gas on the freeway. I doubt you'd say, "What's wrong with this car? I put gas in it a week ago." You know you need a refill.

Are you running out of gas, so to speak, in your Christian life? Perhaps things aren't going so well for you. It seems as if you have no power, that you're barely limping along. If that's your problem, you need a refill. Go back to God and say, "Lord, I ask that You would refill me with the Holy Spirit." John was filled with God's Spirit and that's what gave him boldness. He shone because he burned.

Is your heart burning for God right now? Maybe you need a good case of heartburn. I don't mean the kind you get from eating pizza that has too many anchovies. I mean spiritual heartburn, which comes from a passion for Jesus Christ.

Is your heart burning? If it is, your light will be shining. The light results from a burning heart . . . and it's people with this kind of heartburn who set their world on fire. Just like John.

The story is told of three demons who were trying to figure out how to make Christians ineffective. One said, "Let's just tell them there's no hell, no possibility of punishment. That'll keep them quiet." The second demon disagreed: "Oh, no, let's just tell them there's no heaven, no possibility of reward." The third demon won the day with his suggestion: "Let's not be theologically unsound here. Let's not tell them there's no heaven or no hell; let's just tell them there's no hurry."

6

NO COMPROMISE

✍

"In those days John the Baptist came preaching in the wilderness of Judea, and saying, 'Repent, for the kingdom of heaven is at hand!'"

—MATTHEW 3:1-2

HOW OFTEN WE BELIEVERS shoot ourselves in the foot by compromise. A nonbeliever notices we're not practicing what we preach and so turns his back on the Lord. Compromise is a witness-killer.

One of the reasons John the Baptist had such a strong witness in his day was because he did not compromise. The angel Gabriel had prophesied of him even before he was conceived, "He will be great in the sight of the Lord, and shall drink neither wine nor strong drink. He will also be filled with the Holy Spirit" (Luke 1:15). John lived a disciplined lifestyle because he did not want to come under the power of anyone or anything but the Holy Spirit.

People sometimes ask me, "Is it okay for a Christian to drink?" My response is, "Why ask the question? Why would you want to risk bringing yourself under the power of something other than the Holy Spirit?" I don't want something impairing my abilities to think clearly. I don't want something getting in the way of my life or dulling my senses. The Bible says all things are permissible, but not all things build us up (see 1 Corinthians 10:23). All things are permissible, but not all things are good—and we should not be brought under the power of anything.

Scripture says we're free to do whatever God does not forbid. But at the same time, these two questions ought to be at the forefront of our minds constantly:

1. Is this going to build me up spiritually?
2. Does this thing or activity bring me under its power?

I use these tests with people who ask me questions like, "Is it all right for a Christian to listen to this kind of music? Is it acceptable to watch a sexually suggestive movie?" I run these folks through my two-question grid:

1. Does it build you up spiritually? In most cases, I don't think so.
2. Could you be brought under its power? If there is even the slightest chance of that, why risk it? Why fool around with it? Once you've been filled with the Holy Spirit, what do you need with cheap substitutes?

I give these people one other question to consider, too: Might this thing or activity cause someone else to stumble? Could it be a bad witness? If someone you've been trying to reach sees you doing that thing, might he or she ask, "Why are you doing that? I thought you were a Christian!" A lame response like, "It's really okay. I can explain" just isn't going to cut it.

John was a powerful witness because he did not want to come under the influence of anything but the power of Jesus Christ.

What power are you under right now? You might say, "It's all right if I listen to this music" or, "So what if I like to top one off with the boys?" My question to you is, Does it bring you under its power? Is it controlling you? Is it addictive? If so, you ought to break from it.

Even something such as overexposure to television can weaken your spiritual life. I admit I've been mesmerized by TV. My eyes have glazed over and I've gotten that blank look after being glued to the set for too long. I've allowed chunks of my day to be wasted. It's not worth it. There comes a time when we must say enough is enough!

John was consistent and uncompromising. He stuck to his guns, even when severely tested. Herod the king eventually had him arrested and thrown in prison. Yet Herod took a liking to this godly man when he saw how consistent and uncompromising he was.

Perhaps the king was fascinated with John because Herod himself was a study in compromise. He had been captivated by his brother's wife, Herodias, and took her as his own mate. To make matters worse, she was his niece. John was straightforward with Herod and told the king it was a sinful relationship. He told him the truth. The Bible says Herod was afraid of John, knowing that he was a righteous and holy man (*see* Mark 6:20). When Herod heard John he was perplexed, but Herod enjoyed listening to him.

John made a great impact on Herod—though not great enough, because Herod ultimately conceded to John's execution. Until that day, Herod had a great admiration for John. He knew he could always count on John to tell the truth.

That's the power of a holy, uncompromising life. Nonbelievers look at their Christian friends and can see they're righteous. They know their friends are living a holy life, and they grow perplexed. On one hand, they don't understand some of the things their friends do; on the other hand, they have great admiration for them and like to listen to them. They can see their strong convictions. Their moral perimeters are clear and they don't transgress them. As these non-Christians watch their faithful friends, some of them trade in their unbelief for a solid faith in the Lord Jesus Christ.

Does that describe your experience? Are you uncompromising in your witness? Your godly and uncompromising lifestyle won't win everyone, but it can win some. John didn't win Herod, but he did steer countless others to the Lord Jesus. There's no reason you couldn't do the same thing. That is, if you want to.

"A Christian should be a striking likeness of Jesus Christ. You have read lives of Christ, beautifully written; but the best life of Christ is His living biography, written out in the words and action of His people."

—*Charles Haddon Spurgeon*

7

PASS IT ON

✗

"One of the two who heard John speak, and followed Him,
was Andrew, Simon Peter's brother. He first found his own
brother Simon, and said to him, 'We have found the Messiah'
(which is translated, the Christ). And he brought him to Jesus."

—JOHN 1:40-42

WHO DO YOU THINK are the most zealous evangelists for the Lord? Surprisingly, they're usually not people who have followed Jesus for 30 or 40 years, as you might expect. No, I have found that the most zealous evangelists are brand-new converts.

We see this in our evangelistic crusades that we hold every year. Once a person comes to the Lord, he automatically seems to bring out members of his family. In one crusade held in Hawaii, eight members of one family came to the Lord. It started with a son who brought his parents. They came to the Lord; then a couple of brothers joined them, and finally his sisters made commitments.

I found it fascinating that when we held a crusade in Orange County a few summers ago, those who had been Christians for just hours were the ones bringing their friends. The most zealous people to reach out to their non-Christian friends were those who had accepted Christ the night before. They were excited about what Christ had done for them.

This really amazes me. In this crowd are believers who have known the Lord for 10, 15, or 20 years, and they're not bringing anybody. But here's a brand-new believer, just hours old in his faith, and he's reaching the world. Why is that? Why is it that we have so much zeal when we are new in our faith, but once we accumulate a little bit of knowledge and we begin to grow in our walk with Christ, we think we've outgrown the evangelism phase?

It shouldn't be that way. We should always be bringing others to the Lord. If our zeal is not growing along with our knowledge and understanding of God and His Word, something isn't working.

By the way, when was the last time you brought someone to Jesus? When was the last time you reached out and said, "Come and see. Behold, the Lamb of God who takes away the sin of the world! Let me tell you about Him"? When was the last time? Or has there ever been a "last time"? When was the last time you even mentioned the Lord to someone who did not yet know Him?

"But I'm miserable at witnessing," you say. "I tried it and failed." You and me both! All of us have gone out and tried to do something that hasn't worked. But I've found that failure is often a prerequisite to success. First you find out how not to do it; then you find out how to do it.

I remember how excited I was about the Lord as a two-week-old Christian. I wanted to tell people about Him, so I went into the streets of Newport Beach to share my faith. Once I ran into a friend, Greg, whom I had known since elementary school. Now, a few days after I had become a Christian I told Greg, "Don't worry about me. I know you think I'm going to become a wild-eyed, religious fanatic carrying a Bible and saying, 'Praise the Lord!' That won't happen! I'm going to be low-key about this whole thing. I'm not going to go out talking to people about God."

Two weeks later I was walking down the streets of Newport Beach when I met Greg, Bible under my arm. Before I could catch myself, the words, "Praise the Lord!" slipped out of my mouth. He looked at me and I looked at him, and we both started to laugh. I had said this wouldn't happen, but it did.

I thought, *Wouldn't it be great if my friend came to know Christ?* so I started to witness to him. I knew very little; the extent of my theology was comparable to the blind man in John 9. He told the religious leaders that although he couldn't answer their theological questions, he could say, "One thing I know: that though I was blind, now I see" (John 9:25). That was about as much as I knew. Once I wasn't saved, but now I was.

As I spoke with Greg, some guy walked over to us, looked me in the eyes, and said, "I have a few questions to ask you about God." He fired off five questions that I couldn't answer. I was dumbfounded. Greg looked at me and said, "What about those?" I was humiliated. Worse than that, I felt as if I had let God down.

But at the same time, it caused me to want to find the answers so I could respond to such questions in the future. The Bible says, "Always be ready to give a defense to everyone who asks you a reason for the hope that is in you, with meekness and fear" (1 Peter 3:15).

That day I failed. But in another way I succeeded. I learned a valuable lesson. I don't have all the answers and on this earth, I never will. But if my fiasco with Greg made me want to discover the answers to commonly asked questions, it was a good thing. It helped to mold me.

I expect the future holds still more failures for me. I expect you will have them, too. But that doesn't change our responsibility and privilege to point people to Jesus.

Andrew didn't know much, but he knew enough to bring his brother to the Savior. He couldn't keep quiet about what he had found.

Is there any reason why you couldn't do the same thing?

"The Holy Spirit will move them by first moving you. If you can rest without their being saved, they will rest, too. But if you are filled with an agony for them, if you cannot bear that they should be lost, you will soon find that they are uneasy, too. I hope you will get into such a state that you will dream about your child or your hearer perishing for lack of Christ, and start up at once and begin to cry, 'O God, give me converts, or I die.' Then you will have converts."

—*Charles Haddon Spurgeon*

8

THAT'S FINE FOR YOU, BUT . . .

✳

"Those along the path are the ones who hear, and then the devil
comes and takes away the word from their hearts,
so that they may not believe and be saved."

—LUKE 8:12, NIV

HAVE YOU EVER HEARD of the "yelping dog" principle of evangelism? Here it is: Throw a rock into a pack of dogs, and the dog that yelps the loudest is the one that's been hit.

Evangelism is often like that. Frequently it's those who object the most to our presentation of the gospel on whom the Spirit's conviction is falling the hardest.

You can identify these folks by asking a few simple questions: Is there anyone in your life who makes witnessing seem like a lost cause? Do you have a friend or relative who seems totally unresponsive to the gospel? Does this person make you feel like giving up?

If you can answer yes to any of those questions, you need to take a lesson from Jesus, the Master Evangelist.

In Luke 8:5 Jesus begins a famous parable about evangelism: "A farmer went out to sow his seed. As he was scattering the seed, some fell along the path; it was trampled on, and the birds of the air ate it up" (NIV). Jesus then explained the elements of His story. The birds symbolized the devil; the seed stood for God's Word; and the soil symbolized those who heard the Word.

The problem with some people is that the "seed," God's Word, never takes root in their lives. They hear it, but they simply don't believe it. It's not that they hear and believe and then later drift away; but rather, upon hearing the Word, Satan either entices them, blinds them, or deceives them lest the seed take root in their hearts. This seed touches the ground, but before it has a chance to take root, germinate, and bring life, it is snatched away.

We've all met people like this. They basically live for the flesh and for themselves, and the seed of the Word doesn't penetrate their hardened hearts. No matter how long or how diligently you share the Word with them, it doesn't seem to take root. Satan snatches it up before it can sink in. Such individuals are often indifferent to the gospel and say things like, "That's good for you. I'm glad you're happy. I'm glad you found God, but don't bother me." Others show their rebellion through outright hostility and anger against you.

So what do you do? Sometimes people ask me, "I'm trying to reach this one person who is so hardened against the gospel. What is the one thing I can tell him to make him believe?"—as if I had some magical gospel formula whereby this person would be converted on the spot. If I knew of such a formula, I would gladly give it to you. In fact, I would have been using it myself! But there is no such formula. Jesus says, "No one can come to Me unless the Father who sent Me draws him" (John 6:44). Only the Spirit makes it happen. Our responsibility is to present the gospel, to present the truth. Only God's Spirit can bring a real conversion.

Paul made this clear in 2 Corinthians 4:4 when he wrote: "The god of this age has blinded the minds of unbelievers, so that they cannot see the light of the gospel of the glory of Christ, who is the image of God" (NIV).

Paul personally knew the truth of these words. He remembered his own pre-Christian days and recalled how God brought about his conversion. He says that first his eyes were opened and only then was he turned from darkness to light and from the power of Satan to God. *But notice carefully—first his eyes had to be opened!* That's why the most important action we can take before we share the gospel message is to pray, "Lord, open the eyes of this person, that he may see the truth of the gospel." That's the place to start.

If you know someone who is hard-hearted—a person you've shared with many times but who doesn't seem interested—don't give up on him! Keep praying for him! Pray that his eyes will be opened and that he will come to his senses and turn from darkness to light.

And if *you* are such a person, be warned! Every time the seed of the gospel seeks to penetrate your heart and you resist, your heart, like resistant soil, grows harder. You are allowing your conscience to be seared with a hot iron.

Every time you hear God's truth and you resist it, your heart grows a little harder, a little more brittle, a little more antagonistic to God and His ways. And over the course of time, you step imperceptibly over the line . . . and into eternal destruction.

If there is any spiritual movement in your soul toward God, do not put it off for another moment. God's Spirit is seeking to bring you in. If you keep resisting, you may reach the point of no return. You may go too far. It won't be that God will no longer be willing to forgive you, but that you will no longer be interested in receiving His forgiveness.

Don't let this happen to you! Don't identify with the kind of soil that allows God's seed to fall along the wayside and be eaten by birds.

If you want to feed the birds, go to the hardware store and buy some birdseed. But gobble up God's Word for yourself. Your very soul is at stake.

"The Christian ideal has not been tried and found wanting; it has been found difficult and left untried."
—*G.K. Chesterton*

9

A SPIRITUAL LITMUS TEST

⨳

"The ones that fell among thorns are those who,
when they have heard, go out and are choked with cares,
riches, and pleasures of life, and bring no fruit to maturity."

—LUKE 8:14

THERE ARE MANY WAYS to choke out fruit in a believer's life, and most of them are subtle. They don't happen overnight. When you plant a flower, you don't see a weed lunge out of the ground, throw itself around the stalk of the flower, and start shaking it violently. Weeds grow up gradually.

Do you have weeds in your life? Jesus says they are the cares, riches, and pleasures of this world. They don't destroy our fruit overnight, or even in a week's time. But eventually these weeds can choke out our growth so that we bring forth no fruit.

What are the "cares" Jesus mentions? They could include your ambitions, interests and pursuits, career, and your relationships. They may not be evil in and of themselves. Ambition isn't evil if it's channeled in the right direction; a career is not evil, we all have to make a living. But if your career becomes more important than your walk with God, you have a problem.

Jesus warns us that the earthly and the physical can grow to become more important to us than the spiritual and the heavenly. They can become more real to us than our relationship with God and the hope that He is coming back for us.

A second type of weed, "riches," implies the pursuit of earthly things—laying up for ourselves treasures on earth where moth and rust corrupt and thieves break in and steal (*see* Matthew 6:19). This has very little to do with how much we have; it has everything to do with how much has *us*.

The Bible warns that those who want to be rich fall into temptation and a snare and pierce themselves with many sorrows (*see* 1 Timothy 6:9-10). Note that it doesn't talk about those who *are* rich; it talks about those who *want* to be rich. You can have ten dollars in your savings account and be more materialistic than someone with ten thousand dollars. You can have very little, but live to be rich. If you're obsessed with trying to make the big break, for all practical purposes you're more materialistic than a person who has a lot. It all has to do with your attitude.

When the rich young ruler asked Jesus, "What shall I do to inherit eternal life?" (Luke 18:18), Jesus said, "Sell all that you have and distribute to the poor, and you will have treasure in heaven" (Luke 18:22). That man went away sorrowful because he was possessed by possessions. I believe if that man had said, "No problem, Lord; it's a done deal," Jesus might have replied, "Forget it, I was just testing you." If the Lord's all-encompassing ruling for the wealthy was for them to give away their money, He would have said this to every wealthy person He met. But He didn't. His words to the rich young ruler were aimed specifically at the heart of a man possessed by possessions, the very thing keeping him away from God.

Some of us need to say, "All right, Lord, here it is. My career is great, but I don't want to live for it exclusively. These other things in life are fine, but I don't want them to get in the way of You." God may take them away, alter them, or even add to them. Our job is to keep things in their proper place.

"Pleasures" are the third snare Jesus mentions. We live in a society with many creature comforts. We don't have to enter the bank anymore; now we use automated tellers. We don't have to get up and push the button on the television; now we just pull out the remote control. We don't have to wait hours for our meals to cook; we just pop them in the microwave. Everything is so convenient.

I'm not saying that a remote control is evil or that a microwave is of the devil! Rather, I am saying that we live in a society which places tremendous emphasis on comfort and ease. Sometimes we allow our lives to become so pleasure-oriented that we forget God. The Bible says, "She who lives in pleasure is dead while she lives" (1 Timothy 5:6). Some people live for the weekend. They live to party. Solomon said such a life was meaningless, like chasing the wind (*see* Ecclesiastes 2:11). It's empty and worthless.

Don't let pleasures, cares, or riches choke you out. There may be a lot of things we Christians are allowed to do, but the question is, Do they build us up? If you're involved with something that dulls you spiritually or that makes this world more attractive than the hope of heaven, something is wrong. If some relationship or some possession is slowing you down spiritually in the race of life, you're in danger. If something you are engaged in is choking out your walk with Christ, let it go.

Let me suggest one little test for spiritual weeds— a spiritual "litmus test" if you will. If the thought of the soon return of Jesus frightens you or alarms you or seems unattractive, then you have a problem. A Christian who is walking with God should always be longing for heaven and ready to go at any moment. Like John, we should be able to say, "Even so, come, Lord Jesus!" (Revelation 22:20).

Can you say that right now? Or would you say, "Even so, come in a month, Lord Jesus"? Such a response might indicate that something is choking you out, be it ever so subtly.

May God help us to be ready and to look up! As Jesus said,

"Watch therefore, for you do not know what hour your Lord is coming" (Matthew 24:42). He's coming soon! Are you ready?

"Collapse in your Christian life is seldom a blowout; it is usually a slow leak."

—*Paul Little*

10

POSERS

✖

"They led Jesus from Caiaphas to the Praetorium, and it was early morning."

—JOHN 18:28

SUPPOSE SOMEONE VISITED A SURF STORE, bought a surfboard, a wet suit, and a few bars of wax, picked up some surf stickers to put on his car, and started speaking in surf lingo. Would that make him a surfer? Hardly. To be a surfer, you need to surf.

Surfers have a name for people who try to pass themselves off as the real thing: posers. Posers stand around on the beach showing off their stuff. They have a great board, the right wet suit, perfect sticker placement, and speak flawless surf lingo. But they don't surf—they just talk about it. While they watch others surf, they never get out in the water themselves.

When I was younger, we didn't use the word "posers." We called them "gremmies" if they were kids and "hodads" if they were old guys. The name doesn't matter—posers, gremmies, hodads—they all describe people who go through the motions but stay on the shore. All talk but no performance.

There are a lot of posers in church. They bring a Bible like everybody else. Their cars flash Christian bumper stickers. They've got the lingo down and they talk eloquently about the Christian life. *But they don't live it.*

To be a surfer you must surf. To be a Christian you must follow Jesus Christ. You must come humbly before God, admit your sinfulness, turn away from it, and follow His Son Jesus Christ with everything that's in you.

Posers won't do that, and there are a lot of them around. This provokes a question: Why is it that so often we're willing to spend huge amounts of time and energy on things that don't matter, but so little time serving God? How is it that we can convincingly play at the Christian life, but not fully live it?

This has been a problem for a long time. Just before the Lord was taken away to be crucified, Jesus asked three of His most trusted disciples to watch with Him for one hour in the garden (*see* Matthew 26:36-45). They didn't do it. It's ironic that while Peter, James, and John fell asleep, the servants of the devil were working overtime. They were up late at night and early the next morning to do their evil work.

I wish that all Christians would serve the Lord as energetically as they used to serve the devil! Once we served the devil with everything we had. We lived for ourselves, for pleasure, for the buck, for power. Do we serve Jesus Christ with the same fervency? We should serve Him with more!

Jesus once forgave a woman with the words, "Her sins, which are many, are forgiven, for she loved much. But to whom little is forgiven, the same loves little" (Luke 7:47). Later He told His disciples, "To whom much is given, from him much will be required; and to whom much has been committed, of him they will ask the more" (Luke 12:48).

So often we give God our leftovers. We have time for television but no time for the Bible. Time for movies but no time for church. Time for what interests us while God gets the last few minutes of the day—after we've watched all the programs we wanted to watch, read all the magazines we wanted to read, and finally dropped into bed exhausted. "Oh yeah, God. The Creator of the universe. The One who died for me. Oh, Him. That's right." We give Him those last moments as we're ready to drift off into sleep. We collapse with our faces in the Bible.

If only we would serve God with the same zeal that we once reserved for the devil!

I look at what's happening in our world and I see how evil society has become. These are satanically energized times. Blatant evil stares back at us wherever we look. Each year's crime statistics seem to outstrip those of the year before. Deadly epidemics spawned by widespread immorality frighten the population. Television and music both reflect and create a culture on the brink. Evil permeates our society.

It's reached the point where people are getting an appetite for evil. It's harder to shock us, so we have to raise the stakes a little higher. TV has to be a little more violent, a little more gory, a little more sexually titillating, a little more radical. Detestable things are done in the name of artistic freedom. It seems as if there are no more boundaries. Anyone who dares to stand up for morality is mocked and ridiculed.

As we watch this world go down the tubes in hyper speed, how much more should we who are believers pull out the stops and give our all for the Lord! The devil is working overtime. What about us?

It's time for us to get moving. We must work while it is day, for "the night is coming when no one can work" (John 9:4). Romans 13:11-12 says, "Do this, knowing the time, that now it is high time to awake out of sleep; for now our salvation is nearer than when we first believed. The night is far spent, the day is at hand. Therefore let us cast off the works of darkness, and let us put on the armor of light." How true that statement rings even today—*especially* today!

Once and for all, soldiers, cast off the works of darkness and put on the armor of light. Get out of your foxhole and start marching. It's time to quit griping and complaining. It's time to stop losing ground and start regaining ground. Many years ago the enemies of the Lord were up early while His people were in hiding. There's no reason to repeat their mistake today.

"Dim eyes cannot read fine print. Let your testimony for Christ be written in large letters that the world may see."

—*William Ward Ayer*

11

CHOOSING TO STAY UPRIGHT

❧

"If anyone walks in the day, he does not stumble, because
he sees the light of this world. But if one walks in the night,
he stumbles, because the light is not in him."

—JOHN 11:9-10

SOME OF US MAY WONDER if we're going to stumble and
fall one day. We worry that the pressure may get so great that
we'll just cave in. We know that the book of 1 Timothy teaches
that prior to the return of Christ, there will be a great apostasy, a
great falling away: "Now the Spirit expressly says that in latter
times some will depart from the faith, giving heed to deceiving
spirits and doctrines of demons" (4:1).

We know the enemy will be pulling people down in the last
days. In fact, we're already seeing it happen. Are you going to be
among those numbers? Am I?

The truth is, if you don't want to be, you don't have to be. I
don't say that in self-confidence; I'm not so strong the devil
could never get me. I'm not that foolish.

But I do mean that people fall when they choose to fall. No
child of God is taken out of the protection of Jesus Christ
against his or her will. If you fall away from the Lord, if you
stumble into sin, don't fault God and don't put the blame on

the devil. Realize that you cooperated. James 1:14 says, "Each one is tempted when he is drawn away by his own desires and enticed." Jesus calls this "walk[ing] in the night" (*see* John 11:10).

It's like a fishhook with a little worm wrapped around it. Sure, the hook pulled the fish from the water. But he had to go looking for that worm and take a little nibble. It's the same when you give in to temptation. When you take a nibble and fall, you have no one to blame but yourself. Stumbling results from willing cooperation to sin.

That doesn't have to happen. God doesn't give us more than we can handle. He will always give us a way out, according to 1 Corinthians 10:13. If you fall to sin, it's because you've chosen to. You have lowered your guard; you have disregarded His Word to you. In contrast, God always moves on and completes what He starts.

I'm so glad I'm not God. One of the reasons I'm glad is that I have a tendency to start great projects and not finish them.

Occasionally I cook in the morning. Everything is going well; I'm excited about what I'm doing. I have eggs cooking and bread toasting. This, of course, is a gourmet meal for me—actual eggs and toast. I have it all ready and I put it on the plate and I eat it. Then when I am done, I don't want to clean up after myself.

My wife does it much differently. She cleans as she cooks. Even before she will sit down to eat she wants the whole kitchen spotless. I'll say, "Cathe, sit down, let's eat. We'll clean it later." But she knows if she doesn't do it then, it won't get done.

God starts and finishes a project. He completes what He has begun—and that includes you. The writer of Hebrews says He is "the author and finisher of our faith" (Hebrews 12:2). Aren't you glad of that? You see it in His creation. He doesn't begin a beautiful sunset and then just stop, as if He lost interest.

What if God were working in your life to bring you to completion and said, "I don't know; I'm kind of bored with him. I want to work on another project now. I'll get back to him later"? God will never do that; He will finish the job.

The question is, Do you want Him to finish it? Do you want to be completed?

The Bible compares us to a lump of clay and God to a Master Potter (*see* Isaiah 45:9; 64:8). If the clay is unwilling to conform to the design of the Potter, He sets it aside. Are you flexible? Are you willing? Are you allowing Him to do His work? Or are you resisting Him at every turn?

If you want to make it, you will make it. If you don't want to stumble, you don't have to. Oh, you'll probably have lapses here or there. But you won't fall away from the Lord unless you make a determined decision to do so through continual disobedience to His Word. He completes what He begins.

Philippians 1:6 says, "Being confident of this very thing, that He who has begun a good work in you will complete it until the day of Jesus Christ." This is a message of great comfort and consolation for all true followers of Jesus.

I don't know what the future holds, but I know who holds the future. I don't know what's going to happen tonight or tomorrow or next week or next month. If I allow myself to be gripped by fear and anxiety, I can drive myself crazy. What if this happens? What if that happens? But Jesus has promised that He will be there with me. He didn't promise that He would remove all the storms and difficulties in life, but that He would be with me through each one of them.

The Lord has promised us, "When you pass through the waters, I will be with you; and through the rivers, they shall not overflow you. When you walk through the fire, you shall not be burned, nor shall the flame scorch you" (Isaiah 43:2).

Do you want to walk and not stumble? Then fix your eyes on the light of this world. Take Jesus' hand and walk with Him in the bright Sonlight. Not only will you stay upright, but the view will be spectacular!

Consider the apostle John's advice on stumbling: "He who

loves his brother abides in the light, and there is no cause for stumbling in him. But he who hates his brother is in darkness and walks in darkness, and does not know where he is going, because the darkness has blinded his eyes" (1 John 2:10-11).

12

SPIRITUAL HEARTBURN

✍

"They said to one another, 'Did not our heart burn within us while He talked with us on the road, and while He opened the Scriptures to us?'"

—LUKE 24:32

EVERYONE GETS DISCOURAGED. Things don't turn out the way they had hoped and suddenly they find themselves sinking into a pit of discouragement.

That was certainly true of the two disciples on the Emmaus Road. They were two discouraged people. Their faith had cooled down, their spiritual fervor no longer burned as brightly as it once had, and they had lost their spiritual passion. They thought God had let them down, that He had not done what they thought He should have done. Their hopes and dreams lay shattered.

Of course, in reality they had no reason to be discouraged. Already they had heard reports that Jesus was risen again. But they rejected those accounts. The real problem was not in their heads but in their hearts. They had forgotten what they needed to remember—the words of Jesus to them.

Perhaps you are beaten down, overwhelmed. You feel as if God has let you down. If you are discouraged right now, it may be that you need the same treatment these disciples received.

239

How did Jesus reignite the hearts of these two discouraged men?

1. *He made their hearts burn when He talked to them.* Their hearts did not burn when *they* talked to *Him.* Their hearts did not burn when they talked *about* Him. Their hearts burned when *He* talked to *them* and they listened.

G. Campbell Morgan wrote, "Not in their questioning concerning Him was the fire rekindled. Not in their pouring out of complaint to Him did it burn, but when they ceased talking to or about Him. When they were silent and listened, the fire burned."

Perhaps you can say, "I prayed about it." Did you really? Consider this: Have you ever had a "conversation" with someone who did all the talking? It's impossible to get a statement in edgewise. Maybe he is talking about himself. Then after a while he says, "I'm tired of talking about myself. Why don't you talk about me now?" That's just the way some people are. They dominate a conversation.

Sometimes in prayer we do the same thing. We lay our petitions before God and tell Him what we need and what we want. But there is a time in prayer to be quiet, to be still, and to know that He is God. To listen.

Ecclesiastes 5:1 tells us to be silent when we go before God and to be more ready to listen than to speak. It is when we listen and hear His voice that He can reignite our hearts and we become encouraged. Jesus made His disciples' hearts burn when He talked with them.

2. *He spoke using the Scripture.* Jesus reignited the hearts of His disciples through His use of Scripture. He could have told them something "new and improved"—being God, anything He would have said would have been divine revelation—but He chose to use the Word to encourage His downcast children.

Many today are looking for new revelations from God. I think it's good to look to the Lord for direction, but some people get so hung up on new revelations they forget the one right before them. They want to hear new messages from God but they haven't even discovered the old truths He spoke. They haven't read the Bible cover to cover, and yet they want a new revelation.

These folks need to get acquainted with Deuteronomy 29:29: "The secret things belong to the LORD our God, but those things which are revealed belong to us and to our children forever, *that we may do all the words of this law*" (emphasis added).

3.*He reignited them by reminding them of what they already knew.* Jesus made their hearts burn by reminding them of what they already knew. He rebuked them in Luke 24:25 for failing to believe what He had said already. In their case, the promise was, "I will rise again." In our case, the promise is, "I will come again." We are to look beyond our circumstances and remember His promise.

Let's be honest: We don't really know as much as we think we do. We forget a lot of what we learn. Often when I return to a passage of Scripture on which I've already taught, I discover I've forgotten some of what I once knew. I need to be refreshed over and over. Paul wrote to the Philippians, "For me to write the same things to you is not tedious, but for you it is safe" (Philippians 3:1).

On the other hand, there are many things I know intellectually that I don't know experientially. The question is, Do I apply to my life the truth I know? Sometimes I need reinforcement. I need to be taught, retaught, and taught again.

Perhaps, like the two discouraged disciples on the Emmaus Road, you cannot understand the circumstances of your life. All you can see are your problems, your disappointments. Luke 24 reminds us that Jesus is deeply concerned about your hurt and pain. He wants your heart to burn for Him again.

Was there a time when your heart burned more for Him than it does now? Do you need Him to reignite your heart today? Are you discouraged and downcast? If so, let the Master do for you what He did for the disciples on the Emmaus Road. All He waits for is your invitation.

Consider the words of Jesus to the lukewarm church of Laodicea (*see* Revelation 3:14-22). He wants us either hot or cold. It is interesting that He would actually prefer coldness to lukewarmness. May God ignite our hearts with a burning passion for Him!

13

WHAT ARE YOU WAITING FOR?

✍

"Then they came to Jericho. And as He went out of Jericho with His disciples and a great multitude, blind Bartimaeus, the son of Timaeus, sat by the road begging."

—MARK 10:46

BARTIMAEUS WAS A VERY LONELY MAN. He was a man waiting for a miracle that never seemed to come . . . until the day Jesus passed by.

Jesus had time for this man when no one else did. Everyone else was too busy. In fact, the crowd tried to silence him when he called out for Jesus. But the Lord took time for this man. He always has time for any person who is truly in need. He always has time for the person who is truly seeking Him, who wants to know Him, and who will take His hand.

Psychologist William Moulton Marsten asked 3,000 people, "What are you living for?" He was shocked to find that 94 percent of the people polled were simply enduring the present while waiting for the future. They said they were waiting for something to happen: Waiting for children to grow up and leave home; waiting for next year; waiting for another time to take a long-awaited trip; waiting for tomorrow. It's amazing! They could not live in the present because they were waiting for the future.

I read about a psychiatrist who was asked, "What is the greatest problem of those who seek your help?" Do you know what his answer was? Loneliness. "In fact," he said, "when you get down to it, it's a loneliness for God." Some others in his field agree.

Loneliness is the most devastating malady of our age, the most dangerous and widespread illness in our land. Millions of people are desperately lonely in America. Some experts say this problem has reached epidemic proportions and continues to spread, already affecting 75 to 90 percent of all Americans.

You probably know what it is like to be lonely. You can be in a crowded room and suddenly a momentary loneliness sweeps over you. You feel as if you are all by yourself. The Bible says that even in laughter the heart can have sorrow (Proverbs 14:13). It's amazing how you can be surrounded by people and yet feel alone.

Loneliness is cited as one of the primary reasons that teenagers commit suicide. One survey found that 90 percent of suicidal adolescents or teenagers believed their families did not understand them. They felt isolated and anonymous. These teenagers felt their efforts to communicate feelings of unhappiness and frustration and failure were ignored or denied by their parents, who were striving for their children to achieve the success they themselves were unable to gain.

Is that how you feel right now? Alone? You thought a friend or a spouse would meet all of your needs, but still there's a loneliness deep inside of you.

Loneliness is a frequent reason that people get sexually involved with one another. It's been said that boys give love to get sex and girls give sex to get love. In other words, a guy will say to a girl, "I love you so much. You're the girl of my dreams. I'll marry you." He says it to get sexual favors. On the other hand, many girls give sex to get love. They really want to be appreciated and cared for. They want someone to be concerned about them. They are motivated by loneliness.

The cries of Bartimaeus 2,000 years ago are still audible today. We still hear their echo. Abandoned by everyone on the side of the road, this blind man called out to Jesus for divine mercy. And to this lonely, rejected man, Jesus responded.

Jesus said to him, "Go your way; your faith has made you well" (Mark 10:52). And immediately Bartimaeus regained his sight *and began following Jesus on the road.*

Christ reached out to this lonely man and changed his life. He can do the same for you. Are you alone right now? Perhaps you have no close friends. Maybe you could use a friend. The Bible says there is a friend that sticks closer than a brother. Jesus can be that friend for you. He'll stand by you no matter what you go through. When you are all alone in your room and the door is shut, you can reveal your deepest secrets to Him.

"But I already have such a friend," you say. Really? Has such a friend ever broadcast your deepest secrets? How embarrassing. But God will keep your confidence. He will give you answers. He understands what you're going through. There has never been a man who experienced loneliness as deeply as Jesus did. He will be your friend, but He will be more than that. He will be your Lord and your Savior. He will be your God.

You may be a very popular person. You may have a boyfriend or girlfriend or a couple of each. You may be married. You may have a big family. But still there is a void in your life, a loneliness that just won't go away.

Do you know what that hollowness is? It's a loneliness for God. No mere human can meet this deep need in your life. You were created with a void and an emptiness that only God can fill.

Do you want to leave behind your life of loneliness? Then what are you waiting for? Don't let anything hold you back any longer. Jesus can fill that loneliness and void in your life; come to Him.

Bartimaeus entered this story lonely but left with Jesus. The same can be true for you. The Master is calling you to follow

Him just as surely as He called this lonely blind man 2,000 years ago.

The next time you feel lonely, consider the statement of Jesus in Hebrews 13:5: "I will never leave you nor forsake you." In the original language that verse could be translated, "I will never, no never, no never leave you or forsake you."

Get the point? I think He is trying to tell us something.

14

THE BIGGER PICTURE

✦

"Lazarus was sick. Therefore the sisters sent to [Jesus], saying,
'Lord, behold, he whom You love is sick.' When Jesus heard that,
He said, 'This sickness is not unto death, but for the glory of God
that the Son of God may be glorified through it.'"

—JOHN 11:2-4

SOMETIMES IT IS HARD FOR US to understand why God allows sickness. There are some among us who say that God wants every Christian to be in perfect health. If you are sick or if your health isn't perfect, they would insist you lack faith or that there is sin in your life.

That's nonsense.

Did you know that God can use sickness in the life of a believer? There are times when sickness can be God-sent. It can be what brings us to our senses. It wakes us up when everything is going well and the bills are paid and our health is good . . . and we forget about God: "I don't need God. Everything is going great." And we push Him out of our schedule.

That is, until the bottom drops out. You get fired from your job or get sick. The doctor tells you that your problem is more serious than you thought. Suddenly you turn back to God: "God, help me!"

As horrible as sickness can be, if it brings you back to God, it is a wonderful tool in His hands. In Psalm 119, David wrote, "Before I was afflicted I went astray, but now I keep Your word. . . . It is good for me that I have been afflicted, that I may learn Your statutes . . . . I know, O LORD, that Your judgments are right, and that in faithfulness You have afflicted me" (verses 67, 71, 75).

Of course, not all sickness is of God. Not all sickness is always good; many times sickness can be dreadful. When I'm sick, I ask God to heal me; sometimes He does, sometimes He doesn't. But in general, there are times when God uses sickness to bring us back to Him. Jeremiah wrote in Lamentations 3:31-33, "For the Lord will not cast off forever. Though He causes grief, yet He will show compassion according to the multitude of His mercies. For He does not afflict willingly, nor grieve the children of men." Tragedy, sickness, and hardship are not necessarily God's first choice for us; but often they are the only ways He can bring us to our senses and motivate us to return to Him.

That's exactly what happened in John 11. When Jesus heard that Lazarus was sick, He *purposely* stayed where He was for two more days. Why? Was it because He was angry with Lazarus? Because He didn't love him? Because He didn't care?

No. It was *because* Jesus loved Mary, Martha, and Lazarus that He delayed His arrival. God is interested in long-term benefits, not short-term successes.

My son Jonathan may not like all the things we ask him to eat. He may not like the medicine we give him when he is sick. But we, as his parents, understand that his medication will help him get well. We see that the diet we have established for him will help him grow strong. He may not like it, but as his parents we're interested in the big picture, not childish preferences.

The same is true about our relationship with God. Many times we don't like what God brings into our lives. We don't appreciate the difficulties or the hardships. But God is looking at the big picture.

Joseph had to learn this hard lesson. How he could have despaired and given up when everything seemed to go wrong! As Genesis chapters 37–50 tells the story, young Joseph was the apple of his father's eye. One day he was parading before his jealous brothers in a coat of many colors given to him by his dad; the next day he was sold into slavery by his brothers. He wound up in the house of an Egyptian man named Potiphar. Within a short time, however, he was put in charge of that home and things began to look better. But one day Joseph refused the sexual advances of Potiphar's wife. He was falsely accused of rape and thrown into prison. But God had not forgotten him. Over the course of at least two long years, a series of events finally elevated him to the second-most powerful position in all of Egypt.

One day Joseph's wicked brothers appeared before him, seeking food for their starving families. Joseph now had the power to put them to death, but instead he said to his brothers, "You meant evil against me; but God meant it for good, in order to bring it about as it is this day, to save many people alive" (Genesis 50:20).

Perhaps right now you can't understand why God is allowing affliction in your life. You're having trouble figuring out why God has permitted certain circumstances. All I can say is, hang in there. It ain't over till it's over. Wait awhile. You may be able to look back in a month, a week, maybe even a day, and say, "God meant it for good." Then again, it may take years. And yet again, it may not be until you get to the other side in heaven that you'll understand why God allowed certain difficulties. But be confident of this: He loves you.

The reason Jesus delayed His arrival to Bethany was not because He hated Mary, Martha, and Lazarus. It wasn't that He was disinterested. He delayed his arrival because He loved them with *agape* love and was interested in the glory of God. He waited for their sake, to show them unmistakably that He was the God-man who could command even death to move aside. He waited so they might believe.

It was worth the wait, don't you think?

Sometimes God allows certain problems, tragedies, or unexplained circumstances in your life so that you will be more effective in comforting others. Read 2 Corinthians 1:3-7, then ask God to bring people into your life who need to be comforted in a certain area, just as you have been.

15

THE GOOD SHEPHERD

"I am the good shepherd.
The good shepherd gives His life for the sheep."

—JOHN 10:11

HAVE YOU EVER NOTICED how often in Scripture God calls Himself a shepherd? Isaiah 40:11 says of God, "He will feed His flock like a shepherd; He will gather the lambs with His arm, and carry them in His bosom, and gently lead those who are with young."

Jesus once compared Himself to a shepherd who cared for a hundred sheep, one of which went astray (*see* Luke 15:4-7). Instead of abandoning the sheep to its deserved fate, He sought it out and returned it to the flock, rejoicing in His precious find. Peter's first epistle tells us we were like sheep going astray, but now we have returned to the shepherd of our souls (*see* 1 Peter 2:25).

It is comforting to imagine God as a shepherd, but it is not so flattering to think of ourselves as sheep. If you know anything about the woolly animals, you know they are among the most stupid animals walking God's green earth, ranking way down on the intelligence scale. Sheep are prone to wander and require more care than most other animals—and we're just like them.

Isaiah 53:6 gives us a startlingly accurate assessment of human-ity when it says, "All we like sheep have gone astray; we have turned, every one, to his own way."

Stupid sheep need smart shepherds, and Christians have the wisest in Jesus. The Good Shepherd cares deeply for His sheep and knows each one by name. John 10:3 says, "He calls his own sheep by name and leads them out."

God knows you! In fact, God knows you better than you know yourself. Not only does He know your name, He also knows your temperament and even your quirks.

All sheep share the same basic nature, but each one has its own distinctive personality. A loving shepherd recognizes these individual traits. One sheep may be afraid of heights, another may fear dark shadows, while yet a third may be terrified of jag-ged boulders. The shepherd knows how to watch out for each of his sheep. His intimate knowledge of his flock allows him to be more effective in the care and nurture of his sheep.

I've never owned sheep, but I've had many dogs. Every dog had a distinct personality. One dog named Charmagne (my wife named him) should have been called Charmagne the Cowardly. He looked like a collie but must have been part chicken—he was afraid of everything. Another one of my dogs, a tiny mutt named Sport, couldn't have been more different. He was fearless, un-afraid of anything.

One day I took these two dogs out for a walk at a construc-tion site. We came to two trenches that had been dug in the ground for some pipes yet to be laid. My huge dog Charmagne was afraid to walk over these gouges in the earth, but my little mutt Sport took flying leaps over them—hitting the side, rolling into the ditch, climbing out again. Charmagne the Cowardly. Sport the Fearless.

Jesus knows His sheep and recognizes their differences in temperament and personality. Look at His own apostles. Have you ever noted how different these men were from one another? Peter the impulsive. Thomas the skeptic. Then there were the twin thunder boys, James and John, who wanted to call fire down on anyone who was inhospitable toward them. We're all different—God knows that about us and treats us accordingly.

But that's not all. The Good Shepherd not only knows our natures, He also knows our needs. Don't forget that this One who says He is a shepherd is also, in a sense, a sheep or a lamb. He was the Lamb of God who took away the sin of the world. Isaiah 53:7 says "He was led as a lamb to the slaughter, and as a sheep before its shearers is silent, so He opened not His mouth."

Jesus walked among us in a human body. He understands the frailties and limitations and problems that we face as human beings. He knows our needs. Hebrews 2:17 tells us, "In all things He had to be made like His brethren, that He might be a merciful and faithful High Priest in things pertaining to God, to make propitiation for the sins of the people."

But even that pales beside the greatest way our Good Shepherd cares for us. Jesus told us, "The good shepherd gives His life for the sheep." He came to earth to die for our sins.

You may be that lost lamb mentioned earlier. God has been seeking you out. He's been tapping on the door of your life, eager to demonstrate His love for you. God laid down His life on your behalf so you could live with Him forever in heaven. Not only that, but He also promises you life abundantly, here and now—a dimension of life that is worth living. Not just existence, but real life.

God wants to protect you. He longs to watch out for you as your Shepherd. In these frightening and uncertain times, how good it is to know we have a Good Shepherd who is looking out for us!

The Good Shepherd holds out His hands to you today and says, "I love you so much that I went to a cross and laid down My life for you. I bore your sin and rose again from the dead. Why don't you place your future in My hands so I can give you abundant life?"

Don't be a stupid sheep; accept His offer! It's the smartest move any lost lamb can make.

As our Good Shepherd, Jesus is also our Guardian, so to speak. Read Jude 24-25, then take some time to ask God to truly be the Shepherd of your own life.

16

THE SHEPHERD'S VOICE

*"When he brings out his own sheep, he goes before them;
and the sheep follow him, for they know his voice."*

—JOHN 10:4

I'LL BE HONEST WITH YOU. Many people who say God speaks to them are often the oddest birds in the zoo. It is easy to mistake the voice of God for our own. It is easy to act on our emotions and say God is telling us to do something when God never spoke a single word.

And yet, it is also true that God's people *can* hear their Master's voice.

In John 10:4, Jesus says His sheep hear His voice. Are you hearing His voice? Do you know His will? Perhaps it seems to you as if God is silent. You don't sense any direction or guidance from the Lord—just an icy silence. It's not meant to be that way!

Sheep know that their shepherd calls, and that it's always worth coming when he does so. He is always there with a specific purpose. He has their best interest in mind—to bring them fresh food or to lead them to a stream or a new pasture.

How do you learn to follow the shepherd's voice? In the beginning, baby lambs follow the others. They haven't yet learned to hear the shepherd's voice for themselves, so they follow the more mature lambs. In time, they will learn how to recognize the shepherd's voice for themselves. And when they hear it, they must obey it.

It's not enough merely to hear God's voice and to know His will. We must act on it. The word translated "follow" in John 10:4 could be rendered "one who deliberately decides to comply with instructions." We hear His voice and know what He wants us to do, so we comply. We must obey. If we refuse to follow Him, we may not hear His voice for awhile—not so much because He isn't speaking, but usually because we're not listening.

How does God speak to us today? I wish I could tell you I have ongoing conversations with God in which He speaks to me audibly. But He doesn't. I have never heard the audible voice of God . . . and I doubt most people have. I generally don't believe those who claim to have extended conversations with God. Of course, God could speak audibly if He wanted to; but generally He speaks quietly in the depths of the heart.

Sometimes it's more an impression than a voice. Elijah learned this. When God needed to get the prophet's attention on one occasion, the Scripture says, "The LORD passed by, and a great and strong wind tore into the mountains and broke the rocks in pieces before the LORD, but the LORD was not in the wind; and after the wind an earthquake, but the LORD was not in the earthquake; and after the earthquake a fire, but the LORD was not in the fire; and after the fire a still small voice" (1 Kings 19:11-12). The reason we oftentimes don't hear God's voice is that we're not listening. We're not paying attention.

Many times I have sensed a tug from God's Spirit to share my faith with a certain individual. At other times He burdens me in some way for another person. The point is, He leads me to do specific things at certain times. He will do that with you, too.

You must be careful, however, because impressions can be misleading. The one sure way to test these voices is by matching them with the Word of God. The primary way God speaks to you is through the Bible, whether in a sermon or through personal study.

People have come up to me after I've delivered a message and said, "You were preaching to me." Some time ago a discouraged lady suffering with a bad illness wrote to me after church. The opening words of my sermon that day were, "Have you ever doubted the promises of God in your life?" It was as if that message was meant just for her, she said; it was almost as if I had been with her all week, listening to her doubts and problems. I marvel, because there is no way I could have known about her circumstances. That is God's Word, not me!

The Bible has an amazing way of getting through our defenses and speaking directly to us, as though a verse were custom-written just for our situation. Often a passage seems to jump out as God speaks to our heart.

Circumstances are another way God speaks to us. Though I don't like to direct my life by circumstances, many times they can be a way to confirm that the Lord has indeed spoken to me, as if a door were being opened or closed.

How can you be sure you have heard God's voice? I have found that God's peace floods my soul when I am in His will. God's Spirit reassures me I am doing what He wants me to do. Colossians 3:15 says, "Let the peace of God rule in your hearts." That word "rule" comes from a term that means "let it act as a spiritual umpire, settling with finality all matters that arise in your mind."

There have been times when a certain course of action looked good but because I didn't have God's peace about it, I didn't do it. Later I was thankful. At other times another action looked appealing and even though I didn't have God's peace, I did it anyway—and lived to regret it.

If you are one of Jesus' sheep, you can learn to recognize His voice. If you're a baby lamb, watch the mature sheep for clues about how *they* listen. God does indeed speak to us; we simply must learn to listen. His sheep hear His voice *and know it*. Our job is to recognize that voice and act on it.

For examples of God speaking to a person, look at the stories of young Samuel in 1 Samuel 3:9 and Elijah the prophet in 1 Kings 19:12. Remember, to know God's choice, you must hear God's voice. Is He speaking to you today?

17

LIFE ABUNDANT

⨞

*"I have come that they may
have life, and that they may have
it more abundantly."*

—JOHN 10:10

SHEPHERDS WANT THEIR FLOCKS TO FLOURISH, to be well fed, to be cared for, to be content, and to be satisfied. Our Good Shepherd, Jesus, came to give us the abundant life. He delights in blessing you!

I like to give gifts to my kids. It makes me happy to see them happy. In the same way, God loves to bless you. He delights in it; it's a joy to Him. While the abundant life Jesus promises is not necessarily a long one, it is certainly a full one. Breakthroughs in medical science can add years to one's life, but they can't add life to one's years. Only Jesus can do that.

The abundant life is life at its best, life as it was meant to be lived. It is marked by contentment and satisfaction, regardless of your circumstances. The apostle Paul said, "I have learned in whatever state I am, to be content; I know how to be abased, and I know how to abound" (Philippians 4:11-12). Godliness with contentment is great gain. Hebrews 13:5 says, "Be content with such things as you have. For He Himself has said, 'I will never leave you nor forsake you.'" Contentment does not come from what you have; it comes from who you know.

Are you content? Are you satisfied? Or are you thinking, *If I could just get married, I would be content. If I could just get unmarried, I would be content. If I could get this new car, I would be content. If I could make a little more money, I would be content. If I were a little thinner, I would be content. If I were a little heavier, I would be content. If I could just make this one change, I would be content.*

The Bible teaches that contentment is within our grasp regardless of our circumstances—whether we're in a palace or in a prison, whether we're making a lot of money or a little, whether our health is good or bad. Contentment comes from *who* you know; it comes from your relationship with Jesus.

Psalm 23 explains this as well as any passage in Scripture. Each movement of that wonderful psalm tells us something about the relationship of the shepherd and his sheep or of people and their God.

First it says, "The LORD is my shepherd; I shall not want" (verse 1). This is a picture of satisfied sheep content in the Good Shepherd's care. They don't crave or desire anything else. They are not looking for greener grass on the other side of the fence.

Then David writes, "He makes me to lie down" (verse 2). Sheep are so stupid sometimes you have to make them eat. We can be the same way. Sometimes we don't know what is good for us.

Next he writes, "He leads me beside the still waters" (verse 2). Witless sheep will keep eating and not have the good sense to walk over to a nearby brook to take a drink. The shepherd has to bring his sheep to the water.

Then David said, "Yea, though I walk through the valley of the shadow of death, I will fear no evil; for You are with me" (verse 4). David was protected by his Shepherd in times of danger. Likewise, when we go through life's valleys, or hardships, or difficulties, we can be assured that God is with us. Even when we go through that final valley of death, we know that He will see us into His very presence. When we stand at death's door, we won't have to be afraid because our Shepherd will be there with us.

David also wrote, "Your rod and Your staff, they comfort me" (verse 4). A shepherd uses two primary tools with his sheep. The staff is a long pole with a crook at one end; it is used to snag sheep when they go astray. If a sheep continues to go the wrong direction, the shepherd uses the rod. Sheep are so stupid they have been known to walk over the sides of cliffs to their deaths. And amazingly, other like-minded sheep will blindly follow the first one and tumble over the side. One after another, the sheep will fall to their deaths.

Some sheep are more rebellious than others. A shepherd may notice that one sheep is always wandering and leading others astray. So the shepherd reluctantly uses the rod. He'll give that sheep a good whack with a short, club-like instrument. It's not very sophisticated, but it's quite effective.

God does the same thing with us, and it should comfort us to know we have a heavenly Father who loves us enough to discipline us when we go astray. Hebrews 12 says if you are not disciplined, you are fatherless—you are not a child of God (see verse 8). But if you sense the Spirit of God warning you, trying to bring you back when you stray, rejoice in it. It means your Father loves you, that the Good Shepherd is looking out for you.

God might use the rod of sickness or the rod of tragedy—anything to jolt us out of our sin-induced insanity. It is far better to have a bruised leg than to be a dead sheep! It is far better that God discipline you than that you plunge over some cliff to your destruction!

Are you living an abundant life? Jesus came to give you one, and as your Good Shepherd, He knows just what you need. He desires to bless you more than you want to be blessed! If an abundant life is what you want, there's only one place to find it: in the green pastures of the Good Shepherd.

"The overflowing cup is meant to be shared. Why does my Shepherd cause my cup to run over? In order that I might give some of this life-changing power to others. The anointed head is for me. The overflowing cup is for others."

—*Don Baker*

18

NO TIME OFF

"My Father has been working until now, and I have been working."

—JOHN 5:17

I'M SO GLAD GOD DOESN'T TAKE TIME OFF.

Have you ever really needed to see someone, only to find he has left for the day? How would you feel if you prayed and an angel responded, "I'm sorry. God is unavailable. He has taken the day off"? But that will never happen. God is always available, always on call, always working.

Jesus, too, is always on duty, whether it be in the middle of the day or deep in the night. He's available. He's there. He's listening. Psalm 121:4 says, "He who keeps Israel shall neither slumber nor sleep."

And don't think this diligence is haphazard! In the Gospels, Jesus always acted according to a plan and purpose. The Lord did not wander about Judea without direction. He had an agenda, a plan, a schedule. There were no accidents. Everything transpired according to His perfect plan. The Master had appointments to keep, settled long ago in the counsels of eternity, and He was never late. He had one with Nicodemus at night; He had one with the woman at the well. And in John 5, He kept an appointment with a poor, rejected, paralytic man who had no one to help him.

Maybe you know what it is like to be a reject. Maybe you weren't the big man on campus when you were in high school. Maybe you weren't Mister or Miss Popularity, the center of attention. Perhaps your parents moved around a lot and you changed schools and neighborhoods often and never had long to enjoy the same set of friends. Perhaps more people knew you as "the new kid" than by your first name.

That describes my own upbringing. I lived in New Jersey, Hawaii, California, and Texas. I know what it is like to walk into a classroom where everybody knows one another . . . except me. It's okay on the first day of school because there are a lot of other new kids. But after school has been in session for awhile and you appear on the scene, everyone stares at you to size you up. You hear them whisper, "New kid" as you walk to your desk.

Does that describe you? Maybe you know what it is like to be that new kid. Perhaps you were always the last one picked for a team sport. At school the other kids always chose me for first base—not to man first base, but to *be* first base.

Are you an outcast? Lonely? That was this man in John 5.

Jesus' question to this man almost sounds insulting: "Do you want to be made well?" (John 5:6). I can almost hear the man replying, "No, I have really enjoyed sitting around the well for 38 years. Do fish swim? Of course I want to be made well!"

Why would Jesus ask such a question? Was He making fun of the man? Not at all. The Lord was asking an honest question. He was saying, "Are you content with your condition? Do you really want to change? Are you willing to put yourself in My hands? Are you ready for Me to do what you are unable to do for yourself? Do you really want to be made whole?"

Some people don't want to change. They don't want to be made well. There are people on the streets who like it there. They have chosen to become drug addicts or alcoholics and refuse treatment whenever it's offered. Some people like their life, even though they are miserable. They don't want to change. Some people like sin and don't want to turn from it.

Jesus knew you can't change a person who doesn't want to change. There's nothing you can do for him. He must be willing to cooperate, to respond.

How about you? Are you satisfied with the way you are? Do you really want to change? Do you want your life to be different?

The paralytic man to whom Jesus asked this question replied, "I have no man" (John 5:7). He had no friend to help him, but there was something in the look of Jesus' eyes, something in the tone of His voice, that drew this man out of his shell and caused him to speak of the deepest things in his life. All he wanted was a lift to the water; little did he know the gift Jesus was about to give him.

"Rise, take up your bed and walk" Jesus commanded (John 5:8). Does this sound like mockery? It wasn't. God will never call us to do a task that He will not give us the strength to accomplish. The calling of God is the enabling of God. "Do what you cannot do because I tell you to do it," Jesus was saying. "Take up your bed. Make no provision for a relapse. Walk! Don't expect to be carried. Don't leave your mattress so that if this doesn't work out you can return home. Burn your bridges! Break free from your past! Get up and walk!"

Jesus speaks to us today just as He did to that man. When Jesus commands us to follow Him, He means it. He doesn't want us to keep one foot in our faith and another foot in the world. He doesn't mean we should try to live two lives. He demands that we follow Him. Make a clean break with the past and put it behind you.

Jesus said, "No one, having put his hand to the plow, and looking back, is fit for the kingdom of God" (Luke 9:62). Don't look back. Let it go! Make no provision for a relapse.

The man in John 5, of course, got up and walked. He recognized the power of Jesus at work in his life and he jumped to follow the Savior's word.

The question now is, Will you?

Take a look at the miserable life of Lot, who tried to live in two worlds. What a contrast to his uncle Abraham, who made his choice for righteousness. Compare the angels' visit to Abraham's house with their visit to Lot's house in Genesis 18 and 19. Note the differences between the life of the committed believer and the compromising one.

19

WHEN GOD WEPT

"Jesus wept."

—JOHN 11:35

THE SHORTEST VERSE IN THE BIBLE displays the heart of God perhaps like no other. "Jesus wept," John tells us—and in those two short words, we learn volumes about the kind of God we serve.

Why did Jesus weep? I'll list some possibilities in a moment, but first let's consider *how* Jesus wept. In John 11:33 we read that everyone—all of those connected to Mary and Martha—wept over the death of Lazarus. The word used to describe their weeping could be translated "groaning." They were wailing in anguish. In the midst of this groaning and wailing and anguish, Jesus Himself wept.

But His weeping was different from theirs. We don't read that He groaned audibly. The phrase could be translated "the tears just streamed down His cheeks." As Jesus looked at the scene around Him, the tears began to flow down His face.

What caused Him to weep? We can only guess, but I offer three possibilities. First, they were tears of sympathy for Mary and Martha. Jesus identifies with us in our times of sorrow. The Bible says He was a man of sorrows and acquainted with grief (*see* Isaiah 53:3). When you are hurting inside, when you've lost someone dear to you or a tragedy has befallen you, God and God alone understands the deep pain inside your soul. People may never understand your sense of loss, but Jesus does. In a sense, He weeps with you. He is there, identifying with you. He knows what you're going through.

Second, they were tears of sorrow for Lazarus. Sorrow because Lazarus was dead? No, because the moment Lazarus left his mortal body and was welcomed into eternity, he was more alive than he had ever been. Lazarus was *alive*! Jesus wept because He was about to bring him back again. His were tears for a man who had known the bliss of heaven and now would have to return to a wicked earth.

We feel great sorrow when a Christian loved one dies, and there's nothing wrong with that. Some people say, "He is with the Lord, don't be sorry." But I *am* sorry—I miss him and I wish I could reach out and touch him, hear his voice. I'm sorry for *me*, not him, because I wish I were with him in the presence of God. There is nothing wrong with feeling sorrow when you've lost someone you love. But don't feel sorry for him if he was a Christian. Jesus felt sorrow for Lazarus because He was going to return His friend to this earth.

Last, I think they were tears for unbelief. No one in the crowd, including Mary and Martha, demonstrated faith in Him. Tears flowed down the Master's cheeks because no one seemed to believe His words that He could do the miraculous.

Jesus did more than weep in this passage, however. He also grew angry. John 11:33 says, "Therefore, when Jesus saw her weeping, and the Jews who came with her weeping, He groaned in the spirit and was troubled." A better translation might be, "He was angry and troubled Himself, and was moved with indignation." Not only was Jesus sad, He was also angry. He was indignant. Jesus was angry at something He should have been angry about.

What made Him angry? I think it was the ravages of sin in the world He had created. Here at the tomb of Lazarus He witnessed the result of Adam's wrong choice in the Garden of Eden. Prior to the eating of the forbidden fruit, there was no death. People would have lived forever. But death entered the human race when Adam sinned and we've been reaping the consequences ever since. I believe it angered Jesus to see the devastation that sin had wreaked upon His creation.

Oh, Jesus was going to remedy this shortly. He was about to go to the cross, die for us, bear our sin, and rise again from the dead so from that day forward no child of God would have to fear death. But on this day, death made Him angry.

For death, it was a fatal mistake. Jesus approached the tomb and called out, "Lazarus, come forth!" (John 11:43). What a dramatic moment that must have been! What a thrill it would have been to have heard those words and watched the sight of a dead man wrapped in burial clothes coming to life and lurching to his feet.

Don't forget—Lazarus had been dead four days. His spirit had left his body. He had passed beyond the veil that separates time and eternity. But as though Lazarus were napping, Jesus said, "Lazarus, come forth!" And His friend woke up and came to life.

Only Jesus could call over to the other side of eternity and be heard. Many have tried to contact deceased loved ones, but none have succeeded. Only Jesus can call over the gulf of eternity. Only He can call over to the other side and have His voice be heard and obeyed.

It's a good thing Jesus said, "*Lazarus*, come forth!" Had He simply said, "Come forth," every body in every grave would have resurrected instantaneously. The One who cried, "Come forth!" is the same One who said, "Let there be light" and there was light. Jesus was the Creator. When He commanded Lazarus to come out of the grave, His voice was heard on the other side of eternity and Lazarus had to return.

So take heart. Jesus understands what you're facing, and He sympathizes with you.

Meditate for a few moments on the unbelievably good news of 1 John 3:1 (NIV): "How great is the love the Father has lavished on us, that we should be called children of God! And that is what we are!"

20

GOD'S CURE FOR HEART TROUBLE

✖

"Let not your heart be troubled; you believe in God, believe also in Me."

—JOHN 14:1

HAVE YOU EVER BEEN stressed out, agitated, and troubled? Or uncertain about your future? Perhaps you've felt as if your world had been turned upside down. Maybe that's how you feel right now—it seems as though God isn't aware of your problems, that He isn't paying attention, that He isn't seeing you or hearing you.

Life is filled with troubles, beginning with the day we are born. There are health troubles, family troubles, troubles with our parents, troubles with our kids, husband and wife troubles, financial troubles. Disappointments are another kind of trouble. We're disappointed with ourselves because we don't always measure up to what we want to be. We want to be strong and we're weak. We want to be successful but we fail. We want to be liked and people are indifferent toward us. Circumstances bring yet another kind of trouble. It might be the loss of a job, the sickness of a loved one, uncertainty about the future, or a million other things. Life assails us with a million kinds of troubles.

If we were to choose one word to sum up our times, "trouble" would be a good pick. We live in times of great anxiety where people are tremendously concerned about the future. Their hearts are troubled.

That's certainly how the disciples felt that lonely night when Jesus announced He was about to leave them. They were terribly concerned. In fact, we read that Jesus Himself was troubled in heart. He was agitated as He prepared to identify the one who would betray Him. He was troubled as He was about to predict that Peter would deny Him three times. And He was restless, stirred up, as He got ready to tell the disciples He was about to leave them.

And when *He* got agitated, they *really* got agitated.

You know how that can be, don't you? My wife is like the Rock of Gibraltar for me. When she comes unraveled, I really come unglued. Now try to imagine how the disciples felt when the Lord Himself showed great anxiety. It undoubtedly frightened them.

But, of course, Jesus would never let it rest there. He gave His followers a prescription for their frightened hearts. He gave them His cure for heart trouble.

What cure did Jesus give to His disciples? That's more than just an idle question, because the words He gave His men 2,000 years ago fit the troubles we are facing today.

Jesus' cure for heart trouble is found in John 14:1, which says, "You believe in God, believe also in Me." *The cure for a troubled heart is to believe in God—to take Him at His word.* It was the cure for the disciples, and it's the cure for us.

In essence, Jesus was saying, "Believe that I know what I am doing and that I will certainly return for you, so that we might be together forever." His words take on special significance when you remember that He said this in the face of His own execution. Jesus reminded His followers that their agitation resulted from not believing what God said in the Scripture. They had forgotten God's word to them. The Scripture had spoken not only of Jesus' impending crucifixion, but also of His resurrection. Somehow they had missed that. And because they had failed to take God at His word, they were frightened.

The same thing can happen to us. God has given us His

Word to believe, to take at face value. It may not always be the easy thing to do when circumstances seem to overwhelm us, but we can *choose* to believe the Word of God. In fact, we must.

The disciples failed to do that. They didn't see the big picture. To them, it seemed as if everything were falling apart. They did not realize that everything was exactly on track, perfectly on schedule. Jesus was moving in the same direction He had been moving from the very beginning. Yet they could only hear that He was leaving them.

Unfortunately, we're not so different from them. We can't seem to grasp the big picture, either.

You might be going through difficult times right now and thinking, *God, do You know what You're doing with me? What is going on?* Yet God is still in control; He still sees the big picture. While we think of the temporal, God thinks of the eternal. We think about today; God is thinking about tomorrow. We think of comfort while God thinks of character. We think of an easy time but God is thinking of making us into better people.

God is in control! Romans 8:28 is still operational in your life, if you are a child of God: "And we know that all things work together for good to those who love God, to those who are the called according to His purpose." It may not seem like it, but ultimately everything will all work together.

So during this difficulty, during this time of hardship, whatever it may be—if you want the Master's cure for heart trouble, you're going to have to act on the remedy given to us in John 14:1. Take God at His word, even if you don't feel like it.

And when you do, believe me, you'll feel better in the morning...and for every morning thereafter for the rest of your life.

God has been faithful to His Word in the past, and will continue to be so in the future. God's words to the nation of Israel in Isaiah 43:1-3 are just as true today as they were the day they were written. Take them as your hope today.

21

AFTER THE MOUNTAINTOP

✄

"Now it happened on the next day,
when they had come down from the mountain,
that a great multitude met Him."

—LUKE 9:37

IT'S GREAT TO HAVE mountaintop experiences. But Luke 9 proves that God never allows His people to build their tabernacle in the place of glory when the world is in flames. We are always sent down from the mountain into the real world to carry out the mission God has given us.

Peter, James, and John had just enjoyed a profound experience with Jesus, Moses, and Elijah on the Mount of Transfiguration. They saw Jesus in all His glory. They heard God speak audibly from heaven. How did this affect their day-to-day living? Luke tells us that immediately after these disciples came down from the mountain, they were confronted with a demon-possessed boy. The child's father asked them to cast out the demon but they could not do so, even though Jesus earlier had given them the necessary authority (*see* Luke 9:1). Their faith was too weak.

Imagine: The same men who had just basked in the glory of God and reveled in a thrilling experience were unable to translate it into practical use. Hours after seeing the unveiled deity of

Jesus Christ, they were unable to help this boy. How feeble was their faith. How typical their unbelief.

How much like them we are!

It sounds familiar, doesn't it? We have a problem translating the divine into the day-to-day. We struggle to find a faith with feet, a faith that works.

Oh, we may raise our hands higher in a worship service than everyone else. We may speak of God's grace and power in our lives more than all others. The real question is, How does it affect our day-to-day living? That's the bottom line.

It's great when we go to church and have a wonderful time in the presence of God. Perhaps God speaks to us in a special way. Maybe there's a certain aspect of the message that grips our heart. We say, "That's it. That's what God is telling me. I need to put this into practice." We are moved in a wonderful way.

But right after the last prayer is prayed and we're dismissed we turn around and start gossiping about someone in the church. Or perhaps we go out into the parking lot and into our car to go home and we begin arguing with our wife or husband. In just seconds we go from the pinnacle to the pit, from the top to the bottom. That's how quickly it can happen.

It's not how high we can jump that counts. It's how straight we walk when we hit the ground again. I don't care much about how fervent we are in church. The only thing that matters is, How does it affect the way we live in the world? What we need is more day-to-day obedience—walking by faith, not by feeling.

Don't get me wrong; I thank God for our mountaintop experiences. It's wonderful when we have an emotional encounter with God during prayer or worship or reading the Word, when something comes home to us and God's Spirit overpowers us. It's a wonderful reminder of how much He loves us.

The problem is that some people think that's the way the Christian life should be every day. They're always seeking such experiences and if they don't find them in one church, they go to another and then another. They begin to hurt themselves spiritually.

God has not designed us to have continuous mountaintop experiences. When they come, enjoy them. But they are temporary. They are meant to prepare us for living in the valleys. We must remember that God is constantly seeking to change us into His image, to enlarge our faith, to make us stronger. Therefore we cannot stay in one place and become static. At the bottom of every mountain there is usually a valley or a test.

Guess who was waiting at the foot of the hill after the disciples' great experience on the Mount of Transfiguration? The devil. You find this pattern often in Scripture. Where did Jesus go after He was baptized? Into the wilderness to be tested for 40 days by the devil. After the dove came the devil.

We should anticipate and brace ourselves for attack after times of great blessing. It almost inevitably comes. I have come to expect it in my own life. There will be those difficulties. The valleys are coming.

You might be on a mountaintop right now, thinking, *Man, I love this!* But the Lord says to you, "See that mountaintop over there, the one that's even higher than this one? That's where we're going." "Great!" you say, "but Lord . . . where are You going? You're walking down. It's up." And the Lord replies, "The way to up is down. The way to that mountain is through this valley."

If you want to reach that other mountaintop, you have to go through the valley. Fruit doesn't grow on mountaintops; fruit grows in valleys. It is there we become like Jesus. The mountaintops prepare us for the valleys.

God is changing you into His image and it takes time. It doesn't happen overnight. It's going to take mountaintops as well as valleys. It's going to take a lifetime. Keep moving, because every step you take—up or down—helps you to change and become more like Jesus.

"Studying the life of the Savior, the greatest Teacher, makes it clear that he didn't cram a lot of heads full of a collection of theological facts. No, he involved his disciples in the process so that later the pagan world was compelled to testify, 'These are they who have turned the world upside down.' That's our challenge as this century draws to a close."

—*Howard Hendricks*

22
REAL SUCCESS

✄

"And He said to them, 'Cast the net on the right side of the boat,
and you will find some.' So they cast, and now they were
not able to draw it in because of the multitude of fish."

—JOHN 21:6

FROM ALL OUTWARD APPEARANCES, the ministry of
missionary George Smith was a failure. He had been in Africa
only a short time when he was driven from the country, leaving
behind only one convert, a poor woman. He died not long after
that, while on his knees, praying for Africa.

Years later, a group of men stumbled onto the place where
George Smith had prayed. They also found a copy of the Scriptures he had left behind in Africa. Then they met the one convert
of Smith's ministry. A hundred years afterward, a mission agency
discovered that more than 13,000 converts had emerged from the
ministry George Smith began.

Now that's what I call a successful ministry! But I'm sure it
didn't seem so successful to George Smith. To all outward appearances, his ministry was a failure. One convert, that's all.

What if George had thrown in the towel before the woman
came to Christ? What if he had fled the country without bothering to leave behind a copy of the Scriptures? What if he hadn't

taken time to pray for those in Africa and had chosen instead to keep them out of sight, out of mind? But he remained faithful in the little things, and reaped a reward he would not see until he reached heaven.

John 21:6 reminds us of the importance of obeying Christ even in the little things. The disciples had gone fishing on the Sea of Galilee shortly after Jesus' death and resurrection. They were probably discouraged, confused, and frustrated. Their beloved leader, Jesus, had been crucified just days before, many in the group had deserted Him, and most recently, Jesus had surprised them all by appearing to them in His resurrected body. Yet He didn't stick around.

They were plainly confused. You might have expected that Jesus' miraculous appearance to them behind locked doors would have given the disciples renewed zeal and excitement in their work for the Lord, but instead the group decided to go back to their old jobs. Jesus wanted them to be fishers of men; they decided to be fishers of fish.

Perhaps they thought they were no longer qualified for serving and representing Him. Or maybe they thought Jesus would never forgive them for deserting Him in His time of need. Whatever the case, they soon discovered that fishing wasn't as easy as it once was. They fished all night and caught nothing.

Then Jesus showed up on the shore and told them to try fishing on the other side of their boat. They took His advice—without yet realizing it was their Master—and when they did so, they quickly caught so many fish that the nets could barely contain their catch!

I think it would have been fascinating to eavesdrop on their discussions before they followed Jesus' advice. I'm sure that Peter, the professional fisherman, thought the instructions were downright ridiculous. Put their nets down one more time on the right side of the boat? They had tried that side before! Why would doing it again give them any different results? But for some reason, the disciples complied with Jesus' command—and reaped a blessing so huge they knew in an instant that it had been Jesus who had given the order.

The disciples found success that day because they listened to and obeyed the Lord. By being faithful to His one simple request, they received above and beyond what any of them thought was possible.

There are times when God calls us to the simple. The mundane. The ordinary. Our willingness to do those things may well qualify us for greater service later on. Scripture reminds us not to despise "the day of small things" (*see* Zechariah 4:10).

Jesus Himself taught us, "He who is faithful in what is least is faithful also in much; and he who is unjust in what is least is unjust also in much. Therefore if you have not been faithful in the unrighteous mammon, who will commit to your trust the true riches?" (Luke 16:10-11).

Think of David, whose place as a young man was in the pasture with smelly sheep. But one day God plucked the shepherd boy from obscurity and decided it was time for him to slay a giant. And so began the public career of Israel's greatest king.

Or think of Stephen in the New Testament, who was chosen by the disciples to wait on tables. In time, God said to him, "Stephen, it's time to stop waiting on tables and to serve the Word of God." His sermon recorded in Acts 7 is the longest message in the whole book.

Like David, Stephen, and even George Smith, God may be asking you to do things that seem mundane, unnecessary, or even impractical. But I guarantee that God will use you in ways you never dreamed of if you just let Him be the One in charge. Yes, He may call you to even greater work for His kingdom. But He may also call you to a task that will not bear fruit until years down the road.

Do you want to be successful? Then follow the advice of the Master Fisherman, Jesus, no matter how trivial or humbling that advice might seem. His directions might seem simple, but remember that the One who gives it is the fountainhead of all wisdom.

Read 1 Corinthians 3:5-17. There you will find what is needed in your work for the Lord for it to be of any lasting value. Will your life's work stand the test of time? If you have any doubt, begin making some changes right now.

23

HOW TO WAIT FOR THE LORD'S RETURN

"Let your waist be girded and your lamps burning."

—LUKE 12:35

SOME PEOPLE ARE what you might call prophecy buffs. They love to study Bible prophecy. They love to comb their newspapers and magazines and watch the news for world events that might fulfill Bible prophecy. I admit that I'm always on the lookout for these things, too. Whenever I read a paper or a news magazine or watch a news telecast, I always ask myself how current events might fit into the prophetic scheme.

The problem is, some people study prophecy as a hobby but are never personally gripped by it in a practical way.

But prophecy is utterly practical. First John 3:2-3 tells us that the Lord is coming back and that everyone who has this hope purifies himself, even as He is pure. Believing that Jesus could come at any moment should cause you to live right before God. You should want to use the gifts and abilities He has placed in your care and desire to reach other people with the gospel message.

Jesus insisted that we "be like men who wait for their master" (Luke 12:36). Are you such a man or woman? Are you looking for Him? If so, that will have a dramatic effect on the way you live.

The members of the early church certainly kept this teaching at the forefront of their minds. They believed that Jesus could come at any moment and lived in anticipation of that fact. As a result, they turned their world upside down.

Some people think that because the Lord did not return in the first century, this anticipation by the early church was misplaced. It's true Jesus did not return then, but this hope certainly gave those believers an added zeal and excitement. It purified them. Ultimately, they *will* see His coming; right now they are finding their reward in heaven.

This is why I can say that anyone who believes in the soon return of the Lord is not misplacing his or her faith. We do not place our hope in the coming of the Lord as much as we place it in the Lord who is coming.

The fact that He *could* return at any moment keeps me on my toes. It keeps me alert. It keeps me ready. When we are looking for our Lord, everything else in life changes—even the boundaries of life are altered dramatically.

Before we're Christians, in our estimation life begins at birth and ends at death, so we try to pack as much as we can into the time we have. But when we become Christians, the boundaries are altered and everything changes. Suddenly life did not begin at birth as much as at the day of our *re*birth. We look back at life beginning on the day we found Jesus Christ. That is when we really started living as life was meant to be lived.

And for us, life doesn't end at death. Death is merely a transition—if we taste death at all. The Bible teaches that there is a generation of believers who will not see death. They will be "caught up . . . to meet the Lord in the air" (1 Thessalonians 4:17). We could be that generation! But one thing is certain: One way or another, by death or by rapture, we will see Him. They are merely forms of transportation. The destination is what is important: heaven! Life begins on the day we find Christ and it culminates on the day we see Him face to face at His return.

And how, in practical terms, does our belief that Jesus could come at any time affect the way we live? The answer is found in

Luke 12:35. Jesus says, "Let your waist be girded and your lamps burning." Men in those days wore long, flowing garments similar to a long dress—not the best thing to wear when you want to move quickly. To be dressed in readiness meant that you pulled up that long garment above your knees and tied it into a belt around your waist, giving you more freedom of movement.

Let's consider a modern equivalent of this picture. If I were going to run a 10K race, I wouldn't show up in a three-piece suit. A suit isn't designed for freedom of movement. If you're a woman, you wouldn't come dressed in high heels and an evening gown.

It's not uncommon in New York City to see well-dressed businesswomen, armed with attaché cases, briskly walking in track shoes. They carry their dress shoes until they get to work, where they take off their track shoes and put on the dress shoes. They do that so they can move quickly. They need to be able to run from muggers chasing them through Central Park or from crazy taxicab drivers who like to drive on the sidewalks! They want to move fast. That's what Jesus was talking about in Luke 12:35; we must be ready to move quickly.

Then the Lord uses another illustration. He says, "Have your lamps burning." This lamp was a small piece of pottery with a wick floating in the oil, the equivalent of a first-century flashlight. The psalmist had this in mind when he wrote, "Your word is a lamp to my feet and a light to my path" (Psalm 119:105). It would give light so the user could find his way in the dark.

Taken together, these pictures instruct believers to be unhindered, ready to go, their feet free from encumbrances and their lights shining in a dark world, unashamedly following Christ. We must be ready to go. We should allow nothing to slow us down and we should keep our lamps burning.

Maybe Jesus will come today. But then again, maybe He'll

come a hundred years from now. Whenever He returns, we're to be ready. Are you?

Read 2 Peter 3:10-15. According to the apostle, how should the knowledge of prophecy help shape our character and change our lives? Would you say this is true of your own life?

24

LIKE A THIEF

"But know this, that if the master of the house had known what hour the thief would come, he would have watched and not allowed his house to be broken into. Therefore you also be ready, for the Son of Man is coming at an hour you do not expect."

—LUKE 12:39-40

IT'S UNFORTUNATE that every so often some nut case comes down the pike who says he has figured out the exact day Christ will return. Even though Jesus said, "But of that day and hour no one knows, no, not even the angels of heaven, but My Father only" (Matthew 24:36), there's always one person who thinks he is the exception to the rule.

It doesn't so much amaze me that these people come along. What does amaze me is that so many naive Christians subscribe to what these people say.

For example, someone claims that with the help of ancient Babylonian calendars and obscure mathematic equations, he has uncovered the exact date of the Second Coming. His followers get excited . . . until the day comes and goes and the Lord still hasn't returned.

Jesus told us not to look for a day or hour. He said, "It is not for you to know times or seasons which the Father has put in His own authority" (Acts 1:7). But we are to be watching. We are to be ready. And in Luke 12:39, the Lord used a rather unusual illustration to describe how we are to prepare ourselves for His arrival: that of a thief breaking into a house.

I think it's fascinating that Jesus uses the illustration of a thief to describe His coming. The analogy of a thief introduces a note of danger.

If a thief were to call and tell you that he was coming to break into your house, and he were dumb enough to give you the exact time of his arrival, no doubt you would be ready. Of course, no thief in his right mind would call ahead and announce his time of arrival. You would be waiting for him with a hand grenade, a bazooka, the Marine Corps, the police department, and five rabid German shepherds. You'd be ready. Of course, no thief in his right mind would tell you his plans, because he doesn't want to be caught breaking into your home.

Most thieves are smarter than the one I read about from West Haven, Connecticut. In November of 1991, he was stopped by police near a convenience store that had just been robbed. According to the officer who made the arrest, when the thief was asked what he had been doing, he replied, "I just left the store that I robbed." No kidding!

Most thieves have a lot more on the ball than that bumbler. Therefore they'll case your house. They'll watch the movements of your family. They'll find a time when you're not home and then they'll hit.

In Luke 12:38, Jesus said, "And if he should come in the second watch, or come in the third watch, and find [His servants ready], blessed are those servants." The Jews divided the night into three watches, the third one being very late in the evening. Jesus taught that even if He comes in the latest part of the evening, we should be ready.

Interestingly, many thefts don't happen late at night but in the middle of the afternoon when both husband and wife are at work and the kids are in school. I've heard of thieves who dress up as employees of a moving company. They'll pull up in a moving truck, enter a house, empty it, and drive off. The neighbors think, "Look, our friends are moving. I didn't know that." Can you imagine coming home to an empty house? Everything you own has vanished. The thieves struck at an unexpected hour.

To the nonbeliever or the Christian who is not ready, the arrival of Christ will be like the appearance of a thief. It will strike terror in their hearts. But to men and women looking for Him, His arrival will prove to be a blessed interruption. They will welcome it and be glad to see Him.

Until He comes, we are to be watching and working. If watching is the evidence of faith, working is the evidence of faith in action. Watching for the Lord's coming may prepare our soul for that great day, but working for the Lord's coming is a sure way of bringing additional guests to the wedding feast.

Are you a man or woman looking for your Lord? Are you one who doesn't just theologically agree with this teaching or intellectually accept it as valid, but who has been gripped with its meaning in every fiber of your life? If that describes you, your overwhelming passion in life will be to seek Him first and to be ready for His return. You will do what you can to reach others until that day.

Is there anything in your life you need to change in case Jesus were to appear right now? Are there any passions in your life that are stronger than your passion for Him? If so, they need to be dealt with—not next week, not next month. Now. He can come at any moment.

I hope you're ready to meet the Lord. And I hope when He comes He will find you and me looking for Him. May we remember and act on the words of the apostle Paul: "For you yourselves know perfectly that the day of the Lord so comes as a thief in the night. . . . But you, brethren, are not in darkness, so that this Day should overtake you as a thief" (1 Thessalonians 5:2, 4).

We may not know when the Lord will return, but that Day

doesn't have to overtake us as a thief. To be ignorant does not mean to be unprepared. Are you ready?

Take a look at those who were prepared for the Lord's return and those who were not, as described in Matthew 25. What were the differences?

25

SIGNS OF THE TIMES

✦

*"Take heed that you not be deceived. For many will come in My name,
saying, 'I am He,' and 'The time has drawn near.' Therefore do not go after
them. . . . Now when these things begin to happen, look up and lift up
your heads, because your redemption draws near."*

—LUKE 21:8, 28

WE ARE LIVING in truly exciting times. All around us we are
seeing Bible prophecies fulfilled. Dramatic changes are occur-
ring around the globe, and we all watch with great interest any
new developments in the Middle East, where history both began
and will one day end.

A few years ago one leading rabbi made the following statement to his followers as they witnessed troubling events in the
Middle East: "What's going on now is like labor pains. It looks
pretty messy, but in the end what will come out is a new, living
light. The Messiah may just be an eye blink away."

What a fascinating statement—it's "like labor pains." That's
exactly the analogy the apostle Paul used in 1 Thessalonians 5:3
to describe this time! And Jesus used similar language in Luke
21, a passage often called the Olivet Discourse. In that chapter,
Jesus gives us an overview of the events that will take place prior
to His return to the earth.

The first and perhaps most important labor pain to signal His return will be a widespread deception of false Christs and messiahs. We don't have to look far to see scores of fulfillments to this prophecy. In addition to the constant parade of self-proclaimed messiahs and gurus, New Age teachings have exploded in recent years. With so many religious options, Satan has "flooded the market" with his imitations.

That has been Satan's ploy for years. He figures, "If it ain't broke, don't fix it." He might slap a little paint on here and there, develop a new slogan, and print a revised advertising brochure for his product, but it's the same basic model he has always used. And it still seems to sell well.

All around us we see his strategy at work. Second Peter 2:1-2 says, "There will be false teachers among you, who will secretly bring in destructive heresies. . . . And many will follow their destructive ways." That is why Jesus says, "Take heed that you not be deceived." That phrase "take heed" means "keep your eyes open" or "beware." He is warning believers to beware of false teachings that can infiltrate even their own ranks.

When Paul was leaving the church at Ephesus, he warned its elders, "I know this, that after my departure savage wolves will come in among you, not sparing the flock. Also from among yourselves men will rise up, speaking perverse things, to draw away the disciples after themselves. Therefore watch, and remember that for three years I did not cease to warn everyone night and day with tears" (Acts 20:29-31).

And John wrote, "Little children, it is the last hour; and as you have heard that the Antichrist is coming, even now many antichrists have come, by which we know that it is the last hour. They went out from us, but they were not of us . . . but they went out that they might be made manifest, that none of them were of us" (1 John 2:18-19).

Jesus will not let this go on forever, of course. One day He will return to set everything right. Luke 21:25-27 says, "And there will be signs in the sun, in the moon, and in the stars; and on earth distress of nations, with perplexity, the sea and the waves roaring; men's hearts failing them from fear and the expectation of those things which are coming on the earth, for the powers of heaven will be shaken. Then they will see the Son of Man coming in a cloud with power and great glory." Jesus is going to return to the earth to establish His kingdom and reign in righteousness.

So what should we do in the meantime? Our task is very simple: We must be looking for Him. In Luke 21:28 Jesus says, "When these things begin to happen, look up and lift up your heads, because your redemption draws near." Even today we see the pieces beginning to fall into place: turmoil in the Middle East; economic troubles around the world; the outbreak of violence; sexual perversion. Jesus specifically prophesied that these latter two trends would increase before His return.

In Matthew 24:37 He said, "But as the days of Noah were, so also will the coming of the Son of Man be." If you go back to Genesis 6 and read the story of Noah, you will discover that excessive violence characterized the people. Now fast forward to today—violence is everywhere. Murder rates continue to rise in every major city in the United States. Terrorism rages around the globe. The regard for human life continues to erode.

Then consider what Jesus said in Luke 17:28, 30: "As it was also in the days of Lot. . . . Even so will it be in the day when the Son of Man is revealed." What do we remember about Sodom and Gomorrah? Sexual perversion. And what do we see all around us today? The same thing.

Don't allow these things to drive you to despair, however. Remember: He is coming back to take you home to be with Him forever. This world is not your home. As a Christian, you are a stranger, a sojourner, a pilgrim. You are a visitor looking for a better city, whose builder and maker is God (*see* Hebrews 11:10).

And you'll soon be home!

"If you read history you will find that the Christians who did most for the present world were just those who thought most of the next. The Apostles themselves who set on foot the conversion of the Roman Empire ... the English Evangelicals who abolished the Slave Trade, all left their mark on earth because their minds were occupied with Heaven. Aim at Heaven and you will get earth 'thrown in'; aim at earth and you will get neither."

—*C.S. Lewis*

26

THE PARABLE OF EQUAL OPPORTUNITY

"A certain nobleman went into a far country to receive for himself a kingdom, and to return. And he called his ten servants, and delivered them ten pounds [minas, NKJV], and said unto them, Occupy till I come."

—LUKE 19:12-13, KJV

HAVE YOU EVER WONDERED what God expects of us as we await His return to the earth? What our focus, our purpose, and our goals should be? This parable helps to answer those questions.

A historical footnote adds to the intrigue of this parable. A similar story had played out in real life during the childhood of Jesus. As Herod the Great saw his death approaching, he wrote in his will that his kingdom should be divided among his four sons. Before his wishes could be honored, however, Rome had to ratify the will. One of Herod's sons, Archelaus, traveled to Rome to be named ruler of Judea, the area his father had governed. But several Judeans did not want Archelaus as king, so they followed him to Rome and protested his appointment. They were overruled and Archelaus was given the kingdom.

Prior to his departure from Judea, Archelaus had gathered his servants and gave to each a measure of money and told them to occupy—to do business—till he came. When he returned, those who had wisely invested the money were re-warded. Those who had opposed his appointment as king were executed.

Quite possibly, Jesus alluded to this familiar story point by point to draw a spiritual analogy. He says, "Occupy till I come."

The nobleman gave to each man a mina, the equivalent of a hundred days' wages—a considerable amount of money. The servants had many options. For example, they could give the money to investors and earn interest on it. Or, they could purchase goods and sell them at a profit. The important thing was to give back to their master more than he had given them. How they did it was up to them, as long as it was legal and profitable.

One man took his mina, invested it, and got ten more. Another took his mina, invested it, and got five more. A third man took what he had and hid it in the ground.

This is a parable of equal opportunity. Every man was given a single mina. Jesus is not showing us how to play the stock market or invest in real estate and realize a great return; He's talking about the investment of our lives into His kingdom.

To what do you think He was referring? Each man was given a common responsibility. What common responsibility do all Christians have? What duty is the same for every follower of Jesus Christ? I believe it is the simple commission to go into the world and proclaim the gospel. God has given this sacred trust to every believer.

He's given you a mina, so to speak. What are you doing with it? Are you multiplying it? Or have you hid it in the ground?

The first man succeeded more than the second; he got ten when the second only got five. What accounts for the difference? Undoubtedly, it was his determination and commitment. Perhaps the second man was content and believed that he was doing a fine job. Certainly he was doing better than the man who hid his mina in the earth.

There are many people like this in the church. They are more or less satisfied with the status quo. They just plod along. They are content to earn five minas—unlike some turbocharged believers. While we're still looking for a match, they're setting cities on fire.

Why do they enjoy more success? Why do some excel while others don't? Undoubtedly, it's because they utilize their resources. The Bible says that God has given us all things that pertain unto life and godliness (*see* 2 Peter 1:3). All the power that you need is given to you as a Christian. Are you taking advantage of it?

Sometimes we attempt to do great things for God in the energy of our flesh and see nothing but failure. God isn't asking you to work *for Him*; He's asking to work *through you*. The difference is obeying His Word and working in the power of the Holy Spirit. The Bible says, "'Not by might nor by power, but by My Spirit,' says the LORD of hosts" (Zechariah 4:6).

Maybe that's what some of us need. Maybe we need to say, "Lord, empower me with the Holy Spirit and show me how to do this effectively. Put Your words in my mouth and use me."

Please don't mimic the man mentioned in Luke 19:20. He received the same instructions as the others, but wrapped his mina in a handkerchief and hid it in the ground. He put it away and played it safe.

God doesn't want you to play it safe. He has harsh words for the man who plays it safe. Better to try and fail than never try at all. So give it a shot! Try to make a difference!

The worst option of all is to do nothing, to refuse to take chances, to attempt nothing because you're afraid of failing.

God expects fruit from His people. Jesus said in John 15, "By this My Father is glorified, that you bear much fruit; so you will be My disciples. . . . You did not choose Me, but I chose you and appointed you that you should go and bear fruit, and that your fruit should remain" (verses 8, 16). To fail to bear fruit is, in essence, to hide your mina in a handkerchief. The man who did it in Luke 19 was called a "wicked servant" and was stripped of even the one mina he had.

There's no reason his destiny should become yours.

Take a look at Luke. Notice the difference when Jesus came on board the disciples' boat. Is He on board with you?

27

JUDGMENT DAY

✄

"I say to you, that to everyone who has will be given; and from him who does not have, even what he has will be taken away from him."

—LUKE 19:26

THE BIBLE TEACHES there is coming a day when all Christians will stand before God to be held accountable for their deeds. God will judge us according to how we used the abilities and gifts He entrusted to us. He will judge us based on what we did with the "mina," the equivalent of 100 days of wages. He will also judge our motives. Sadly, many in that day will see their work burned and will suffer loss, even though they themselves will be saved (*see* 1 Corinthians 3:10-15).

The third servant mentioned in Luke 19 was ineffective because his heart was not right toward his master. He had a false perception of him. He said, "I feared you, because you are an austere man. You collect what you did not deposit, and reap what you did not sow" (Luke 19:21). He considered his master unfair, harsh, demanding. The servant wasn't motivated by love.

Some people feel this way about God. They are afraid of Him. They think whatever they do for God must be done out of duty or God will nail them. How far from the truth that is! Paul wrote, "The love of Christ constrains us" (2 Corinthians 5:14).

Any service we attempt for God, any work we seek to do for Him, must be motivated by love.

Our love for Him should be in response to His love for us. As you read the Scriptures and get to know the character of God and His love for you—when you fail as well as when you succeed—and you realize His love is everlasting and that He has drawn you with cords of lovingkindness, your rebellious heart will melt and you will begin to respond to Him in love. The Scripture says, "We love Him because He first loved us" (1 John 4:19). Love will begin to overflow from your life and any work you do will be a delight, not a drudgery. You will eagerly ask, "Lord, what can I do for You?"

That was Paul's experience on the Damascus Road. He was a murderer, a persecutor of the church. Yet Jesus stopped him in his tracks by knocking him to the ground in a blinding light. Paul then had just two questions: "Who are You, Lord?" and "Lord, what do You want me to do?" (Acts 9:5-6). That's the response of a man who has truly met God. And those are two questions every believer should ask Jesus.

If we're reluctant to serve Him, maybe we need to spend more time getting to know Him for ourselves. Maybe there's no overflow in our lives because there hasn't been enough intake. Perhaps we're trying to get by on the bare minimum. Peter and John said, "We cannot but speak the things which we have seen and heard" (Acts 4:20).

Luke 19 reminds us that judgment is coming—but that doesn't have to fill you with dread. God loves to reward faithful servants. One of the most thrilling verses in all the Bible is found in Luke 19:17, where the master says, "Well done, good servant; because you were faithful in a very little, have authority over ten cities."

That man's reward was equal to what he had accomplished. He had gained ten minas and was made ruler over ten cities. The other man gained five minas and so was made ruler over five cities. Each man's reward fit his accomplishments. The measure of our authority and our rewards from Jesus will be proportionate to our devotion to Him now. To be faithful in small things means the chance to serve the Lord in a greater capacity.

I don't know what form this reward will take. It appears from this text and other scriptures that part of our reward will include the right to rule and reign with Him. It may be that we will oversee a certain province or country or region.

The thought of being privileged to serve Christ and rule with Him under His authority boggles the mind. It's an opportunity we should desire intensely, for in His presence is fullness of joy and at His right hand are pleasures forevermore (*see* Psalm 16:11). Whatever God would call us to do is well worth it. It staggers the imagination to think that He would ask us to do anything on His behalf. What a joy!

Serving the Lord is a great joy. It's exciting and fulfilling. Don't ever think that those of us in full-time ministry are making some great sacrifice. What I do, I love. I do it because I love Him, and I love Him because He first loved me. I can't even take credit for my love for Him. It is so wonderful to have God work through you. And you know, it's just as rewarding to me to be used of God to minister to one person as it is to many people. Just the thought that God would call upon me thrills my soul.

God wants to call upon you, too. Don't think of it as a duty. It's a privilege, the highest privilege. Don't take this sacred trust and bury it in the ground. Multiply it. Use it. Be diligent. Yield to the power of the Holy Spirit and ask God for directions as to how you can be used by Him. Then stand back and watch the results!

Until that day when the Lord returns, let's keep our focus clear and our eyes single and occupy till He comes. Jesus says in Revelation 22:12, "Behold, I am coming quickly, and My reward is with Me, to give to every one according to his work."

What sort of reward awaits you?

For a closer look at rewards in the believer's life, look at 1 Corinthians 3:11-17. See if you can discover the basis on which God will test His children.

28

SERVED BY THE KING

"Blessed are those servants whom the master, when he comes, will find watching. Assuredly, I say to you that he will gird himself and have them sit down to eat, and will come and serve them."

—LUKE 12:37

WHEN WAS THE LAST TIME you were served by a king? I doubt most of us can point to even one incident—but there is coming a day when the King of kings and Lord of lords will seat some of His children at His banqueting table and will *wait on them*!

Jesus used the picture of a Jewish wedding to relay this startling revelation. Jewish weddings were held primarily at night. A bridegroom's servants would wait for their master to come home with the bride, and when the new couple arrived, they would open the door and welcome them.

What is unique here is Jesus' declaration that the master himself "will come and serve them." The idea of the master serving his servants was unheard of in Jewish culture. But that's exactly what Jesus promises to do for those who eagerly await His coming. There is a special reward for the vigilant servant, a unique blessing to the individual who anticipates and waits for the return of his Lord.

It is as if Jesus says to us in this passage, "I would like you to be ready. Wait to hear the sound of My footsteps. And when I come walking up to the doorway, open that door! Be ready for Me and I will come and serve you."

Some Christians will not be living as closely to the Savior as they should be when He comes back, and yet they, too, will be taken. If He were coming only for perfect people, we would all be left! Jesus is going to come even for those of us who could be doing better than we are. We're all saved by grace.

Lot is an example of this. When the Lord came to deliver him from Sodom and Gomorrah prior to the destruction of those cities, Lot was not living a model life for a believer. He had lowered his standards; he was compromising. He was even a bit reluctant to leave when the angels escorted him out. But he *was* taken.

In the same way, some weaker believers will be taken when the Lord comes back. It will be a sad day for them, though. They will stand before the Lord and will have accomplished absolutely nothing with their lives. Of them the apostle Paul's words will ring true: "If anyone's work is burned, he will suffer loss; but he himself will be saved, yet so as through fire" (1 Corinthians 3:15). You can say of such believers that they had a saved soul but a lost life.

Is that a good description of you? Does that picture your Christian experience? Do you have a saved soul but a lost life? Do you know you're going to heaven yet are doing nothing for the Lord in the meantime? If so, make a change! There is a special blessing promised to the vigilant servant, to the one who gladly anticipates the return of the Lord.

Does the old expression, "When the cat's away the mice will play" describe you? Some people live their Christian lives with the same mind-set that characterizes lazy employees. Think of an unproductive construction site. When the boss is gone everybody takes it easy. Then all of a sudden he drives up and a scout shouts, "The boss is coming!" Everybody pulls out their hammers and starts pounding away. There may be nothing to pound, but they pound anyway, just to look busy. The boss sees activity and people moving about, gets back in his truck, drives off . . . and the site returns to inactivity once more.

But over in one corner, there is one guy working hard. He was working before his boss came, working when his boss arrived, and continued working after his boss left. Some of the other workers say to him, "Will you lighten up? If he sees how productive a person can be, he might be angry with the rest of us and dock our pay or tell us to work harder." But the man continues to work.

We are to be like the hard worker as we wait for the coming of the Lord. We are to work hard, laboring for the Lord at our designated tasks.

Though it is true that our employers on earth may not know all that we do, your Father in heaven does know. He will reward you publicly in that day. Jesus said, "Your Father who sees in secret will Himself reward you openly" (Matthew 6:4).

Maybe nobody knows about the service you do for your Lord. They don't know about the hours you spend in prayer. They don't know about the time you spend witnessing. They don't know about the sacrifice and commitment you've made. When you give a gift, you don't make a big show of it. You don't want your name on a wall plaque at church because you gave x amount of dollars. When you give, you do as Jesus said: "Do not let your left hand know what your right hand is doing" (Matthew 6:3). You do it quietly, discreetly.

One day your heavenly Father, who is taking note of everything you've done for Him, will reward you openly. The Bible says, "Let us not grow weary while doing good, for in due season we shall reap if we do not lose heart" (Galatians 6:9).

Will you be one of the blessed ones who are served a lavish dinner by the King of kings Himself? Or will you be on the sidelines, watching but not participating? The choice is yours.

Make a fresh commitment to Jesus Christ. Rededicate yourself to finding and effectively using the gifts, talents, and abilities He has given you. Commit yourself anew to spend Every Day with Jesus!